Moms Gone Mad

Motherhood and Madness, Oppression and Resistance

edited by

Gina Wong

DEMETER

DEMETER PRESS, BRADFORD, ONTARIO

Published by:
Demeter Press
140 Holland Street West
P. O. Box 13022
Bradford, ON L3Z 2Y5
Tel: (905) 775-9089
Email: info@demeterpress.org
Website: www.demeterpress.org

Demeter Press logo based on Skulptur "Demeter" by Maria-Luise Bodirsky <www.keramik-atelier.bodirsky.edu>

Cover Artwork: "Hatching the Universal Egg: Birth Power" ©Judy Chicago, 1984, Embroidery on silk, 20.25" x 20.25", Embroidery by Sandie Abel. Collection of The Albuquerque Museum of Art and History. <www.judychicago.com>. Photo: Michele Maier.

Printed and Bound in Canada

Library and Archives Canada Cataloguing in Publication
        Moms gone mad : motherhood and madness, oppression and resistance / Gina Wong, editor.

ISBN 978-0-9866671-7-6

1. Motherhood--Psychological aspects. 2. Motherhood--Social aspects. 3. Mothers--Psychology. 4. Women--Psychology. 5. Feminist theory. I. Wong, Gina, 1971-

HQ759.M59 2012   306.874'3019   C2012-905377-5

To Iris, my heart;
Cassie, my soul fire

Table of Contents

Acknowledgements
ix

Introduction: Moms Gone Mad:
Motherhood and Madness, Oppression and Resistance
Gina Wong
1

MOTHERHOOD: MADNESS AND OPPRESSION

Chapter 1
Mothers, Madness and the Labour of Feminist Practice:
Responding to Women in the Perinatal Period
Jules E. Smith and Marina Morrow
21

Chapter 2
"The First Rule Is that a Mother Should Govern Her Own Feelings":
Modern Childrearing Advice and the
Discipline of Maternal Emotions
Roblyn Rawlins
35

Chapter 3
The Persistence and Destructiveness of Mother-Blame
in Psychological Theory
Regina M. Edmonds
48

Chapter 4
Fractured Motherhood: The Insanity of Reproduction
in Australia in the 1930s
Alison Watts
64

Chapter 5
Who Decides If Mothers Are Crazy?
From Freud's Mother to Today's
Paula J. Caplan
79

MOTHERHOOD: RESISTANCE AND EMPOWERMENT

Chapter 6
Matroreform:
Toward Collapsing the Mother's Panopticon
Gina Wong
95

Chapter 7
Cultural Representation of Childlessness:
Stories of Motherhood Resistance
Grace Bosibori Nyamongo
108

Chapter 8
The Space Between:
Mothering in the Context of Contradiction
Joanne Minaker
124

Chapter 9
Reconceiving and Reconceptualizing Postpartum Depression
Gina Wong and Kathryn Bell
141

CONTENTS

Chapter 10
Postpartum Depression and Caregiving:
Beyond the Developmental-Inadequacy Discourse
Nicole Letourneau and Gerald F. Giesbrecht
165

NARRATIVE VOICES: MAD MOMS

Chapter 11
Creating a Space for Mothers Who Have
Lost a Child Through Suicide
Donna F. Johnson with Helen Levine
185

Chapter 12
Daughters of Depression: Breaking Free from the Bell Jar
Nancy Gerber
195

Chapter 13
Postpartum Psychosis: A Mother of Madness
Gina Wong and Teresa Twomey
205

Chapter 14
Envious Mothers, Beautiful High-Spirited Daughters:
The First Step Towards Woman's Inhumanity to Woman
Phyllis Chesler
219

Contributor Notes
225

Acknowledgements

I want to feel what I feel.
What's mine. Even if it's not happiness,
whatever that means...
Because you're all you've got.

It may have been Andrea O'Reilly who posted this quote of Toni Morrison's (see Brockes) that lingers in my thoughts as we bring *Moms Gone Mad* to completion. In many ways, in tandem to producing this book, my own life journeyed new roads as has the editing of this book taken me on different paths of discovery, adventure, and insight. But, simultaneous challenges, struggles, and difficult decisions such as what to include and what goes into a next book shadowed the path. Likewise, mothering is fraught with a web of complicated emotions, trials, and tribulations. All of it: personal life, editing a book, the experience of mothering—honouring the good with the bad and seeing the value in all of it, has been for me recognizing a deep call to respect life and all her mysteries, beauties, warts, boldness, and fragility. Most profoundly, this book dovetailed with the ending of a 15-year relationship to a life partner and through this most difficult time, for which the development of this book was slowed, I thank all those who supported and believed in me and this project.

A heartfelt thanks goes to Andrea O'Reilly, Renée Knapp, and Tracey Carlyle within the organization of Demeter Press and ARM/MIRCI, who were pillars of support.

Likewise, Athabasca University granted me the 2011 President's Award for Research and Scholarly Excellence for editing this book which allowed time from my academic position to devote to this book. The sixteen contributors of this book, each and every one of you sharing your experiences, ideas, and profound concepts of motherhood empowerment, oppression, and resistance moved me and I thank you for your patience and dedication to bring this collection to bear.

Just this evening, as I write these final words, I visited with my dearest friend Danya Handlesman for whose nineteen-year friendship deeply nourishes me. There is a sacred space between intimate friends who just know you, accept you, and whom you can be most candidly genuine with. Cathryn Goodman, Ann Hollifield, Sandra Collins, and Tamara Hanoski are other such dear friends—many despite geographical distance. The contributors in this book all dance in this sacred space and invite readers into this place of intimacy with life. I am awe-inspired at collectively what we achieved and reveal about moms gone mad, motherhood, and mothering. As well, my clients are a true inspiration and share in this vulnerable space of speaking the at-times unspeakable. Saying out loud all the mothering complexities and deconstructing the 'good mother' is profoundly courageous and quiets the madness. I also wish to acknowledge the Belgravia community of families, namely the women Claudia Garros, Elizabeth Yih, and Tamara Nicholson who laugh with me in motherhood and sisterhood.

Finally, the new road has taken me to a place of depth in joy, love, and friendship. Tom Bechthold, you are the grounding light in me. Our children, Kieran, Cassie, Iris and our life together are an abundant gift. And all of it … even if not always happiness, I want to feel because that's the grace and full etching of life. The meaning of it made more splendid because of you all.

REFERENCES

Brockes, Emma. "Toni Morrison: 'I want to feel what I feel. Even if it's not happiness." *The Guardian* 13 April 2012. Web.

Introduction

Moms Gone Mad:
Motherhood and Madness, Oppression and Resistance

GINA WONG

WRITING THE INTRODUCTION to this collection takes me back to the roots of my involvement in motherhood scholarship, which began in 2005 when I presented at the *Association for Research on Mothering* conference (ARM, known since 2010 as MIRCI: *Motherhood Initiative for Research and Community Involvement*) in Toronto, Canada. As a psychologist specializing in women's issues and in particular, maternal mental health and wellness, and as a mother with two young daughters, I was compelled to broaden my knowledge base in the area. At the conference, I experienced a profound sense of affinity and coming home engendered by listening, presenting, theorizing, critiquing, and dialoguing about motherhood scholarship, activism, agency, feminism, and much more. Unique to this organization and conference (and the only gathering at the time of its kind internationally), was the sole impetus to deconstruct, understand, and give meaning to the work and process of mothering as an individual, social, political, economic, and global endeavor and from an array of disciplinary perspectives, scholarly and community understandings, and from first person accounts of mothers. I had a deep thirst that was thoroughly quenched with my involvements with ARM/MIRCI.

Nevertheless, while finding refuge in maternal scholarship, the increased awareness, critique, and reflection on motherhood oppression and subjugation became for me deeply troubling and maddening. Consequently, my fervor intensified over the years to increase my advocacy for mothers' empowerment. In 2009, I presented at the *Moms Gone Mad: Motherhood and Madness, Oppression and Resistance* international conference (hosted by ARM and Mamapalooza) in New York. This book was inspired and conceived from that conference which expounded on motherhood and mothering as a site of powerlessness, oppression, resistance, and empowerment.

Fundamental to this collection and to the aim of the *Moms Gone Mad* conference as noted by Andrea O'Reilly (founder and director of ARM and MIRCI) is the seminal and classic work by Adrienne Rich entitled *Of Woman Born:*

Motherhood as Experience and Institution. Rich is a forerunner in revealing that maternal experiences and motherhood are chiefly defined through male-centered institutions. Indeed, Adrienne Rich, Sara Ruddick, and Andrea O'Reilly (2006) distinguish between motherhood and the experience of mothering. They separate *motherhood* (the male-centered institution and ideology, which are oppressive) from *mothering* (the act of mothering and motherwork that has the potential to be empowering). Inherent in this distinction is the recognition that we maintain some power and that maternal resistance and empowerment are possible amid oppressive forces. O'Reilly advances that "mothering seeks to undermine patriarchal motherhood by exposing, tracking, and eventually countering the ways that patriarchal motherhood functions as a master discourse or hegemonic narrative that defines how women must mother" (13).

In editing this book, I am inspired by *Motherhood: Power and Oppression* an edited collection by Andrea O'Reilly, Marie Porter, and Patricia Short. From a feminist perspective, they capture the duality in that mothering is simultaneously a site of power and oppression. In the current volume *Moms Gone Mad*, we strive to advance the essential work of these scholars and of many maternal theorists by exposing the oppressive breadth of motherhood and the empowering possibilities in mothering.

The seventeen contributors to this volume convey a multiplicity of ways that mothers, even in the midst of maddening experiences are not passive bystanders nor victims. As O'Reilly, Porter, and Short write:

> Oppression does not equate to the absence of agency…. It is possible to see that mothers are victimized and influenced by societal, and their own, expectations. There is a vast difference between being victimized and being a victim. (9)

Likewise, this collection while attending to oppression and madness, simultaneously highlights the agency, legitimacy, and power of mothers. For example, Joanne Minaker judiciously explores the blending of oppression and empowerment for mothers in Chapter 8.

MOMS GONE *MAD*

Phoebe Eng in *Warrior Lessons* describes a phenomenon whereby women exhibit sudden volcanic eruptions of anger and madness described in modern history called "running amok" (64). The term originates from Asian cultures. It appears that women gone *amok* notably occurs among communities where normative codes of behavior dictate female practices of honor, duty, deference, and submission; and where assertiveness and aggressiveness are regarded as dishonorable behaviors. These women are extraordinarily hemmed in—and then one day uproariously explodes with uncontrollable rage. The behavior, almost animalistic is completely understandable from a feminist lens. Eng explains, "[a]nger tells us and those around us where our innate boundaries are, what we instinctively feel is tolerable or intolerable, and can signal when those limits have been trespassed" (65). Nevertheless, for the women in oppressive societies it is doubly problematic as they are further disparaged and judged for acting up and this additionally confirms and reinforces them as the problem.

Considering this phenomenon in a general sense, it is natural and understandable that women and mothers go *mad* or run *amok* within the context of cultural oppression and subjugation. Our alarm bells have gone off and Eng aptly states, "[a]s is only sensible with alarms, it makes sense to acknowledge and respond" (65). Many of us mothers are MAD, we are angry, and we are acting up in ways to fight against standards of expectation that are impossible and crazymaking. This book illustrates moms gone *mad* and *amok* as a result of overly constraining societal forces. There is an urgent need to acknowledge and respond to the madness to which this book aims to contribute.

Many authors in this collection explore how and why mothers are easily reduced and dismissed by the simple label of *mad* and/or *insane, crazy* either diagnostically, institutionally, or individually by those around them and by mothers themselves. Such a misnomer arises predominantly from fear of the mother's power or the unknown, and many contributors in this volume describe ardent attempts to push against such labels. Nevertheless, while moms gone *mad* or *amok* elucidates our oppression, "mad" also captures empowerment. The terms *mad, misfit,* and *outlaw* depict outliers from the conventional norm. Exactly what we strive to be: mothers acting up in ways to fight against the grain of expectation and conformity to rigid ideological norms. As such, *Moms Gone Mad* as a collection in this book represents resistance to the oppression and is a site of empowerment.

MADNESS IN PATHOLOGIZING WOMEN

Historically, Phyllis Chesler, a renowned author and psychotherapist, first published the book *Women and Madness* in October of 1972, selling nearly three million copies and exposing the patriarchal bias in psychiatric diagnosis. It includes her important illumination of the ubiquitous yet often covert maligning and pejorative views of women and mothers. In her revised and updated 2005 edition of *Women and Madness*, Chesler imparts:

> ...although there has been enormous progress—a sea change even—the clinical biases that I first wrote about in 1972 still exist today. Many

clinical judgments remain clouded by classism, racism, anti-Semitism, homophobia, ageism, and by cultural and anti-immigrant biases as well. I have reviewed hundreds, possibly thousands, of psychiatric and psychological assessments in matrimonial, criminal, and civil lawsuits. The clinical distrust of mothers, simply because they are women, the eagerness to bend over backwards to like fathers, simply because they are men is mind-numbing. Mother-blaming and woman hatred sizzle on each clinical page. (15)

The continued psychiatric control Chesler denounces is emblematic of general views of women and mothers in contemporary society that were formally highlighted at the May 2009 conference. Chesler delivered the keynote address at the *Moms Gone Mad* conference, and it is reprinted in the Narrative Voices section of this book.

Likewise, Paula J. Caplan and Lisa Cosgrove address in their book *Bias in Psychiatric Diagnosis* the constructions of mental illness and psychiatric disorder that disadvantages and harm women (see also Caplan 1995). Furthering the discussion of the oppressive forces for women and mothers within psychiatric diagnosis, many of the authors in this volume, including Caplan (Chapter 5), continue to elucidate this alarming reality.

MOTHERING DISCOURSES

This book is intended to expose and deconstruct damaging institutions and ideologies that are toxic to motherhood. Through a critical lens and feminist examination of forces that impinge on mothers, this collection systematically exposes ideologies and hegemonic forces that regulate mothers' lives in impossible ways. The core premise of this book is that moms are *mad* and *run amok* in reaction to sociological pressures and expectations promulgated for mothers. These myths and ideologies are so deeply ingrained that they are the set standards and norms that regulate mothers' existence. Each chapter in some way captures the insidious way the impossible standards induce madness in mothers. Some chapters focus more on the oppression of mothers such as the chapters contained in *Section I: Motherhood: Madness and Oppression*; other chapters focus on resistance and empowerment (*Section II: Motherhood: Resistance and Empowerment*); and final chapters emphasize the narrative voices of *mad* mothers (*Section III: Narrative Voices: Mad Mothers*).

Madness stems from a multiplicity of toxic ideological principles surrounding motherhood. Some of these predominant discourses include the good/sacrificial/perfect mother, intensive mothering, new momism, and the bad mother myths. What follows is a brief description of these major discourses, which thread throughout the chapters in the book, and delineates how these ideologies function to create the "observational gaze" described by Foucault (1979, 1989). Discourses of mothering are ostensibly invisible and overlooked; and many women struggle and personalize issues to themselves, remain silent, and internalize madness rather than locating the madness in the institutions and expectations of mothers within our society (see Caplan 1995; Chapter 5). A feminist analysis, specifically a *matricentric feminist* (O'Reilly 2011) critique is required to fully understand the discourses and the implications/consequences of those ideologies for mothers.

THE GOOD/SACRIFICIAL/PERFECT MOTHER

Alyson Schafer describes the prevailing cultural myth of the *good* mother in her book *Breaking the Good Mom Myth: Every Modern Mom's Guide to Getting Past Perfection, Regaining Sanity, and Raising Great Kids.* Similarly, Fiona Joy Green and many other maternal scholars aptly describe the *good mother* (often referred to as the *perfect mother*). Ingrained nearly as tacit understanding, simply hearing "perfect/good mother" quickly conjures her up in our minds. In *Practicing Feminist Mothering*, Fiona Green (2011) discusses the historical development of this term. Likewise, Caplan in Chapter 5 addresses that: "[t]he Good Mother Myths set standards of perfection that are so high that no one could possibly meet them. They include the myth that a good mother never gets angry, is 100 percent giving and nurturing 100 percent of the time, and is by nature capable of knowing everything necessary to raise happy, well-adjusted children."

The sacrificial mother is in many ways a derivative of the good mother ideology. O'Reilly (2004a) relays in *Mother Outlaws: Theories and Practices Empowered Mothering* that the normative discourse of sacrificial motherhood are deeply oppressive to women. These notions further impinge and add multilayer to the good woman expectations. O'Reilly articulates (2004b) in *Mother Matters: Motherhood as Discourse and Practice*:

> I argue that the current dominant discourse of motherhood, what I term sacrificial motherhood, is characterized by six interconnected themes: 1) children can only be properly cared for by the biological mother; 2) this mothering must be provided 24/7; 3) the mother must always put children's needs before her own; 4) mothers must turn to the experts for instruction; 5) the mother is fully satisfied, fulfilled, completed and composed in motherhood; and finally, 6) mothers must lavish excessive amounts of time, energy and money in the rearing of their children. (14)

Taken together, the sacrificial mother tenets and the good/perfect mother ideologies prompt mothers to don a *mask of motherhood* described by Susan Maushart in her 2000 book by that name. Maushart theorized a mask of motherhood that must be worn as a direct result of the pressure on mothers to be good, perfect, and sacrificial. Mothers react by eclipsing themselves and hiding from others and denying those parts that do not fit the mould of the perfect mother. The mask or façade that mothers must keep, lest she be judged as bad or incompetent, may keep her from talking, sharing, and getting support for any mothering challenges she experiences. In her book, Maushart attempts to expose the realities of mothering to challenge myths of complete serenity, fulfillment, and enjoyment that *good, perfect,* and *sacrificial* mothers are supposed to embody.

O'Reilly also (2011) asserts an overarching philosophy of *maternalism* (9) that, upon analysis, further entrenches mothers to wear the mask of motherhood. *Maternalism*, O'Reilly theorizes, is like paternalism; it asserts that, "mothers know best" (9). It stands as a prescribed ideological belief that mothers have unique, natural, and special abilities to mother. Furthermore, this promulgated myth suggests that, "women are (and should be) the moral conscience of humanity and asserts women's legitimate investment in political affairs through this emphasis" (9). From patriarchal perspectives, *maternalism* could mistakenly be seen as respectfully making way for the power and authority of mothers and finally giving mothers the credit they deserve. Notwithstanding, a mother-centred feminist analysis identifies *maternalism* as a continued reification of the perfect/good and sacrificial mother and recognizes such things as the complete absurdity/madness with enlightening mothers with copious amounts of mother-expert literature while at the same time expecting mothers to "know best." *Maternalism* is not a gain for women. It furthers the oppression because, yet again, it prescribes how mothers should be and defines her worth and status strictly by the singular role.

INTENSIVE MOTHERING

Another outcrop of the good, perfect, and sacrificial standards for mothers is the *intensive mothering* philosophy. Sharon Hays introduced this term in *The Cultural Contradictions of Motherhood* where she defined how mothers particularly in the 1980s, but truly over the past century, have been tasked with being everything for their vulnerable and sacred children. To be good mothers, women must spend countless hours stimulating their children, feeding them what is best, making painstaking decisions implied to determine the success or failure of the child. In effect, *intensive mothering* requires every ounce of energy and insists on the guidance of experts. Furthermore, mothers are expected to love every minute of it.

Feminist Elizabeth Badinter's book, *The Conflict: How Modern Motherhood Undermines the Status of Women,* addresses the mother's entrapment (mother's panopticon as discussed below) although not from this specific conceptualization. Badinter poignantly articulates what MIRCI and maternal scholars and activists are advancing—that unrealistic standards and expectations on modern mothers have increased over time and in fact set mothers further back and to an extent not seen since the 1950s (Badinter). Badinter describes how attachment parenting, with the same tenets as intensive mothering, tethers mothers to the home and children; and as a result modern mothering expectations have regressed the status of women. She writes that "for a majority of women it remains difficult to reconcile increasingly burdensome maternal responsibilities with personal fulfillment" (2). Reactions to Badinter's explosive bestseller include heated debates about whether feminism is antithetical to modern mothering. Critics also make ruthless and disparaging remarks about Badinter herself, which unfortunately happens when people feel judged and threatened about their mothering practices.

NEW MOMISM

Susan Douglas and Meredith Michaels coined the term "new momism" to represent the overarching ideal surrounding motherhood and the myth that women are incomplete beings unless they bear children and devote themselves endlessly to mothering. New momism implies that utter fulfillment for women comes only from motherhood (and in the doting, sacrificial, and perfect way); and that any other role she has in her life is superfluous. Women are defined chiefly by whether they have children and then how perfectly they mother. The twenty-first century ideology of *new momism* goes together with the previous discourses addressed. In combination with other discourses a mother's panopticon is constructed (see below).

THE BAD MOTHER

Caplan specifically draws out the difference between the good mother and bad mother myths. The bad mother myths directly contribute to the damning of mothers. No matter what they do it always leads to the inevitable conclusion that they are deficit, mad, possibly even pathological. Each choice, decision, action, inaction of a mother regarded through the bad mother lens is proof of her inadequacies. Consequently, the bad mother myths summons mothers to monitor and regulate their behaviors because they can never be good enough (Caplan 1989, 2000; see Chapter 5). The inevitable bad mother verdict constantly undermines women and regardless of how tightly the mask of motherhood is worn she will be scorned or criticized by others, and/or herself, for failing.

MOTHER'S PANOPTICON

The ideologies explored and the many others that exist for women and mothers create what Foucault (1979, 1989) conceptualized as the "observational gaze" or a panopticon, which is a figurative representation of a prison. The prison guards are unknown and faceless to mothers as the observational glass is one-way thereby creating a sense of omnipresence. Mothers are confined, watched, regulated, adjudicated, and punished not just externally. Self and other-surveillance occurs and mothers regulate and delegitimize other mothers as well as themselves as we co-exist in the prison. An onslaught of guilt, shame, and self-repudiation are only some of the consequences of not being a good, perfect, sacrificial, intensive, mask wearing, fully realized and fulfilled mother. Sociocultural norms and oppressive motherhood ideologies as described earlier as well as others (e.g., embodiment, sexuality) define the observational gaze upon which we judge ourselves and other mothers (see Chesler, Chapter 14 on women's inhumanity to women).

Without feminist analysis and critique, our imprisonment in this Alcatraz would not be realized nor understood. A mother-centred feminism that O'Reilly demands in *The 21st Century Motherhood Movement* is necessary to fully deconstruct and dismantle the panopticon. While maternal activism has burgeoned in the last decade, O'Reilly states that "the 21st century motherhood movement has become a social movement with its own specific mandate and objectives, one that is distinct from the larger feminist movement" (3). However, while these advancements have been made she argues that maternal activism is marginalized because mothers are marginalized and because the motherhood movement has occurred, for the most part within social media (also marginalized). As such "maternal activism is often not recognized... or [is] dismissed" (3).

O'Reilly aptly expresses the urgent need for social change and empowerment of mothers. With respect to the turning of the tides engendered by the twenty-first century motherhood movement, she posits that this movement:

> ...makes possible and gives rise to a specific and much-needed theory and politic of feminism for mothers that I have termed "matricentric feminism." I use the term matricentric to denote a mother-centred standpoint and to emphasize and designate it as a particular, long overdue, and urgently needed mode of feminism. This is not to suggest that a matricentric feminism should replace traditional feminist

thought; rather, it is to remind and emphasize that the category of mother is distinct from the category of woman, and that many of the problems mothers face—socially, economically, politically, culturally, psychologically and so forth—are specific to women's role and identity as mothers. (2011: 25).

In order for mothers to recalcitrate from the confines of the panopticon, matricentric feminism is imperative. We urgently need a formal and specific theory and politic of feminism explicitly devoted to the emphasis on motherhood and mothering (O'Reilly 2011). And in order to incite change and continued revolution, matroreform is called for. Matroreform (Green 2008; Wong-Wylie, 2006, 2010; see Chapter 6) is described as a transformative maternal practice that is "an act, desire, and process of claiming motherhood power…a progressive movement to mothering that attempts to institute new mothering rules and practices apart from one's motherline (Wong-Wylie 2006: 739). In original writings, I describe matroreform as a psychological, spiritual, and emotional reformation of mothering from within including removal and elimination of obstacles to self-determination and self-agency as a mother and woman. As such, matroreform, which is a reformation of mothering, is best realized through matricentric feminist awareness, and is an essential transformative process that will dismantle the mother's panopticon.

Strategies to shred damaging ideologies that buttress the mother's panopticon can be explored once the contours of the prison are understood and realized. The dominant discourses are so prevalent, ubiquitous, and automatically promulgated that it impedes our awareness and insight into the mere existence of a panopticon. But, when we step back and examine the deeply ingrained ideologies, the imprisonment of mothers is apparent. At this stage, awakening to the observational gaze and mother's panopticon, and generating meta-understandings to what drives how we feel and what we do as mothers, are the first steps. Overall, the mother's panopticon is illustrated in some way by each chapter in this collection either directly or indirectly. This book contains three sections that loosely organize chapters by their emphasis on madness and oppression; resistance and empowerment; and narrative accounts of madness. A brief summary of each chapter and their linkage follow.

SECTION I: MOTHERHOOD: MADNESS AND OPPRESSION

In the first chapter in this collection, Jules Smith and Marina Morrow succinctly address the madness and oppression, particularly in the perinatal period and surrounding women's reproductive health. They advance that "our very notions of mental health, mental illness, and madness arise from discursive and clinical practices that have positioned women as more vulnerable to mental instability" and they outline how mental health overall is a gendered concept. Factors influencing women's mental health include the dominance of biomedicine in mental health and adoption of neoliberal discourses that reinforce an individual approach to complex problems experienced by women in the perinatal period. They suggest that a neoliberal approach does not begin to address "the interplay of biology, psychology, and the social worlds of women." The authors use an institutional ethnographic method of analysis that "starts with people's lived experiences and then aims to understand them in the context of larger social and institutional processes."

Smith and Morrow deconstruct the stories of three fictitious mothers. By doing so, they demonstrate the multiplicity of factors involved and the multi-layered aspects of mothers' lives that so easily are reduced to her own problem had she only been strong enough, independent enough to find herself in different circumstances (neoliberal understandings). Smith and Morrow (as well as authors in Chapters 4 and 5) vehemently critique psychiatry and the mental health system for its "abuses, including challenges to the diagnostic categories of the *DSM* and illustrations of how women's so-called madness is often an understandable response to wider social conditions."

In Chapter 2, the evidence of the mother's panopticon is clearly substantiated. Roblyn Rawlins discusses the panopticon and poignantly discusses the oppressive nature of childrearing "expert" advice touted as far back as 1856. She states that "[t]he story of childrearing from the nineteenth century until today is replete with self-appointed childrearing experts proposing to guide mothers in making the best choices for their children." In her chapter, Rawlins candidly depicts how childrearing "experts" regulate mothers' emotions. She lays the "historical groundwork for the discourses of emotional regulation of mothers and mother-blaming that are still so ubiquitous and so oppressive today."

Rawlins, in a different way than Smith and Morrow, outlines the control of mothers by "experts." This author expresses that "[t]he childrearing experts exhorted mothers to control their feelings of anxiety, worry, maternal love, and especially anger, or risk serious physical, emotional, and moral harm to their children." To even further oppress and subjugate mothers with impossible standards—mothers were advised to control and regulate any feeling or demonstration of anxiety about not being able to regulate their emotions with their children. The "perfect emotional self-control" (contained in the *good mother* ideology) demanded of mothers is certainly, as Rawlins states, "a cruel irony" and perpetuates the notion of female emotionality as needing expert control. Running *amok* as a normal reaction may be better understood given the oppressive and maddening context of overruling mothers' emotions. Once again, the fortress of the mother's panopticon becomes obvious.

In Chapter 3, Regina Edmonds articulates the stronghold of mother-blame in our culture and how it reduces women to the one role of mothering. Edmonds' discussion underscores the notion of *new momism* (Douglas and Michaels) that equates women's value and worth to her status and ability to mother. Edmonds continues to shed light on the enormity of burden and pressure on mothers. Whereas Chapter 2 describes the need for maternal regulation of emotionality in raising healthy, well-adjusted children, Edmonds illuminates that "we begin to search for those responsible for the child's distress, and too often find it dwelling within the child's mother. She should have protected the child more fully, she should have been more present to her child's needs, she should have put her children first. This oppressive mantra of "shoulds" is learned early and well, especially by girls, our future mothers."

The impossible standards for a *perfect mother* are contradicting, maddening, and oppressive; yet are so deeply entrenched and wholeheartedly internalized. Central to this chapter, and in nearly every other chapter in this book, is the bad mother myth (see Caplan, Chapter 5) and the "pervasiveness and persistence of automatically blaming mothers for the difficulties, large and small." In particular, this conviction is shared by Letourneau and Giesbrecht in Chapter 10, who discuss postpartum depression and the automatic blame and inadequate-status that are cast onto depressed mothers for inevitably victimizing their children because of their mental health. Such views are short-sighted and disregard the array of societal factors and the influence of other caregivers involved.

I can relate to Edmonds as she poignantly shares how she herself, a psychologist, is not immune to the mother-blaming discourses and that she "continues [to] be undermined by an unconscious internalization of its central and highly judgmental premises." Once again, we see the confines of the mother's panopticon. That is, mothers regardless of who we are, what we do (even feminist maternal scholars) cannot exist outside the fortress of constraint and self-surveillance.

Alison Watts' (Chapter 4) coincides with Smith and Morrow (Chapter 1) in depicting the madness and oppression mothers encounter at the start of the perinatal and postpartum period. Herein, Watts examines the patient records of a family member, Ada, whose life is spent over a 40-year period in three Australia mental institutions that began 14 days after delivering her baby. Coming alive on the pages, Ada's most tragic story of oppression and disempowerment in the mental health system is woven together and vividly recounts a fractured motherhood. Tragically, Ada endures admission and discharges from mental institutions over several decades at the hands of her husband and the psychiatric community. Similar to arguments advanced by Rawlins in Chapter 2, Watts highlights that the 1920s and '30s "proliferation of advice books and manuals on child rearing and mothercraft produced a governing and civilizing trend upon mothers as prescriptive ways to raise children." Like

Rawlins (Chapter 2); Smith and Morrow (Chapter 1) and many other chapters in the book, Watts cogently illustrates through the story of Ada how "power relations, social conditions, and material reality of mothering" is ignored and patriarchal constructions dominate.

Chapter 5 is a contribution by Paula J. Caplan, a renowned psychologist for her brilliant work in fighting against the psychiatric biases against mothers in our culture. As noted earlier, she describes two sets of dominant North American myths ubiquitous in our culture that impede a mother's sense of adequacy and esteem: the *good mother* myth and the *bad mother myth*. To elucidate these myths further, Caplan shares excerpts from three of her previous works: "Mocking Mom: Joke or Hate Speech?" which depicts the oppression at the hands of society that mother's experience; "Call Me Crazy," which is a play that further illustrates how psychiatric diagnosis in the early twentieth century perpetuates the bad mother myth; and "What Mommy Told Me," which is a play that demonstrates the oppression that children bear at the hands of the court system and how sexual abuse by a father can be construed in a way to blame the mother and punish her for the accusations in the first place. The assumption is that "mothers are either mentally ill or pathological liars or both." Caplan goes on to identify that as feminists we need to examine the experiences of mothers and the myths that define mothers as mad, inferior, and incapable (bad mother myth) all the while expecting them to be everything for their children (good mother myth).

SECTION II: MOTHERHOOD: RESISTANCE AND EMPOWERMENT

In Chapter 6, I explore the transformative process of matroreform (Green 2008; Wong-Wylie 2006, 2010) that represents mothers coming into their own apart from oppressive confines and societal constraints. Matroreform is an act of resistance and empowerment on a personal level to refuse replication of our mother's oppression; and it also captures the process to collective resistance against the subjugation of mothers in the panopticon. I theorize about matroreform using matricentric feminism and the social ecological model to capture how a revolution and reformation of mothering ideally involves change on all levels that influence mothers including personal, familial, societal, and global scale (microsphere, mesosphere, exosphere, macrosphere). Social ecological theory goes hand in hand with Institutional Ethnography (IE) developed by Canadian Sociologist Dorothy Smith. It is an approach that studies women in their environment and the interrelationships that abound; and IE is a fitting method of research to understand the process and experiences of matroreform.

At first glance, Chapter 7 appears to be about the oppression of African mothers particularly within the Gusii society. Grace B. Nyamongo thoroughly exposes the cultural subjugation of women that exists within the societal preference for male sons. However, Nyamongo does so in a way that gives voice to Gusii mothers' perspective and experience. Nyamongo reveals that in the Gusii society childlessness refers most notably to not having had a male child. That is, sonlessness in this society equates childlessness which negates the existence, importance, and value of females and renders girls and women invisible. Women in this society are worthy and valued only by virtue of the sons that they produce. Nyamongo describes the "cultural madness entrenched in society's perception about sonlessness" and the gender inequity and "discrimination against women at all levels in contemporary society." In revealing the cultural practices and values of the Gusii society, Nyamongo gives voice, life, and empowerment to Gusii mothers who live in such entrenched and oppressive ideological contexts. She reveals the acts of resistance and measures of self-preservation that women employ to live, cope, and survive in this culture.

In Chapter 8 by Joanne Minaker and Chapter 9 by Gina Wong and Kathryn Bell, a similar theme of recognizing binaries or divides in mothering is at the core of both chapters; however, each chapter focuses on different aspects of mothering. Minaker emphasizes mothers' agency and experience and the contradictions that exist within mothering practices. In a shrewd way, Minaker reinforces the notion that other maternal scholars have described— that mothering and motherhood is not monolithic; rather, they can be both empowering and oppressive. She shares that "mothers' narratives reveal that rather than standing in opposition to one another, oppression and resistance blend.... Rather than inevitable contradictions that women must work against, mothering is a negotiation of tensions in the spaces between oppressive constraint and empowering possibility." Drawing on the work of Adrienne Rich (1986), Minaker reminds us of the origins of maternal feminist thinking and that motherhood is both a site of power and of resistance "rather than simply a patriarchal bastion of male domination and oppression."

Likewise, in Chapter 9, Bell and I challenge a static and binary view of postpartum depression (PPD). We reconceptualize the etiology of maternal depression through a lens that resists strictly adhering to a psychiatric definition that disregards cultural influences. Rather than debating whether factors that underlie PPD are biological, psychological, or sociocultural in nature, we propose that it involves a confluence of all these factors to varying degrees and is different for each mother. While examining mainstream sociocultural contexts that breed PPD in mothers, Bell and I recognize that "sociocultural perspectives ha[ve] been largely negated in North American patriarchal reification of PPD." Such a view of PPD "removes the origins of *madness* from the mother [and] locat[es] it rightfully in the sociocultural landscape that we live within." Highlighting cultural promulgations such as the *good mother, good woman*, and the *silencing of the self* theory of depression, Bell and I recommend counselling treatment strategies that can empower women and mothers to resist these ideologies.

Continuing a discussion of PPD in Chapter 10, Nicole Letourneau and Gerald Giesbrecht argue against the "inaccurate and damaging discourse about mothers with depression that characterizes them as inadequate to support the development of their children," which they coin the developmental-inadequacy discourse. Similar to Wong and Bell, these researchers highlight factors that contribute to the development of PPD. Originating from a culture so engrained with the *good mother* ideology and *intensive* and *sacrificial mothering* expectations, mothers are besieged with blame when they are depressed as they are found automatically culpable for developmental and psychological harm in their offspring. Letourneau and Giesbrecht's resistance and outcry is that the "the evidence of negative effects of depression needs to be recast."

Consistent with Wong and Bell's ideas, these researchers examine social inequities and economic factors that play a tremendous role in the complexity of PPD and the outcomes for children and families—but that are so often habitually overlooked or disregarded in medical and psychiatric circles. Letourneau and Giesbrecht empower mothers and assert that "blaming mothers for the developmental outcomes of their children unfairly ignores the complex social and relationship factors that both give rise to symptoms of depression and influence children's development."

SECTION III: NARRATIVE VOICES: MAD MOTHERS

In Chapter 11, Donna Johnson with Helen Levine poignantly reveal the extraordinary gulf of grief and self-blame/hatred that mothers experience when they lose a child to suicide. It is atrocious that as a culture we work against mothers; and instead contribute to reifying ingrained ideologies and discourses that usurp the growth, development, and confidence of mothers. *New momism* (Douglas and Michaels 2004) offers an understanding to why a mother, despite being told countlessly that her child's suicide is not her fault, feels broken, "unworthy to walk the earth," and that she "[is] going insane." The pain of the women can be understood when we comprehend the imprisonment of mothers within the panopticon—where her worth is legitimized by enacting the role of mother perfectly.

Johnson and Levine describe a program they developed that brought together five mothers grieving the loss of their child from suicide. They shared: "[n]o existing program addresses the cultural prescription for perfection in motherhood that gives rise to feelings of inadequacy in most mothers and which, when a child commits suicide, can lead to despair." Over time, and with the gentle brilliance of Helen Levine's feminist analysis, the group shifted from a focus on self-blame, guilt, and inadequacy to examining the societal "prescriptions for perfection in mothering." While the mothers were neither guilt nor grief-free at the end of the program, Johnson and Levine recognized that by analyzing the impossible societal pressures on mothers, it began to shape an understanding that motherhood is a cultural construction in which mother-blame is deeply embedded. This analysis opened the door, if only by a crack, to self-compassion and gave way to understanding the social construction of motherhood that promote self and other recrimination.

Nancy Gerber's chapter (12) is a personal narrative account of the author's own struggle with depression. Gerber ties her experience of depression to her motherline and provides the backdrop to depression by examining the context of these women's lives. From inside the story, Gerber achieves what Smith and Morrow describe in Chapter 1 of an institutional ethnographic approach that invites us to draw on lived experiences and understand them in the context of larger societal and institutional processes. Like Smith and Morrow, Gerber demonstrates the multiplicity of factors influencing and shaping the experience of depression over the three generations, including her own.

Indeed, Gerber speaks about depression as an "umbilical cord" connecting her and enabling a common ground between herself and her mother. Gerber, while suggesting an intergenerational transmission of depression, does so in a way that does not contribute to mother-blaming. Mother-blame is vehemently and aptly disputed in many of the contributions in this book. Specifically, in Chapter 10, Letourneau and Giesbrecht critique the automatic blaming of mothers for harming their children when they suffer from PPD. As a psychologist in clinical practice working with mothers who are depressed, I see first-hand the shame, guilt, and self-repudiation that internalized mother-blaming does to women. Accordingly, as editor, it was intentional to include these chapters with keen awareness of addressing the prevailing and destructive dominant discourse surrounding PPD that overtly and covertly emphasize the victimizing of children and blaming of mothers. In Chapter 12, Gerber strives to empower other mothers through her own demonstration of vulnerability to speak about and find support for depression.

In Chapter 13, Teresa Twomey and I dialogue about the experience of post-partum psychosis which we coin a *mother of madness* because it is so feared and misunderstood by mainstream medical practitioners and the general public. Our aim in this chapter is to demystify postpartum psychosis through a personal interview between Twomey and I. We focus the interview on her experience of writing and gathering other women's stories for her groundbreaking book *Understanding Postpartum Psychosis: A Temporary Madness* published in 2009. Twomey unabashedly shares her ideas and perspectives, which is also informed by her own experience of postpartum psychosis after the birth of her first child and her advocacy work ever since. Twomey vividly describes in a narrative account what it was like, what her thoughts, worries, and concerns were when she was in her the depth of psychosis. We "illuminate[s] postpartum psychosis from an understanding and empathetic perspective which contrasts with the system of oppression and judgmental lens through which *mad* mothers are often viewed. We provide awareness about the experience of postpartum psychosis in order to push back against the oppressive forces of stigma, ignorance, and prejudice..."

It seems fitting to end this collection with a reprint of Phyllis Chesler's keynote speech at the 2009 *Moms Gone Mad* New York conference. In chapter 14, Chesler covers taboo topics such as women's inhumanity to women, which includes how mothers can judge other mothers; and how mothers can apply insidious cruelty, be competitive, and ousting of mothers. This speech illustrates *moms gone mad* and *women gone mad* not attributed only to patriarchy but triggered by insidious hurt and harm from other women and mothers. Herein patriarchy, the good and perfect mother myth, the bad mother myth, new momism, and so forth rage in such a way that women and mothers regulate and judge other mothers against the promulgated norms. Once again, we see evidence of imprisonment in the Alcatraz of a mother's panopticon where we have turned on everyone including ourselves for survival.

In effect, women have internalized these myths and isms and do not respect, trust, or like other women—or themselves. Chesler brazenly speaks out about competition between mothers and daughters, and that mothers can be cruel, envious, disparaging, and controlling of daughters. She suggests, "women with low self-esteem are more hostile to other women." Indeed it *is* difficult to hold one's esteem in high regard in the face of impossible standards and *madness* in our culture. The gaze and watchful eye in the mother's panopticon turns women not just onto themselves but we begin to regulate other women to deal with the trapped confines of the prison and perhaps in self-preservation. Chesler boldly illustrates the self-destructive and other-destructive coping defenses women and mothers have adopted that, no less, serve to chip away at womanhood and motherhood at our own hands.

CONCLUSION

The chapters in this book attest to the urgent need for a mother-centered feminist movement or *matricentric feminism* as O'Reilly implored in *The 21st Century Motherhood Movement*. There is an urgent need to enhance dialogue about revolutionizing understandings and constructions of motherhood that serve as our confinement in the mother's panopticon. A central aim of this collection is to further highlight those ideologies and discourses that reify and encourage us to label mothers as *mad*. This book compassionately demonstrates why mothers are running *amok* in ways that may not be as overt as a volatile explosive tantrum; but in subtler, covert, and more internalized forms of self (and other) destruction. From a mother-centered feminist consciousness and matroreform we push against ideological forces that convince mothers of their weakness, madness, and culpability.

For this and so many reasons we need to recognize the oppression of mothers and turn our madness into uniting, resisting, and furthering the empowerment of motherhood. Limitations in this book are that other dominant patriarchal discourses surrounding women's beauty, size, shape, and sexuality (to name a few) that further add to the pressures and expectations in the mother's panopticon could not be covered. In other writings, I address issues of *embodiment* and sociocultural influences on adolescent girls and women (see Wong-Wylie and Russell-Mayhew). While this book could not address all topical matters related to mother's oppression and subjugation, I believe this volume contributes to underscoring the profound ways that motherhood as an institution is oppressive and damaging and at the same time honors the empowering practices of mothering. This book draws out the mother's panopticon and both highlights our madness and celebrates our evermore resistance.

REFERENCES

Badinter, E. *The Conflict: How Modern Motherhood Undermines the Status of Women*. Toronto: HarperCollins Publishers, 2011.

Caplan, P. J. *Don't Blame Mother: Mending The Mother-Daughter Relationship*. New York: Harper and Row, 1989.

Caplan, P. *THE NEW Don't Blame Mother: Mending The Mother-Daughter Relationship*. New York: Routledge, 1989.

Caplan, P. *They Say You're Crazy: How The World's Most Powerful Psychiatrists Decide Who's Normal*. Jackson, MI: Da Capo Press, 1995.

Caplan, P., and L. Cosgrove, eds. *Bias in Psychiatric Diagnosis*. Lanham, Maryland: Jason Aronson, 1992.

Chesler, P. *Women and Madness*. New York: Palgrave Macmillan, 2005.

Douglas, S. J., and M. W. Michaels. *The Mommy Myth: The Idealization of Motherhood and How It Has Undermined Women*. New York: Free Press, 2004.

Eng, P. *Warrior Lessons*. New York: Pocket Books, 1999.

Foucault, M. *Discipline and Punish: The Birth of the Prison*. Harmondsworth, UK: Penguin, 1979.

Foucault, M. *Madness and Civilization: A History of Insanity in the Age of Reason*. New York: Vintage Books, 1989.

Green, F. J. "Matroreform: Feminist Mothers and Their Daughters Creating Feminist Motherlines." *Journal of the Association for Research in Mothering,* 10 (2) (2008): 11-21.

Green, F. J. *Practicing Feminist Mothering.* Winnipeg, Manitoba: Arbeiter Ring Publicating, 2011.

Hays, S. *The Cultural Contradictions of Motherhood.* New Haven: Yale University Press, 1996.

Maushart, S. *The Mask of Motherhood: How Becoming a Mother Changes Everything and Why We Pretend It Doesn't.* Toronto: Penguin Books, 2000.

O'Reilly, A. *Mother Outlaw: Theories and Practices of Empowered Mothering.* Toronto: Women's Press, 2004a.

O'Reilly, A. *Mother Matters: Motherhood as Discourse and Practice.* Toronto: Association for Research on Mothering, 2004b.

O' Reilly, A. *Rocking the Cradle: Thoughts on Motherhood, Feminism and the Possibility of Empowered Mothering.* Toronto: Demeter Press, 2006.

O'Reilly, A. *The 21st Century Motherhood Movement: Mothers Speak Out on Why We Need to Change the World and How to Do It.* Bradford, ON: Demeter Press, 2011.

O'Reilly, A., M. Porter and P. Short, eds. 2005. *Motherhood: Power and Oppression.* Toronto: Women's Press.

Rich, A. *Of Woman Born: Motherhood as Experience and Institution.* London: Virago Press, 1986 [1977].

Ruddick, S. *Maternal Thinking.* Boston: Beacon Press, 1989.

Schafer, A. *Breaking the Good Mom Myth: Every Modern Mom's Guide to Getting Past Perfection, Regaining Sanity, and Raising Great Kids.* Mississauga, ON: John Wiley and Sons Canada, 2009.

Twomey, T. *Understanding Postpartum Psychosis: A Temporary Madness.* Westport, CT: Praeger Publishers, 2009.

Wong-Wylie, G. "Images and Echoes in Matroreform: A Cultural Feminist Perspective." *Journal of the Association for Research on Mothering,* 8 (1,2) (2006): 35-146.

Wong-Wylie, G. "Matroreform." *Encyclopedia of Motherhood.* Ed. Andrea O'Reilly. Thousand Oaks, CA: Sage Press, 2010. 739-740.

Wong-Wylie, G. and S. Russell-Mayhew, "No 'Body' to Blame? Sociocultural Influences on Girls and Women." Ed. L. Ross. *Counselling Women: Feminist Issues, Theory and Practice.* Toronto: Canadian Scholars' Press/ Women's Press, 2010. 195-219.

I. MOTHERHOOD:
MADNESS AND OPPRESSION

1.
Mothers, Madness and the Labour of Feminist Practice

Responding to Women in the Perinatal Period

JULES E. SMITH AND MARINA MORROW

A S FIRST DESCRIBED by Susan Penfold and Gillian Walker (1983, 1986), the psychiatric paradox positions psychiatry as an institution that maintains and reinforces women's oppression by propping up longstanding beliefs about women's status and roles in society. That is, although psychiatry purports to help women, it actually socially regulates them (Penfold and Walker 1986). This critique drew on the work of early second wave feminists in the United States (e.g., Chesler) and in Canada (e.g., Smith and David) who showed how medical science and psychiatry, in particular, pathologized femininity. Feminists were not the first or only group to critically assess psychiatry. The roots of such an assessment are traceable to Michel Foucault (Lagrange) and, later, to critics writing from both inside the discipline (e.g., Szasz) and outside, including those disenfranchised or damaged by psychiatry (e.g., Burstow and Weitz; Capponi 1992, 2003; Shimrat). But feminists were the first to specifically articulate that mental health is a gendered concept (Barnes and Bowl). That is, our very notions of mental health, mental illness, and madness arise from discursive and clinical practices that have positioned women as more vulnerable to mental instability (Morrow). Nowhere has this insight proven more salient than in discussions about women's reproductive mental health, where, beginning with Freud's work on hysteria, women's reproductive organs and hormones have been tied to women's emotionality, volatility, and madness (Ussher 2006).

Although the place of women in relation to psychiatry and the mental health care system has evolved, we argue that the psychiatric paradox remains a highly useful concept, particularly for understanding women's distress and their reproductive mental health. Indeed, feminist critiques have become adept at excavating the broader structural and institutional factors that shape approaches to women's mental health (e.g., Appignanesi; Caplan and Cosgrove; Chan, Chunn, and Menzies; Morrow 2008). In particular, they have demonstrated how the continued dominance of biomedicine in mental health and the adoption of neoliberal discourses reinforce individualistic responses to the complex problems experienced by women during the perinatal period. Neoliberal discursive strategies work against social and structural understandings of women's mental health and impede the implementation of programs and supports that recognize the interplay of biology, psychology, and the social worlds of women (Morrow 2008; Morrow, Wasik, Cohen and Elah Perry). In our efforts to understand the disjunctures between official scientific discourses about women's mental health in the perinatal period and women's complex experiential knowledge of that time in their lives, we have been influenced by the work of Dorothy Smith (1987, 2005, 2006) and the analytic contributions of institutional ethnography (Mykhalovskiy; Roth; Townsend). Institutional ethnography starts with people's lived experiences and then aims to understand them in the context of larger social and institutional processes (Smithß 1987, 2006). In this instance, we are concerned with how women's lives as mothers are organized through multiple social practices and institutions (Weigt). Our intention is to inform feminist clinical practice as well as service and policy development in the area of reproductive mental health. Smith reminds us that through identifying problematic institutional practices, there are possibilities for change from within (Smith 1987).

In what follows we use institutional ethnography to analyze the stories of three women (Lucia, Grace, and Rani[1]) reporting emotional distress or maternal unhappiness during pregnancy and after the birth of their babies. These stories are drawn directly from one of the author's clinical practice, and in composite represent a variety of women's reactions and experiences. The author used her extensive experience of counseling women and drew on approximately ten women's cases to develop the composite stories. The composites were also developed to accurately represent a range of diverse social locations and intersecting forms of oppression in the lives of women. Although the emerging information is not necessarily generalizable to all women, it reveals how the change in social location experienced by women entering motherhood subjects them to multiple institutional discourses (medical, psychiatric, social welfare, immigration). We then link the everyday experiences of these women to the larger political and policy context and the discursive practices in this realm that shape mental health care for women. We argue that analyses that foreground the social and structural determinants of mental health are imperative for understanding women's diverse experiences and needs.

EXPLORING TENSIONS WITHIN THE PARADOX

The feminist response to the psychiatric paradox has resulted in two strategies for undermining it to women's advantage. The first is a vibrant critique of psychiatry and the mental health system for its abuses, including challenges to the diagnostic categories of the *DSM* and illustrations of how women's so-called madness is often an understandable response to wider social conditions. The second is a movement to work within the mental health system to address the needs and concerns of women.[2] Specifically with regards to reproductive mental health, the task has been to challenge traditional pathologizing dis-courses about women, madness, and reproduction while keeping the very real mental health issues associated with the perinatal period (pregnancy and postpartum) on the mental health agenda. Maintaining simultaneous attention to the relevance of both for the support and care of women is what Jane Ussher refers to as a "material discursive intra-psychic approach" (2005: 19). Recent writings highlight the challenges in developing an agenda that negotiates between, on the one hand, the individualistic discourses of bio-psychiatry and psycho-social approaches to care; and, on the other, socio-political framings of the causes of mental illness, which situate women's experiences of pregnancy, postpartum, and motherhood in a profoundly sexist social context that also fails to recognize or support the work of mothering (Landy; Morrow, Smith, Lai and Jaswal; Ussher and Perz). Indeed, there are few direct accounts of feminist approaches to perinatal depression, as most of the current research comes out of the medical field. In response to this dearth, Ruth Cain calls for a "feminist reassessment of maternal distress" and argues for postpartum depression to be "analyzed in bio-political terms" (123). Cain's analysis of the consequences for women of reproducing include: lower status; entry into a privatized space of mothering without macro-structural supports; and negative impact on work choices resulting from the need for flexible and/or reduced work hours. Yet the loss of status, financial independence, and career mobility are rarely included in an analysis of perinatal depression. The construction of perinatal depression as a collection of symptoms that have a purchasable cure, results in mothers' self-regulation rather than social or collective solutions to the problems of childcare and rearing. But Cain also warns that feminists who follow a social constructionist version of depression may minimize "the huge physical, emotional and social shifts experienced differently by every woman who has or rears a child" and the need to pay attention to the impact this has psychologically as well as "the chemical changes which narrate an embodied range of potential responses to social and cultural pressures" (136).

Daniel Stern writes about the intra-psychic aspects of mothering and how they are shaped by cultural and political contexts through the concept of the motherhood constellation, which encompasses the intricacies of mother/infant relations and women's identities as mothers. Factors that influence the formation of the constellation include the contradiction of the value placed on babies and their desirability, and the expectation that mothers should care for babies without experience, training, or support (Stern). One outcome of this is self-regulation by mothers themselves on the continuum of good to unfit mothering (Cain). Feelings and activities on the negative end of the continuum are those associated with maternal mental illness (Cain). The narrative of mothering then becomes biomedicalized and elides the social and cultural conditions that are part of a mother's everyday/everynight life (Smith 1987).

The Canadian Mental Health "Recovery" Study Working Group contextualizes self-regulation in a global market economy that demands a flexible self that can change according to the demands of social and economic orders. This self-reflexivity is experienced differently depending on one's social location. Privilege begets privilege, as the person with greater resources can take advantage of changing conditions, while marginalized persons must fit themselves to circumstance. They are also assigned a moral duty to take personal responsibility for structural forces affecting their well-being (Mental Health "Recovery" Study Working Group). Thus, women who have privilege may benefit from an official diagnosis of perinatal depression, as this may enable them to select from a range of resources that could improve their personal well-being. Women who occupy a social location of oppression will often find themselves subject to the further intrusion of institutional intervention and case management. The Mental Health "Recovery" Working Group calls for a move away from the privatization that Cain terms "the maternal habitus of depression" (Cain 123) and highlights the need to constitute the self as social, in that it cannot be known outside of its relationship with others. Citizenship and, by extension, the role of mother, are not universal definitions but dialectic, "informed by difference defined by distinct social experience according to social location" (Mental Health "Recovery" Study Working Group 33). This approach invites women to become producers and interpreters of knowledge emerging from their experience, rather than placing their experience within predefined and increasingly medicalized concepts such as perinatal depression, which may, in turn, regulate their lives. The reality is that "speech may be free but the means of making one's self heard and having one's position given credence are not equally available to all" (Coates and Wade 511).

The dominant discourse of the medical establishment regarding maternal unhappiness has also been challenged by the emergence of memoirs by mothers. Ivana Brown examines the public discourse on gender, reproduction, and motherhood as revealed through recently published memoirs, personal short stories, and essays. Women's stories reveal how the social practices of mothering are structured to distort natural differences between mothers and fathers; and to justify current gender relations and inequities. In the memoirs Brown analyzed, women who identified as feminists were unhappy with the social position they found themselves in as new mothers: isolated, exhausted, left alone all day with a baby, and having to adjust their lives far more than men. In this light, postpartum depression can be understood as the expression of feelings of inequality, injustice, and powerlessness: the three conditions that are most likely to make women angry (Petrachek). The women in Brown's analysis felt relief when baby care was divided equitably among themselves and others. Unsurprisingly, this was often dependent on their ability to afford paid childcare or domestic labour supplied by racialized, immigrant, or working-class women.

In practice, shifting the question from, "what is wrong with this woman?" (privatized, individualized conception of mental illness) to "what happened to this woman?" (social, shared relations, unequal access to power) generates knowledge that reveals, for example, the mental health implications of violence, social exclusion, and social inequalities (Williams and Paul). Asking women how they orient themselves to the gendered nature of motherhood elicits new narratives. Recall that for Ussher (2005) the material conditions of women's lives (poverty, sexism, racism) must be valued alongside the discursive (language, culture, power, and ideology as it manifests, in this instance, through psychiatry and medicine) and the intra-psychic (individual and psychological aspects of women's lives) to enable adequate support and care of women in mental distress. Each aspect is integrated and grounded in a critical realist epistemological paradigm that can be used to respond to distress without decontextualizing her experiences from the larger social and discursive context (Ussher 2005).

INSTITUTIONAL ETHNOGRAPHY AS A USEFUL ANALYTIC FRAME

As we've highlighted, institutional ethnography begins with women's lived experiences and then analyzes the social and institutional processes that shape that experience (Devault and McCoy; Smith, 1987, 2005). Women themselves are thus not the focus of inquiry, rather institutional ethnography involves the explication of ruling relations that affect her everyday/everynight life to expose the ways in which social relations and the practice of mothering are organized by race, class, and gender (Smith 2005) and translate into experiences of oppression or privilege. For Smith, ruling relations are the forms of consciousness and organization that are objectified in the sense that they are constituted externally to particular people and places—a specialized complex of objectified forms of organization and consciousness that organizes and coordinates people's everyday lives (Smith 1987, 2005).

Institutional ethnography has been applied to the work of mothering (see Griffith; Griffith and Smith) and to analyses of women and psychiatry (Hak; Smith 1978), but less often to the intersections between psychiatry and mothering (Landy). Even rarer are accounts of how the knowledge produced through institutional ethnography can be used by health professionals to work with women in the perinatal period in such a way as to treat this time as an extension of the women's ordinary, everyday knowledge while identifying the relations of ruling that organize their mothering activities (Pozzuto, Arnd-Caddigan, and Averett).

The analysis that follows is a step towards such a guide. It is our contention that the structures and systems in which women's lives become embedded during the perinatal period can make them more vulnerable to oppression. That is, social inequities are exposed as the rigidity of social expectations, thus, roles and labour are accentuated, especially in relation to gender. Whereas a woman may have been able to negotiate social networks in a relatively autonomous way before becoming a mother, she is now more dependent on these networks—family and in-laws, the legal system, social welfare and community resources—which may function in oppressive ways.

The composite stories that follow demonstrate how women get caught in systems of inequity and are vulnerable because of their roles as mothers, and the subsequent effect this has on their emotional well-being. Here, institutional ethnography provides a pathway linking the micro everyday/everynight worlds of mothers and macro institutional practices. Richard Pozzuto, Margaret Arnd-Caddigan and Paige Averett put forward the notion of a macro-practitioner; that is, a health care professional who works on behalf of the woman to help them "understand and repair the ways in which objectification has undermined their identity and well-being" (13).

STORIES OF MOTHERS GONE "MAD"

LUCIA

Lucia is a 21-year-old woman from Chile awaiting approval of her refugee claim. Unable to live with her parents for political reasons, as a child, she lived with different aunts and uncles. She does not feel close to anyone in her extended family except a female cousin who also lives in Canada. She has recently married a man from Spain named Alex. Alex has no legal status as he entered Canada on a student visa that has now expired. Shortly after they met, Alex began requesting that they have a child together, as he wanted to have a family with her. Lucia becomes pregnant, they marry and as the pregnancy progresses Alex's behaviour towards her becomes increasingly abusive, especially after she stops working in her second trimester. Lucia feels traumatized by the difficult labour and delivery she experiences. Her husband continues to isolate, demean and control her. Alex refuses to participate in the care of the baby or do any of the labour in the home, and he gets angry at both the

26

baby and Lucia when his expectations are not met. Lucia is having difficulty sleeping and concentrating, and she is very weepy. She states she never wanted to be a mother and had wanted to continue to study English and pursue a career. She is demoralized by Alex's behaviour and hopes that it is stress that is making Alex act so abusively. Lucia is referred to a mental health program by her public health nurse, and receives a psychiatric assessment and diagnosis of major depressive disorder, relapse in postpartum, post-traumatic stress disorder (PTSD) and substance abuse in remission. She begins medications, which help her sleep, although she still has to attend to her baby at night, as Alex refuses to get up. Lucia feels overwhelmed to be in a situation that she vowed never to find herself in. She alternates between thinking about ending her life and resuming illicit drug use. Her refugee claim is turned down and she is deported to Chile.

In institutional ethnography, texts (such as the DSM-IV-TR) represent the juncture between people's daily lives and the method by which individuals are coordinated extra-locally (Corman). These texts also coordinate and organize the work of mental health professionals as well as the lives of women. Michael Corman produces a map of the regulating discourse to illustrate how psychiatric assessment displaces experiential knowledge of both the mother and the practitioner into a textually mediated form. This framing and organizing leaves the everyday and context-contingent nature of oppression and privilege unaccounted for (Corman; Hulko). Only by using the events of everyday lives to highlight intersectional identities and bring the dynamics of privilege and oppression to life can relations of ruling be made real (Hulko).

In the story of Lucia, institutional ethnography helps to reveal how the funneling of this woman's experience and social relations into a set of symptoms and a diagnosis obscures the multiple domains in which her life is actually lived. Her life and that of other mothers are organized by textual knowledge that reinforce the relations of ruling—in this instance, the intersection of biomedicine, immigration processes and scripts of patriarchy and motherhood—that, in turn, displace Lucia's experiential knowledge of Lucia.

GRACE

Grace is a 34-year-old woman who has been married for several years to Albert. Grace has recently given birth to a baby girl, Lily, after a healthy pregnancy and uncomplicated delivery. They live with Albert's parents. Albert and his parents run a family business. The business has been impacted by the economy. Grace has been requesting that they find their own place to live, but Albert claims they can no longer afford to. He works long hours and spends very little time with his daughter. Some of the supports that Grace had access to (doula support, housecleaning) have been withdrawn based on the change in their financial circumstances. Grace is struggling with managing all the tasks associated with being a mother coupled with constant criticism from her mother-in-law and husband. It is difficult for her to leave the house without her mother-in-law's interference. She is hurt that Albert defers to his mother and feels isolated and powerless in her own home. She misses her work, her colleagues and her financial independence. She would like to go back to work, but her husband does not want her to. She does not know how to get her husband to take her concerns seriously, he feels that they "are crazy" and that most women would be grateful to stay home with their baby and have so much family support. She wonders if her expectations are too high, if maybe she is a perfectionist and has an anger management problem, since she is always irritable. She has also heard that this is a sign of post partum depression (PPD) and wants to know if she is depressed.

Grace's story highlights how the biomedicalized discourse surrounding post-partum depression is often internalized by women and acquires explanatory power. The language surrounding depression and anxiety is often exploited by the perpetrators in abusive relationships to undermine the victim (e.g., what's wrong with you? you are controlling/ irrational/ overly emotional/ unmotivated, etc.). The responses a woman gives to questions from her health care professional may privilege this discourse, locate the problem as situated within her, and minimize or negate her experience of the multiple features of oppression: powerlessness, marginalization, exploitation, and violence (Hulko).

Displacement of subjective knowledge is exacerbated by the fact that violence and abuse often increase in the perinatal period. Linda Coates and Allan Wade argue that misrepresentation in personalized violence is commonplace, but for different reasons for perpetrators and victims. For perpetrators, it is used to manipulate public appearances, entrap victims, conceal violence, and avoid responsibility. Women will use language to escape or reduce violence, conceal all or part of their resistance, retain maximum control of their circumstances, and avoid condemnation and social pressure from third parties (Coates and Wade). Thus, the possibility that women would downplay their experiences of violence during a psychiatric assessment is likely where women are often concerned about the safety of themselves and their babies, including the consequences of judgment regarding their "fitness" as mothers.

Providers need to be aware of this when assessing a woman in the presence of her partner as this may change the representation of her experience. The elaborate network of discursive practices that are used to misrepresent others as deficient and in need of assistance from capable authorities (Coates and

Wade) is where mental health practitioners may unwittingly collude with the perpetrators of oppression.

RANI

Rani is a 30-year-old woman who lives with her partner Kal and their infant son. Rani has been re-experiencing panic and anxiety since the birth of her baby. Kal wants to fully participate in the care of the baby but works long hours to make up for the loss of Rani's income. Rani's parents immigrated from India and worked long hours, leaving her and her sister unsupervised and in the care of older male cousins who abused them from the ages of five to eleven. Her mother was supportive when she disclosed the abuse, but her father denied it (his older brother's sons were the perpetrators), forbade Rani's mother to discuss it and now controls her visits with Rani. Rani has seen a variety of mental health professionals over the years. She has a history of several psychiatric diagnoses including PTSD, Obsessive Compulsive Disorder (OCD), Generalized Anxiety Disorder (GAD) and substance abuse. She is thrilled with her baby and is so concerned about any harm coming to him that she has recurring intrusive thoughts of falling down the stairs with him, dropping him from heights and drowning him in the bathtub. She is worried that she will not be able to protect her son from being abused. She can't sleep and will only leave the baby with Kal, so she does not get many breaks. She loves and cares for her baby well but adds up all the errors she has made and is beginning to feel like a bad mother. She does not want to take medication but has been told by several health care providers who have attended Post Natal Depression training that she will cause her son harm if she does not get her depression and anxiety treated.

In an attempt to raise awareness about mental health among community health care providers, a heavy emphasis has been placed on biomedical discourses that privilege medical approaches to treatment, and the consequences of failing to take mental health seriously. This is particularly true for perinatal depression, where the emphasis is on the impact of depressed and/or anxious mothers on the fetus or infant. The health of the fetus/infant is often the site where differing social locations can have large implications on the outcome of the mother's wellbeing, depending on how closely she is regulated through state and government interventions (e.g., involving Ministries related to children's welfare).

Adele Clarke et al. have noted that "the growth of medicalization—defined as the processes through which aspects of life previously outside the jurisdiction of medicine come to be construed as medical problems—is one of the most potent social transformations of the last half of the twentieth century in the West" (161-162). No one professional group is responsible. Biomedical discourses have become so fully integrated into everyday talk that they appear unproblematic until examined in detail and compared to the experiences they are presumed to represent (Coates and Wade). It is therefore critical that careful consideration of the construction of perinatal depression is given in the education of health care providers. Wolff-Michael Roth has written on the need to include patients in the production and interpretation of data to break open the power/knowledge boundary that currently exists between providers and patients. He reminds us that when "knowledge is articulated collectively, power comes to be enacted collectively as well" (170). The prefigured concept of perinatal depression can permeate and frame a woman's life. The everyday/every night lives of mothers are replaced by conceptual terms that mediate them. That the social, cultural, and individual conditions of a woman's life will be expressed in her (or lack of) mental well-being must be legitimized.

SITUATING MOTHERS' EXPERIENCES IN THE LARGER DISCURSIVE REALM

Mothers' experiences of emotional distress and the professional responses to this distress are taking place within a larger political and policy context. This context includes neoliberal political agendas which favour reduced social welfare spending and individualistic conceptualizations of social problems (Morrow 2006). The struggle to get women's mental health issues on a wider political agenda is thus not only difficult, but also subject to co-optation by the prevailing neoliberal discourses, as mediated through biomedicalism in mental health care. Retaining feminist social and structural understandings of women's mental health requires vigilance on the part of mental health care practitioners so that they do not reproduce negative patterns of ruling relations that objectify women (Pozzuto, Arnd-Caddigan and Averett). Such reframing requires situating women's experiences of pregnancy, postpartum, and motherhood in a social context and working towards recognition and support for the work of mothering.

[1]Composite stories and pseudonyms have been used to protect women's confidentiality.
[2]Examples include the recognition by psychiatrists of battered women's syndrome as a way of understanding women's violent responses to men who have repeatedly victimized them; an expansion of the definition of post-traumatic

stress disorder to account for women's responses to severe childhood and adult abuse (Herman); and the development of women-centred or women-specific services (Haskell). It should be noted that debate continues over whether these steps fully encompass a structural understanding of women's oppression (see for example, Morrow 2008; Becker; Linder).

REFERENCES

Appignanesi, L. *Mad, Bad and Sad: A History of Women and the Mind Doctors from 1800 to the Present.* London: Verago Press, 2008.

Barnes, M. and R. Bowl. *Taking Over the Asylum: Empowerment and Mental Health.* Basingstoke, Hampshire: Palgrave, 2001.

Becker, D. "When She Was Bad: Borderline Personality Disorder in a Post-traumatic Age." *American Journal of Orthopsychiatry* 70 (4) (2000): 422-432.

Brown, I. "Mommy Memoirs: Feminism, Gender and Motherhood in Popular Literature." *Mothering and Feminism* 8 (1/2) (2006): 200-212.

Burstow, B. and D. Weitz, eds. *Shrink Resistant: The Struggle Against Psychiatry in Canada.* Vancouver: New Star, 1988.

Cain, R. "'A View You Won't Get Anywhere Else?' Depressed Mothers, Public Regulation and 'Private' Narrative." *Feminist Legal Studies* 17 (2009): 123-143.

Caplan, P. J. and L. Cosgrove, eds. *Bias in Psychiatric Diagnosis.* New York: The Rowman and Littlefield Publishing Group, 2004.

Capponi, P. *Upstairs in the Crazy House: The Life of a Psychiatric Survivor.* Toronto: Viking, 1992.

Capponi, P. *Beyond the Crazy House: Changing the Future of Madness.* Toronto: Penguin, 2003.

Chan, W., D. Chunn and R. Menzies, eds. *Women, Madness and the Law: A Feminist Reader.* London: Glasshouse, 2005.

Chesler, P. *Women and Madness.* New York: Avon Books, 1972.

Clarke, A. E., J. K. Shim, L. Mamo, J. R. Fosket, and J. R. Fishman. "Bio-medicalization: Technoscientific Transformations of Health, Illness, and U.S Biomedicine." *American Sociological Review* 68 (2003): 161-194.

Coates, L. and A. Wade. "Language and Violence: Analysis of Four Discursive Operations." *Journal of Family Violence* 22 (7) (2007): 511-22.

Corman, M. *Panning for Gold: An Institutional Ethnography of Health Relations and The Process of Diagnosing Autism in British Columbia.* Victoria: Society for the Study of Social Problems, 2007. Web. Retrieved December 13, 2009.

DeVault, M. L. and L. McCoy. "Institutional ethnography: UsinGrifg interviews to investigate ruling relations." Eds. J. F. Gubrium and J. A. Holstein. *Handbook of Interview Research: Context and Method.* Thousand Oaks, CA: Sage, 2002. 751-776

Foucault, M. *History of Madness*. Trans. J. Kahlfa and J. Murphy. Oxford: Routledge, 2006 [1961].

Griffith, A. "Insider/Outsider: Epistemic Privilege and Mothering Work." *Human Studies* 21 (4) (1998): 361-376.

Griffith, A. and D. Smith. *Mothering for Schooling*. New York: Routledge, 2005.

Hak, T. "'There Are Clear Delusions': The Production of a Factual Account." *Human Studies* 21 (4) (1998): 419-36.

Haskell, L. *Bridging Responses: A Front-Line Worker's Guide to Supporting Women Who Have Post-Traumatic Stress*. Toronto: Centre for Addiction and Mental Health, 2001. Web. <www.camh.net>. Retrieved December 13, 2009.

Herman, J. (1992). *Trauma and Recovery*. New York: HarperCollins, 1992.

Hulko, W. "The Time- and Context-Contingent Nature of Intersectionality and Interlocking Oppressions." *Affilia* 24 (1) (2009): 44-55.

Landy Kurtz, C. *Women Who Are Socioeconomically Disadvantaged: Postpartum Experiences, Needs and Use of Services*. Unpublished dissertation. McMaster University, Hamilton, 2006. Web. <digitalcommons.mcmaster.ca/dissertations/?AAINR28216>.Retrieved December 13, 2009.

Lagrange, J., ed. *Michel Foucault Psychiatric Power Lectures at the College de France 1973-1974*. New York: Palgrave MacMillan, 2006.

Linder, M. "Creating Post-Traumatic Stress Disorder: A Case Study of the History, Sociology, and Politics of Psychiatric Classification." *Bias in Psychiatric Diagnosis*. Eds. P. J. Caplan and L. Cosgrove. New York: The Rowman and Littlefield Publishing Group, 2004. 25-40.

Mental Health "Recovery" Study Working Group. *Mental Health "Recovery": Users and Refusers*. Toronto: Wellesley Institute, 2009.

Morrow, M. (with S. Frischmuth and A. Johnson). *Community Based Mental Health Services in BC: Changes to Income, Employment and Housing Supports*. Vancouver: Canadian Centre for Policy Alternatives, 2006.

Morrow, M. "Women, Violence and Mental Illness: An Evolving Feminist Critique." *Global Science/Women's Health*. Eds. C. Patton and H. Loshny. New York: Teneo Press, 2008. 147-174.

Morrow, M., J. E. Smith, Y. Lai and S. Jaswal. "Shifting Landscapes: Immigrant Women and Postpartum Depression." *Health Care for Women International* 28 (6) (2008): 593-617.

Morrow, M., A. Wasik, M. Cohen and K.-M. Elah Perry. "Removing Barriers to Work: Building Economic Security for People With Mental Illness." *Critical Social Policy* 29 (4) (2009): 655-677.

Mykhalovskiy, E. "Towards a Sociology of Knowledge In Health Care: Exploring Health Services Research as Active Discourse." *Unhealthy times: The political economy of health and health care in Canada*. Eds. P. Armstrong, H. Armstrong and D. Coburn Toronto: Oxford University Press, 2001. 146-166.

Penfold, S. and G. Walker. *Women and the Psychiatric Paradox*. Montreal: Eden Press, 1983.

Penfold, S. and G. Walker. "The Psychiatric Paradox and Women." *Canadian Journal of Community Mental Health* 5 (2) (1986): 9-15.

Pozzuto, R., M. Arnd-Caddigan, and P. Averett. "Notes in Support of a Relational Social Work Perspective: A Critical Review of the Relational Literature with Implications for Macro Practice." *Smith College Studies in Social Work* 79 (2009): 5-16.

Roth, W.-M. "Living With Chronic Illness: An Institutional Ethnography of (Medical) Science and Scientific Literacy." Ed. W.-M. Roth. *Everyday Life in Science Education from People for People: Taking a Stand(point)*. New York: Routledge, 2009. 146-171.

Shimrat, I. *Call Me Crazy: Stories from the Mad Movement*. Vancouver: Press Gang, 1997.

Smith, D. "'K' is Mentally Ill: The Anatomy of a Factual Account." *Sociology* 12 (1) (1978): 23-53.

Smith, D. *The Everyday World as Problematic*. Boston: Northeastern University Press, 1987.

Smith, D. *Institutional Ethnography: A Sociology for People*. Victoria: University of Victoria Press, 2005.

Smith, D., ed. *Institutional Ethnography as Practice*. Lanham: Rowman and Littlefield, 2006.

Smith, D. and S. David, eds. *Women Look at Psychiatry*. Vancouver: Press Gang, 1975.

Szasz, T. *The Myth of Mental Illness: Foundations of a Theory of Personal Conduct*. New York: Hoeber-Harper, 1961.

Stern, D. *The Motherhood Constellation: A Unified View of Parent-Infant Psychotherapy*. New York: Basic Books, 1995.

Townsend, E. *Good Intentions Overruled: A Critique of Empowerment in the Routine Organization of Mental Health Services*. Toronto: University of Toronto Press, 1998.

Ussher, J. M. "Unravelling Women's Madness: Beyond Positivism and Construction and Towards a Material-Discursive-Intrapsychic Approach." Eds. W. Chan, D. E. Chunn, and R. Menzies. *Women, Madness and the Law: A Feminist Reader*. London: GlassHouse, 2005. 19-40.

Ussher, J. M. *Managing the Monstrous Feminine: Regulating the Reproductive Body*. London: Routledge, 2006.

Ussher, J. M. and J. Perz. "Empathy, Egalitarianism and Emotion Work in the Relational Negotiation of PMS: The Experience of Women in Lesbian Relationships." *Feminism and Psychology* 18 (1) (2008): 87-111.

Weigt, J. "Compromises to Carework: The Social Organization of Mothers'

Experiences in the Low-Wage Labor Market After Welfare Reform." *Social Problems* 53 (3) (2006): 332–351.

Williams, J. and J. Paul. *Informed Gender Practice: Mental Health Acute Care that Works for Women.* London: National Institute for Mental Health in England., 2008

2.
"The First Rule Is that a Mother Should Govern Her Own Feelings"

Modern Childrearing Advice and the Discipline of Maternal Emotions

ROBLYN RAWLINS

The first rule, and the most important of all, in education, is, that a mother should govern her own feelings and keep her heart and conscience pure. (Child 3)

LYDIA MARIA CHILD advised the above in *The Mother's Book*, one of the most influential childrearing advice books of the nineteenth century. The story of childrearing from the nineteenth century until today is replete with self-appointed childrearing experts proposing to guide mothers in making the best choices for their children. In this chapter, I review how nineteenth- and early twentieth-century childrearing experts constructed mothers' emotions as powerful and pathological forces that could greatly harm children, laying the historical groundwork for the discourses of emotional regulation of mothers and mother-blaming that are still so ubiquitous and so oppressive today.

Advice books for mothers were filled with cautionary tales that represented women as full of dangerous emotions that "good mothers" must control. The childrearing experts exhorted mothers to control their feelings of anxiety, worry, maternal love, and especially anger, or risk serious physical, emotional, and moral harm to their children. Calls for women to control their very thoughts and feelings are *prima facie* oppressive. Even worse, mothers who tried to be "good" by following the experts' advice and denying their own feelings of worry, fear, anxiety, maternal love, and anger must have inevitably failed to achieve perfect emotional self-control. In a cruel irony, these daily failures to control their thoughts and feelings may have caused mothers additional worry, fear, and anxiety and thus been doubly oppressive. Alternatively, one can imagine an empowered mother, filled with anger at the madness of the experts' recursive loops of oppression, throwing her childrearing advice book away—perhaps the ultimate act of resistance within modern motherhood.

By the mid–nineteenth century, there was a broad Anglo-American consensus that the care of young children was an exacting, time-consuming, and important activity that should be at the center of women's lives and that mothers were the most important moral educators of children. Paradoxically, the same processes of modernity that created the image of mothers as ultimately responsible for installing a durable sense of conscience and self-regulation in their children devalued their traditional knowledge of mothering. Expert voices and scientific prescriptions for child rearing rose steadily from the mid-nineteenth century onward (Apple). The changing nature of childrearing expertise is part of the ascendance of specialized knowledge/language/power beginning the nineteenth century (Foucault). Knowledge about the most basic, human activity of caring for a child was no longer considered part of the social stock of knowledge or maternal instinct, available to all mothers, but was becoming the province of specialized experts who made it their business to instruct and discipline mothers.

During the late nineteenth century and early twentieth century, physicians, academic experts, educators, philanthropists, reformers, and women's groups such as the National Congress of Mothers called for the reconstruction of traditional motherhood into what was viewed as scientific, rational, modern motherhood (Apple). According to the experts, mothers needed education and expert guidance. American and English childrearing experts published, and consumers purchased, hundreds of childrearing advice books to instruct mothers in modern motherhood (Apple; Grant).[1]

One of the most striking findings of my broader research into late nineteenth and early twentieth century Anglo-American childrearing prescriptions is that modern childrearing prescriptions, although putatively directed at children, in fact disciplined mothers across more domains of everyday life and in more severe ways than they did children (Rawlins). Childrearing experts articulated and disseminated theories about maternal influence on fetuses and children that led to prescriptions exhorting women to discipline their bodies, behavior, thoughts, and especially their emotions. This work demonstrates that the contemporary practice of mother-blaming (the practice of crediting mothers with much influence over their children and holding them responsible for children who are troubled or who cause trouble) has its roots in the nineteenth century and thus contributes a historical perspective to the current literature on mother-blaming (see for example, Ladd-Taylor and Umansky).

This chapter is based on my analysis of 117 American and 81 English childrearing advice books published primarily between 1850 and 1930. The criteria for selection were that books must: 1) focus specifically on childrearing; 2) be written primarily or exclusively for a lay audience of mothers/parents; and 3) be published by a private author or non-governmental organization (because I was interested in studying expert advice as a consumer good, I examined only those for-profit books published by private authors or organizations and excluded advice published or financed by the state). It is difficult to ascertain the representativeness of the selected manuals: there is no reliable index to the popularity of books during the study period. I sought to minimize this problem by, first, taking the largest available sample. I identified and included books that met the basic selection criteria in the comprehensive collections of the New York Public Library, the Schlesinger Library for the History of Women, and the British Library. Following Stephanie A. Shields and Beth A. Koster, I reasoned that those books that were easily accessible would tend to be those that had been popular and/or widely available. I used multiple indicators to ensure the inclusion of the most popular and influential texts, including those texts with multiple editions, those authors and texts that were cited by the authors of contemporaneous childrearing advice, those texts and authors included in previous studies of the childrearing literature, and texts authored by important childrearing experts as identified in the secondary literature.

Fully three-quarters of the texts I analyzed contained explicit prescriptions for the discipline and self-control of mothers. Childrearing experts urged mothers to control their behavior, to control their bodies through the control of appetites, expression, and demeanor, to control both the experience and expression of emotions, and even to control their thoughts, both before and after their children were born. Some experts indicated this emphasis on maternal discipline in the title of their childrearing manuals. From America came *The Mother's Book of Daily Duties* (Abell), *On the Training of Parents* (Abott) and *Self-Training for Mothers* (Chance), and from England, *The Mother's Thorough Resource-Book: Comprising Self-Discipline of the Expectant Mother* (Anonymous) and *The Mother's Home-Book: A Book for Her Own and Her Children's Management* (Anonymous).

There are no equivalent prescriptions calling for discipline and self-control of fathers in the childrearing advice manuals examined here. The importance of maternal self-control was sufficiently naturalized in childrearing discourse that few authors bothered to include explanations or rationales for their calls for generalized self-control and discipline of mothers, rather the experts took the necessity of maternal discipline and self-control as axiomatic. Winifred Sackville Stoner did buttress her typical call for maternal self-control by citing an expert popular among childrearing authors: "Herbert Spencer said that the training of child implies the most strenuous training of its mother, who must learn to control herself before she can control her little one" (211). Andrea Hofer Proudfoot wondered "how many mothers are thoroughly satisfied that they are capable of governing themselves before they try to govern their children..." and argued that "many of us are whipping out of our children things that we should have whipped out of ourselves before they were here" (122).

"FOR BABY'S SAKE": DISCIPLINING PRENATAL MATERNAL
EMOTIONALITY

The childrearing experts instructed pregnant mothers to control their very thoughts and feelings in order to ensure the well-being of their unborn children. In her 1853 *Mother's Book of Daily Duties, Containing Hints and Direction for the Body, Mind and Character*, Mrs. L. G. Abell listed the following daily duties under the heading of "Ourselves:" "When we are alone we have our *thoughts* to watch; in the family, our *tempers*; in company, our *tongues*" (171). Mrs. L. C. Tuthill warned mothers in 1855, "you cannot say with truth, "my thoughts, are they not mine own? and [sic] they leave no mark behind them" (135). The Englishwoman Emma Churchman Hewitt wrote in 1909 of how the mother's "physical health, her emotions, even her very thoughts, will affect the child she carries beneath her heart!" (10) and suggested that as a result:

> The first thing then toward training the child to a hearty, healthy physical condition and sane views of life would seem to be that the mother should hold a season of serious self-communion. In this, she should lay her heart and soul bare for self-inspection... she may make a list of her faults, her failings and her weaknesses, spiritual and physical... "For baby's sake!" That must be her watchword.... "For baby's sake" she must give up violent tempers and sulky fits, and cultivate serenity of mind. (12)

Emotional self-control is by far the most often called-for form of discipline for mothers in modern childrearing prescriptions. Nearly half of the advice manuals I analyzed contained prescriptions for mothers to control their emotions. According to childrearing experts, mothers had to strive for emotional self-control or else risk physical, moral, and emotional harm to their children before birth, while nursing, and throughout their young lives. The experts constructed maternal emotions as dangerous and pathological, including anxiety, worry, maternal love, and especially anger.

Although a few authors included in my large-scale review of the childrearing advice literature argued that pregnant women could not affect their fetuses through their experience of uncontrolled emotions or thoughts, modern childrearing experts were much more likely to support this model of prenatal maternal influence. The mechanisms by which a pregnant woman's thoughts, actions, emotions, morals, or experiences affected her fetus were not often specified, but some modern childrearing experts nevertheless made strong arguments, often by horrifying anecdote, that they did so (e.g., Bakewell; Bayer; Beecher; Napheys; Usher). The English childrearing expert Mrs. A. M.

Usher gave a typically dramatic rationale for her wide-sweeping prescriptions of self-control for pregnant women:

> The care of a child should begin when a woman first knows that she is going to become a mother … avoid all overfatigue, and, as far as possible, all shocks and disagreeable sights, and controlling the temper. These things make a great difference to the health and strength of the infant when born. The writer has herself seen two children who have had limbs broken before birth through the carelessness of the mother…." (1)

According to the childrearing experts, it was especially important for pregnant women to control their feelings of fear, depression, sadness, worry, and anxiety. For example, Mrs. J. Bakewell wrote in 1862 of "how much the future bodily health, mental vigour, and moral tendencies of their offspring, depend on [the mother's] own conduct and state of mind during pregnancy" (10) and urged pregnant women to "impress deeply on your mind… that by giving way to impatience and despondency, you will most probably entail upon your offspring a fretful and gloomy temper…" (11). Dr. George Napheys suggested a higher cost for babies born to women who failed in emotional control:

> There is now little room for doubt that various deformities and deficiencies of the fetus, conformably to the popular belief, do really originate in certain cases from nervous impressions, such as disgust, fear, or anger, experienced by the mother. Fright, anxiety, or other emotions in the mother, produce idiocy in the offspring. (155)

"OH, THIS RASH HUMOR MY MOTHER GAVE ME:"
DISCIPLINING MATERNAL ANGER

According to the experts, anger was the one emotion that mothers must control above all others. Of the childrearing manuals I analyzed, nearly half of the English texts contained prescriptions calling for maternal anger control, roughly twice the number calling for anger control among children, while over half of the American texts contained prescriptions calling for control of maternal anger, more than quadruple the number containing prescriptions for control of childhood anger. The childrearing experts evaluated maternal anger more negatively than they did childhood anger and included much more detailed and stringent prescriptions for the control of mothers' anger than for the control of children's. Modern childrearing experts argued that maternal anger was a powerful force holding great potential for harm to fetuses and children and that mothers must therefore continually strive to control their anger.

Childrearing experts utilized various rationales for prescribing anger control among postnatal mothers. The most often cited reason is that mothers could thereby help their children learn to control their own anger. For example, Edwina Keasbey wrote in 1886, "You must keep this guard upon your actions, not only in your immediate conduct with your child, but in all your daily life. If you show anger towards others, your children will soon follow your example" (78). According to Alice Acland, "We ourselves may help children to gain, or to retain, self-control by our own mastery of ourselves, because fuss and anxiety, or the reverse, seem to be almost as 'catching' as a bodily disease" (33). Some childrearing advisors argued that children's moral development would be thwarted if their mothers failed to control their own anger. According to Lydia Maria Child, "It is important that children, even when babes, should never be spectators of anger, or any evil passion.... The first and foremost thing ... is that the mother should keep her own spirit in tranquility and purity ... who can tell how much MORAL evil may be traced to the states of mind indulged by a mother..." (3).

According to some experts (see, for example, Bayer), anger in pregnant women could cause miscarriages and physical and mental abnormalities through stunting the normal development of the fetus. Other experts argued that anger in pregnant women would lead to the fetal development of a life-long propensity toward anger. For example, Virginia Terhune Van de Water wrote in 1912:

> The woman who makes her physical condition [pregnancy] an excuse for outbursts of petulance, for fits of hysterical weeping, for impatient speech and look, is injuring her baby as surely as herself. "Oh, this rash humor which my mother gave me!" might be the moan of many a man or woman marred in temper before birth by a mother's lack of self-control. (15)

Similarly, Dr. C. J. Bayer explained, "Dr. Greisner, an authority upon brain disorder, says that such outbursts of temper, or anger, on the part of a child, are a true mania, and are caused by malformation of the brain... because the mother had just such periods of ill-temper while the brain of her offspring was forming" (196).

Likewise, mothers of infants were advised to control any feelings of anger while nursing. The theory that strong emotions in nursing mothers, especially anger, poisoned breast milk appeared in one-third of manuals published through the 1870s and was presented with decreasing prevalence up until 1921, when Mary L. Read wrote of how "anger, worry, excitement produce poisons that render the milk indigestible, even poisonous" (104). For example, Eunice White Bullard Beecher warned mothers in 1873:

> If, unfortunately, you have allowed yourself to be overcome by anger, keep far away from the little one, till you have asked God to still the tempest, and feel that by his grace you are at peace. If in such an unhappy state you dare to perform a mother's sweetest duty, your child will bring you to repentance before many hours elapse. (260)

To illustrate her point, Beecher recounted the didactic story of a mother whose child died of convulsions after she had been "furiously angry with her husband…. The physician knew of her ungovernable temper, and, boarding with her, had been the witness of the morning's tornado. Over the suffering little creature, he sternly told her that her temper had killed her child" (260). This notion was a tremendously powerful discipline of nursing mothers, who were warned that if they failed to control their anger while nursing, their child would be made ill or perhaps even die.

"HERE OF LATE, I'M JUST SICK WITH WORRY:" THE CRUEL IRONY OF MATERNAL EMOTIONAL CONTROL

In what seems a cruel irony, the same experts who supplied the maternal imagination with detailed examples of the great harm uncontrolled maternal emotionality could cause children simultaneously urged mothers to control worry and anxiety. For example, Bayer, after listing many horrific examples of deformed children resulting from their mother's lack of control of her thoughts, warned mothers to not only control their thoughts, but also to control their anxiety about the possible consequences of lapses in their control: "And do not live in continual fear that something is going to happen. Such mental action will produce a nervous temperament, and your child will always live in fear that something is going to happen, and it will become, as it were, a bundle of nerves and be unable to control them" (205).

As the previous quotations illustrate, the mid-nineteenth through early twentieth century childrearing advice literatures of America and England abound with instances of mother-blaming based on inadequate maternal emotional control. For example, in his 1897 book *Maternal Impressions*, Bayer stated unequivocally that, "every case of abnormal mental or physical development is traceable to the mother's mental condition previous to the birth of her offspring" (8).[2] In the same vein, C. Phyllis Armitage, an English official health visitor and advice author, connected prescriptions for maternal control of worry and anxiety to true womanhood and added mother-blaming to punctuate her ideas:

> The mother who is always harassed and worried, nervy over her baby, expecting that he will not be well … has a very adverse effect on the health of her child.…A "womanly" woman, who expects her baby to be normal in every way, who does not worry over-much but 'takes things as they come,' generally does not have trouble with her children. (42)

This implies that women who did have trouble with their children were either not truly womanly or at fault because they failed to control their worry and anxiety, maternal emotions likely at least in part to have been prompted by reading expert advice on childrearing.

A mother who attempted to put into practice the experts' advice by completely denying her own feelings of worry, fear, and anxiety about her child must have inevitably failed to achieve perfect self-control. These daily failures generate their own maternal feelings of worry, fear, and anxiety. The English advisor Eliza Warren acknowledged the difficulties of controlling maternal anxieties when she wrote that "the influence of the mother upon the child begins even during her months of pregnancy; therefore it behooves her to keep herself from vexatious cares and perplexities, even as she would shun pestilence. To do this requires an almost superhuman effort, to be obtained only by prayers for help…" (7).

Current research into cognitive processes suggests that mothers attempting to put into practice these prescriptions to control their thoughts and emotions probably did experience more negative thoughts and emotions than they would have otherwise. A substantial body of experimental evidence collected by cognitive psychologist Daniel Wegner demonstrated how difficult the suppression of unwanted thoughts can be. In a classic study, Daniel M. Wegner (1989) found that when asked not to think of a white bear, people actually end up thinking about the white bear through what he terms an "ironic monitoring process" that searches for mental contents indicating failure to attain the desired state of mind (1994.) Thus, particularly in stressful circumstances, self-consciously trying to avoid unwanted thoughts or emotions often results in one's experiencing more of the unwanted thoughts or emotions (Wegner 1994.)

The advice to pregnant women or nursing mothers to avoid anxiety and worry functioned as a maternal discipline that ironically generated new anxieties and worries for mothers who read these advisors' prescriptions. Molly Ladd-Taylor's edited collection of mothers' letters to the United States Children's Bureau provides us with some insight on how early twentieth-century mothers experienced advice about self-control of thought processes and anxiety. For example, Mrs. O. W. wrote in 1918 that she had asked her physician several times about how to help her baby who suffered from digestive problems and cried a great deal, but "each time he tells me not to worry as it will affect the quality of the milk. Still I feel that my baby is not right and want some good advice. I cannot help but worry and cannot rest, as the Doctor advises..." (cited in Ladd-Taylor 105). (One cannot help but wonder if Mrs. O. W.'s physician may have been unable or unwilling to answer her questions about her child's health and used the proscription against worry to evade them.)

In 1925, Mrs. W. M. wrote to the Children's Bureau asking for advice and vividly illustrating the ironic monitoring process as regards maternal discipline of thought:

> ...I'm just worried sick. Its [sic] on my mind all the time. I wake up nights and think of things to eat; it seems I just can't get that off my mind and what can you do when you long for watermelon or mush melon, or anything out of season? I cant [sic] get these things now. Can that mark or harm the baby in any way? Oh please tell me what to do. All these thoughts about marking the baby when you dont [sic] eat what you think of, or long for, just drive me frantic. I think of one thing, and then I think of something else, but I try to over-come these thoughts ... here of late I'm just sick from worry. (cited in Ladd-Taylor 57)

CHILDREARING ADVICE AND THE DISCIPLINE OF MOTHERS

Maria Scott Chance's 1914 manual entitled *Self-Training for Mothers* exemplifies how prescriptions for maternal self-control of emotions resonated with stereo-types of femininity. By the late 19th century, the dominant conceptualization of the self as naturally based upon one's "innate" femininity or masculinity was firmly entrenched in Western culture and the qualities ascribed to femininity were widely considered inferior to those ascribed to masculinity. Chance wrote of how women's "hereditary faults," including "love of ease, caprice, self-indulgence, vacillation of purpose, indecision, hastiness of speech" are such that the "very simplicity and directness of the child's mind causes him to rebel instinctively against them" (6). Note that the child here is male and his superiority to his mother is that of men over women: the generic child of nineteenth and early twentieth century childrearing advice was a male child. Chance advised mothers to hide their devalued feminine qualities through surveillance and control of the self: "Only by virtue of self-control can the mother keep her vagaries hidden within herself..." (7).

For Maria Scott Beale Chance and other childrearing experts, women's supposedly natural and essential characteristics—emotionality, impulsiveness, weakness, irrationality—stood in opposition to the characteristics of disciplined self-control making up the ideal modern self. Rationality or reason is an integral part of the modern self, and "reason has been constructed as a masculine domain that is divorced from and deemed superior to the senses, emotion, and imagination" (Diamond and Quinby 15). Therefore, maternal self-control of woman's natural characteristics was imperative in modern childrearing and the modern mother had to work to suppress those anti-modern characteristics she was believed to possess by virtue of her womanhood.

As noted, the modern childrearing literature from the United States and England reflects an almost obsessive concern with disciplining maternal emotionality. The construction of maternal emotions as powerful and potentially pathological is part and parcel of a wider cultural concern over female emotion generally. Feminists have argued that the hysteria which was so widespread among middle-class women in the nineteenth century represents "the crystallization in a pathological mode of a widespread cultural obsession" (Bartky 66) with the control of women's emotions. As Carroll Smith-Rosenberg has suggested, for many women the hysterical fit must have been the only possible outburst of rage or despair. This form of emotional release and *madness* was denied mothers by expert childrearing advisors.

The experts' insistence that mothers must control their emotions reflects concern over women's emotionality in general. Childrearing experts believed that women's emotions were powerful forces liable to veer out of control and therefore representing potential threats to the healthy development of fetuses and children. Ulrich Beck argued that the modern sensibility finds the uncontrolled and uncontrollable threatening and anxiety-provoking. This sense of threat, together with the sexism expressed in the nineteenth-century masculinist discourses associated with the "horrors of the half-known life" as discussed in G. J. Barker-Benfield's classic text of the same name, resulted in widespread cultural concern with the control of women's emotions. The childrearing experts studied here represented women as full of dangerous emotions that continually threaten to escape the bonds of self-control within which modern mothers must struggle to contain them, "for baby's sake."

SUMMARY

As this chapter has demonstrated, theories of maternal influence on fetuses and children worked together with older ideas about women's emotionality to give rise to detailed and stringent prescriptions calling for the discipline of mothers across many domains, but focusing primarily on mother's emotional control. Childrearing experts insisted that women who failed to live up to these prescriptions for self-control caused harm to their children and were thus culpable for poor childrearing or birth outcomes, while simultaneously setting into motion what I have called the cruel irony of maternal control of anxiety.

Expert knowledge about childrearing constructed motherhood as both powerful and potentially pathological. Thus, childrearing advice literature functioned as a disciplinary technology for women. The idea of disciplinary technologies is Foucaultian in premise: a disciplinary technology is an institutionalized mechanism that indoctrinates and regulates individuals, social groups, and populations through power/knowledge (Foucault). The childrearing advice literature that I examined constitutes such a disciplinary technology, generating expert knowledge that disciplined mothers by promoting the relentless self-monitoring, self-regulation, and self-control of their bodies, their behavior, their emotions, their selves. A discipline that calls for women to control their very thoughts and feelings demonstrates how modern disciplinary power—how the panopticon, the faceless gaze, surveillance (Foucault)—is far-reaching indeed and unfortunately, is not just a thing of the past.

[1] I use a specifically social scientific definition of modernity here, and exclude conceptualizations of modernity and/or modernism employed primarily in the humanities and elsewhere. Modern, modernity, and modernism are extremely ambiguous terms: modern may be used to refer to anything which is viewed as contemporary rather than traditional; modernity is often equated with modernization or economic and technological development only; and modernism most often refers to a movement in the arts beginning around 1850 and continuing through 1950 (Cahoone). While the period of history that has been termed "Early Modern"—from the end of the Middle Ages until about the seventeenth century—is important formatively, the period in which modern notions of selfhood become well established begins around the mid-eighteenth century and continues throughout the nineteenth and early twentieth century, as the technological, industrial, and political transformation of the world reaches beyond the contours of society and becomes built into the architecture of the modern self (Giddens; Jervis). It is in this sense that I refer to nineteenth and early twentieth century advice literatures and motherhoods as "modern."

[2] It is striking that many if not most of Bayer's and other experts' examples of deformities resulting from maternal negligence during pregnancy—especially facial or cranial abnormalities, paralysis, or broken bones—could be the result of birth accidents attributable to physician negligence or inexperience with forceps-assisted births. If that is so, these attributions on the part of physicians would serve the purpose of enhancing the professional standing of obstetricians through blaming mothers for birth injuries.

REFERENCES

Abbott, E. H. *On the Training of Parents*. Boston: Houghton, Mifflin and Co., 1908.

Abell, L. G. *The Mother's Book of Daily Duties*. New York: R. T. Young, 1853.

Acland, A. H. D. *Child Training: Suggestions for Parents and Teachers*. London: Sidgwick and Jackson, Ltd., 1914.

Anonymous. *The Mother's Home-Book: A Book for Her Own and Her Children's Management. With Hints and Helps for Every-Day Emergencies*. London: Ward, Lock and Co., 1879.

Anonymous. *The Mother's Thorough Resource-Book: Comprising Self-Discipline of the Expectant Mother*. London: Ward and Lock, 1860.

Apple, R. D. *Perfect Motherhood: Science and Childrearing in America*. New Brunswick, NJ: Rutgers University Press, 2006.

Armitage, C. P. *A Handbook for Mothers: Practical Advice on Pregnancy and Motherhood*. London: John Bale, Sons and Danielsson, Ltd., 1929.

Bakewell, J. *The Mother's Practical Guide in the Physical, Intellectual, and Moral Training of Her Children*. 4th ed. London: John Snow, 1862.

Barker-Benfield, G. J. *The Horrors of the Half-known Life: Male Attitudes Toward Women and Sexuality in 19th Century America*. New York: Harper and Row, 1976.

Bartky, S. L. *Femininity and Domination: Studies in the Phenomenology of Oppression*. New York: Routledge, 1990.

Bayer, C. J. *Maternal Impressions: A Study in Child Life*. Winona, MN: Jones and Kroeger, 1897.

Beck, U. *Risk Society: Towards a New Modernity*. London: Routledge, 1992.

Beecher, E. *Motherly Talks with Young Housekeepers*. New York: J. B. Ford and Co., 1873.

Cahoone, L. "Introduction." *From Modernism to Postmodernism: An Anthology*. Ed. L. Cahoone. Cambridge: Blackwell, 1996. 1-14.

Chance, M. S. *Self-Training for Mothers*. Philadelphia: J. B. Lippincott Co., 1914.

Child, L. M. *The Moral, Intellectual, and Physical Training of the Young*. Glasgow: W. R. M'Phun, 1856.

Diamond, I. and Quinby, L., eds. *Feminism and Foucault: Reflections on Resistance*. Boston: Northeastern University Press, 1988.

Foucault, M. *Discipline and Punish: The Birth of the Prison*. Harmondsworth, UK: Penguin, 1979.

Giddens, A. *Modernity and Self-Identity*. Stanford, CA: Stanford University Press, 1991.

Grant, J. *Raising Baby By the Book: The Education of American Mothers*. New Haven: Yale University Press, 1998.

Herrick, C. T. *A Home Book for Mothers and Daughters*. New York: The Christian Herald, 1897.

Hewitt, E. C. *How to Train Children*. London: Stanley Paul and Co., 1909.

Hutchison, A. M. *The Child and His Problems*. London: Williams and Norgate, Ltd., 1925.

Jervis, J. *Exploring the Modern: Patterns of Western Culture and Civilization*. Oxford: Blackwell, 1998.

Keasbey, Edwina. *The Culture of the Cradle*. New York: James Pott and Co., 1886.

Ladd-Taylor, M. *Raising a Baby the Government Way: Mother's Letters to the Children's Bureau, 1915-1932*. New Brunswick, NJ: Rutgers University Press, 1986.

Ladd-Taylor, M. and L. Umansky, eds. *"Bad" Mothers: The Politics of Blame in Twentieth Century America*. New York: New York University Press, 1998.

Napheys, G. H. *The Physical Life of Woman*. Philadelphia: George MacLean, 1870.

Proudfoot, A. H. *A Mother's Ideals*. Chicago: A. Flanagan Co., 1897.

Rawlins, R. D. *Making Moderns: Discipline and Self-Control of American, English, and Irish Mothers and Children, 1870-1930*. Unpublished doctoral dissertation. State University of New York, Stony Brook, 2002.

Read, Mary L. *The Mothercraft Manual*. Boston: Little, Brown and Co., 1921.

Shields, S. A. and B. A. Koster. "Emotional Stereotyping of Parents in Child Rearing Manuals, 1915-1980." *Social Psychology Quarterly* 52 (1989): 44-55.

Smith-Rosenberg, C. *Disorderly Conduct: Visions of Gender in Victorian America*. New York: Knopf, 1985.

Stoner, W. S. *Natural Education*. Indianapolis: The Bobbs-Merrill Co., 1914.

Tuthill, L. C. *Joy and Care: A Friendly Book for Young Mothers*. New York: Charles Scribner, 1855.

Usher, A. M. *Book for Mothers and Nurses on the Management of Children*. London: J. and A. Churchill, 1913.

Van de Water, V. T. *Little Talks With Mothers of Little People*. Boston: Dana Estes and Co., 1912.

Warren, E. *How I Managed My Children from Infancy to Marriage*. London: Houlston and Wright, 1865.

Wegner, D. M. *White Bears and Other Unwanted Thoughts: Suppression, Obsession, and the Psychology of Mental Control*. New York: Viking/Penguin, 1989.

Wegner, D. M. "Ironic Processes of Mental Control." *Psychological Review* 101 (1994): 34-52.

3.
The Persistence and Destructiveness of Mother-Blame in Psychological Theory

REGINA M. EDMONDS

THE ASSUMPTION THAT the emotional health and wellbeing of children is primarily the consequence of how effectively they have been mothered fosters the belief that all misbehavior or psychological distress seen in a child results from poor mothering. This pervasive cultural belief, in turn, sanctions mother-blame as an acceptable explanation for any struggle a child endures. This analysis is a startling over-simplification, as it systematically ignores many other obvious factors affecting child development, such as the impact of fathers, either present or absent, poverty and other pressures which disadvantage families, and the temperament of the child him/herself, to name just a few. Psychologists and other "helping professionals" have participated in mother-blame to a large extent as the brief review, presented in this chapter, of the history of theorizing about the etiology of psychiatric disorder and other troubles children experience indicates. Perhaps what is most important, however, is the fact that mother-blame persists today, not only in the psychological analysis of many forms of distress children manifest, but also within many popular press forays into commentary on "good mothering." This ideology, then, becomes a form of oppression as mothers are systematically held to unrealistic standards of performance regarding their children's behavior and as they, themselves, internalize this pervasive view that they are primarily to blame if their child is unhappy or performing poorly. Two concomitant beliefs, which derive from the original premise that mothers are the single most critical factor in their child's development, are that it is an easy thing to nurture children selflessly because it is "natural"—an aspect of "maternal instinct"—and not a form of demanding work based on complex cognition and tireless labor, and that this care-giving can be provided even when a mother's own needs for things like safety, security, and emotional wellbeing are not adequately met. As conversations with mothers, collected either specifically for this chapter or from myriad informal discussions with mothers over the years indicate, many mothers internalize these beliefs regarding mother-blame and once they do, many begin to experience anxiety, self-doubt, and a pervasive sense of guilt and failure. In this way the oppression of mother-blame moves from the external society into the very heart of each mother and she not only comes to espouse this belief herself and to place its harsh judgment upon other mothers, but she also comes to apply its lash to her own labors as a mother. In the process many mothers lose touch with other dimensions of experience which would allow them to recall that children themselves bring many unique characteristics to all interactions and that external factors, beyond the control of any mother, also shape children's lives.

MULTIPLE FACTORS AFFECT CHILD DEVELOPMENT

One clear truth that is often ignored in the literature on mother-blame is that children are enormously complex beings. From the time they are born most strive to walk, talk, and make sense, however primitive, of the "blooming, buzzing confusion" (James) of people and things swirling around them and the sensations coming from within. Developmental psychologists have invested great energy, thought, and resources trying to map the processes by which children gain mastery of the principles governing their world—its social, linguistic, and physical dimensions—and yet most remain in awe of the seemingly miraculous way most children develop these abilities through the tenacious application of their own agency. The newborn screaming to be fed, the toddler throwing a tantrum that the strongest adult has difficulty controlling, the teenager defying, without a blink, the "law" laid down by a concerned parent, are familiar images demonstrating the independence and inner energy children tap to direct their actions. One woman, who agreed to talk about her mothering for this chapter, described her soon to be three-year-old twins as having "iron wills" and went on to express her relief at this fact by saying, "I love that they have really strong temperaments and do what they want to do because it does take the blame off for me—seeing that they are going to be who they are and they are not my little pieces of clay to mold is actually a massive relief to me."

While, in some cases, mothers themselves and classic texts spanning the developmental sequence all the way from *The Competent Infant* (Stone, Smith and Murphy) to *Identity: Youth and Crisis* (Erikson) demonstrate that throughout the life cycle, children, even infants, bring their own unique talents and formidable motivational energies to the world in remarkable ways, somehow this insight is lost when children experience emotional distress. Suddenly their vulnerability, undeniably another valid dimension of their being, takes center stage. But as an appreciation of this one aspect of a child's being, namely, fragility, emerges, it seems to wash out of our collective consciousness the strength and independent agency children also possess. Once our memory is lost for the ways in which a child "perseveres in its own being" (Ruddick 71), we begin to search for those responsible for the child's distress, and too often find it dwelling within the child's mother. She should have protected the child more fully, she should have been more present to her child's needs, she should have put her children first. This oppressive mantra of "shoulds" is learned early and well, especially by girls, our future mothers. Another mother, who contributed her thoughts for this chapter, says:

> *There was like this one thing that I remember—something that stuck with me. I don't know, I was ... about eight years old and I was playing with my doll and, um, she [my mother] said something to me, she said something like ... your kids always have to come first ... and that just stuck. ... I always think about just this one line that she said and I feel I always have to live by that line—the kids always have to come first.*

Further conversation with this mother indicated that what was implied in the notion that "the kids always have to come first" was the belief, rampant throughout North American culture and beyond, that if a child's needs are put on hold by the mother, even for a short time, then significant psychological harm is likely to result. In this way the oppressive and impossible to achieve standards for "perfect" mothering are internalized and the groundwork for subsequent feelings of failure, guilt, shame and often depression in mothers is established.

Whenever we see a child acting up or in distress we ask: "What is wrong with that child's mother? How could she be so blind?" Once such words are uttered or thought, the dynamic of mother-blame is invoked. To some degree we all do it; mother-blame is everywhere, as Paula J. Caplan (37) says, "like air pollution." It is the contention of this chapter that the pervasiveness and persistence of automatically blaming mothers for the difficulties, large and small, that their children experience is destructive to mothers and children and that it is an extraordinary oversimplification of the multiplicity of factors that contribute to distress in children, none the least of which is the child's own temperament and will.

Other obvious factors influencing a child's well-being, but frequently ignored in our conversations about why a child is having difficulty, include other significant interpersonal relationships, such as those with fathers, both present and absent, and with peers, some of whom demonstrate profound cruelty. Social factors, such as poverty, institutionalized racism, and inflexible educational and welfare systems must also be factored into our explanations. While it is certainly true that mothers are important to the development of their children, so are fathers, siblings, grandparents, teachers, and the vast and complex social milieu surrounding them. Biological factors are also significant in the emotional stability of many children. It is also true that the wellbeing of mothers themselves is crucial to their ability to extend to children the care they need and that attention should be focused, as well, on the forms of support and affirmation mothers require to succeed in their parenting role. As one mother, who reflected on her experiences as a mother for this chapter, insightfully states, "I think, like, it actually matters; it matters whether we're happy or not. Just 'cause we're a mother doesn't mean that it never matters again whether you are having a good life." Implied in her comments and developed further in conversation with her, is her willing embrace of the imperative to mother her children well, but also her understanding that it is nearly impossible to mother effectively when little concern is given to the quality of a mother's own life and her appreciation of society's blindness when it assesses a woman's "success" or "failure" in mothering without looking at the conditions in which she was asked to perform this role.

HISTORICAL OVERVIEW OF MOTHER-BLAME WITHIN PSYCHOLOGICAL THEORY

Despite psychology's relative silence regarding what women who strive to mother well require and its omission of the fact that many factors conspire to form children, an extensive body of literature on what children themselves need in order to thrive, and a companion literature focused on what mothers must provide to prevent psychopathology in their children, exists. This section of the chapter, therefore, will review a number of classic studies in the field of child psychopathology and will provide a brief analysis of a number of recent developments in childrearing practices, promoted by the popular press, with an eye toward assessing the degree to which the emotional stability of children was and continues to be attributed solely to the actions of mothers, without reference to other relevant etiological factors.

Historically, psychologists and psychiatrists have been among those most guilty of mother-blame. Much of the early writing on psychological disorders of all types endlessly blamed mothers for everything from anorexia to school phobia, autism to Tourette's syndrome. While a complete review of the literature on the mother's role in the creation of psychopathology in children is beyond the scope of this chapter, a brief description of some of the best known papers on the topic, especially with respect to the etiology of schizophrenia and other serious disorders establishes, without a doubt, that the focus was on the mother as the primary cause of disturbance in the child. I believe it is important to recount the history of mother-blame in order to undermine its continued destructiveness. As a psychologist myself, I was directly exposed to large quantities of mother-blaming literature during my training and, while I consciously struggled against its impact, I know for a fact that my own mothering was and continues to be undermined by an unconscious internalization of its central and highly judgmental premises.

Silvano Arieti, for example, who was a highly respected authority on the etiology of schizophrenia, developed an impressive catalogue of adjectives that he claimed his schizophrenic patients had used to describe their mothers. He neatly and alphabetically arranged these adjectives into a list and it is overwhelming to read. According to Arieti, his patients characterized their mothers as being:

> barbarous, bitter, blood thirsty, brutal, callous, cold-blooded, cruel, demonic, devilish, diabolical, envious, evil-minded, faithless, false, ferocious, hard hearted, harsh, hateful, hellish, ill-disposed, ill-natured, implacable, infernal, inhuman, maleficent, malicious, malignant, merciless, relentless, revengeful, ruthless, satanic, sinister, stony, unfeeling, unkind, and so forth. (90)

From this list we can see that Arieti's patients were quite creative in the vocabulary they used to describe their mothers and to blame them for their symptoms.

Other professionals within the field of psychology and psychiatry, especially those espousing the psychoanalytic perspective that was dominant in America from the 1940s through the 1970s, also demonstrated ingenuity in the ways they blamed mothers for causing schizophrenia in their children. Frieda Fromm-Reichmann, one of the most empathic and masterful therapists of her time, nevertheless coined the term "schizophrenogenic mother" in one of her much cited papers and it was rapidly assimilated into the lexicon of causal concepts within psychiatry because it was thought to have aptly captured the presumed psychopathological mother-child interactions central to the understanding of schizophrenia.

Two years later, Suzanne Reichard and Carl Tillman made reference to the term and further elaborated it by breaking it down into two sub-types: the "overtly rejecting" schizophrenogenic mother and the "covertly rejecting" mother (251). The overtly rejecting mother was described as having "conceived unwillingly" and was portrayed as "cold and sadistically cruel to her offspring" with "excessive demands for neatness and cleanliness, for politeness and observance of social forms, or for fulfillment of her own unfulfilled ambitions." The covertly rejecting schizophrenogenic mother fared no better in the description given to her. According to Reichard and Tillman:

> She exerts an equally malignant influence on her child's mental development, but in a much more subtle way. She is just as dominating

as the sadistically hostile mother, but her domination takes the form of overprotectiveness—probably a reaction-formation against unconscious hostility—of such an extreme degree as to merit the appellation "smother love." This pattern is most frequently found in infantile, egocentric mothers who batten parasitically on their children and who aim, through babying them, to prevent them from ever becoming independent. (251-252)

In contrast to most psychoanalysts, who characterized the relationship between the mother and her disturbed child as consisting primarily of rejection and hate, Harold Searles focused on the deep and complex bond of love that exists in the mother-child relationship of schizophrenics. In an unusual and moving piece, he describes the tragedy embodied in the confused way in which love is given and received by both the mother and the child. Both fear their feelings of intimacy and have learned no appropriate ways to communicate their mutual love, consequently it must be distorted into grotesque and mystifying manifestations. One of the main ways love for the mother is expressed by the child, according to Searles, is in the child's willingness to experience the schizophrenic break with reality rather than challenge the distorted world view of the mother. This decision is made in order to avoid disrupting the fragile psychological balance of the mother who employs severe distortions of reality in order to achieve her tenuous hold on life. Searles makes the powerful statement that:

The schizophrenic illness now becomes basically revealed as representing the child's loving sacrifice of his very individuality for the welfare of the mother who is loved genuinely, altruistically and with wholehearted adoration which, in the usual circumstances of human living, only a small child can bestow. (220)

An analysis in which intense love, as opposed to deep hatred, is emphasized was a breath of fresh air within psychoanalytic circles, but it nevertheless, once again, indicted the mother in the tragedy of schizophrenia in her child. Whether it was love or hate at the base of the relationship, the mother was nevertheless to blame.

What seems so amazing in the midst of this preoccupation with the mother and her role in the disturbance of the child is the relative lack of attention given to other factors that influence the child. Even if the vituperative comments regarding the mother were accurate, surely a host of other factors are relevant to a child's development. Most notably, what is absent from these early pronouncements is an analysis of the part played by fathers in the development of schizophrenia. A review of the researchers and therapists quoted above, who have characterized the mother so harshly, is interesting with respect to their descriptions of fathers. Some, such as Fromm-Reichmann, make virtually no specific references to the impact of fathers, as if they simply do not exist. While others mention fathers, we find that, in contrast to the scathing descriptions given of mothers, fathers are generally portrayed as passive, hopeless souls requiring compassion since they are dominated by the same infuriating woman as the child. Reichard and Tillman, for example, quoted one researcher as saying "the mother was aggressive, overanxious, and oversolicitous, while the father played a very subdued role" (249) and another claiming that each patient "had a cold, rigorous, sadistically aggressive mother and a soft, indifferent, passive father" (250).

One truly fascinating observation in reading much of the literature on parent-child interactions in schizophrenia is how many researchers use the term "parents" interchangeably with "mother." Referring again to the comprehensive review of the early literature by Reichard and Tillman, they reported on a study entitled *The Parent-Child Relationship in Schizophrenia*, but it is clear that the participants were only mothers and their schizophrenic children. Leo Kanner, another influential early figure in the study of child psychopathology, observed the confusion of the term "parent" with mother and stated: "Parental rejection is treated in the literature mostly as if it were synonymous with maternal rejection" (124). This error continues to exist as a sampling of relatively recent publications on childhood disorders reveals (see, for example, Caron et al., and review articles by Cassano et al.,; Connell and Goodman; and Phares et al.).

An equally interesting phenomenon is the way in which the mother is held responsible for the attitudes of the father too. Even if the father or other family members participate in creating a pathological environment that later results in the disturbance of the child, their behavior is nevertheless the mother's responsibility. Arieti, for example, stated: "It is not just the attitude of the mother toward the child that has to be taken into consideration, but also how the attitude of the mother affects the whole family, and how the result of this attitude toward the whole family indirectly affects the child" (77). Kanner also placed the mother in the center of the family interactions by asserting that fathers often reject their children in order to maintain some relationship with the mother. If the father is rejecting the child

> ...he may do so because, being the less dominant marital partner, he tries to buy his own acceptance for the price of agreeing with his wife's condemnation of the child.... Rejecting mothers often accuse their husbands of being "too lenient" with the rejected child, of not cooperating with their punitive schemes, of "letting the child get

away with murder." Agreement with the wife seems, especially to a submissive man, to be a worthwhile purchase price for domestic tranquility. (125)

It seems as though these authors are asserting that mothers reject and inflict pain upon their children out of some active form of hatred, while fathers, if they do inflict pain, do so out of helplessness and fear of the mother. Theirs are sins of omission, not commission and thereby less heinous is the implication of this literature. The question of the father's responsibility for his own behavior and the way in which his own helplessness adds additional burdens to the mother's world is not raised in these analyses. The fact that the mother too may feel alone, frightened, needy, frustrated, and unsupported is rarely addressed in the body of classic psychoanalytic writings. Mothers are seen as powerful and intentional in their refusal to provide what children need and hence are clearly worthy of the blame placed upon them. The striking absence in this literature of any discussion of male violence within the family as an etiological factor in child distress is also noteworthy.

In reviewing the dynamics presumed to exist in the etiology of other severe disorders during this time period, mothers fared no better. Kanner, for example, credited with identifying autism as a specific disorder in children in 1943, claimed that it was found primarily in upper class, white families where mothers showed a cold, distant, and highly intellectualized stance toward the child. These observations were soon denoted by the label "refrigerator mother," a term picked up by the media and then often associated with the renowned child analyst, Bruno Bettelheim, whose Orthogenic School, associated with the University of Chicago, was viewed as among the most prestigious training centers for child therapists from the 1950s through to the 1970s. Bettelheim, in his book *The Empty Fortress: Infantile Autism and the Birth of the Self*, extended the concept of coldness in the mother and likened the conditions in which autistic children grew up to those found in the Nazi concentration camps of World War II. Throughout the writings of Kanner, Bettelheim, Arieti, and the others described in this chapter, the words used to describe mothers, often in exquisite pain themselves from trying to understand and care for a child struggling with an extremely serious disorder, such as schizophrenia or autism, are extremely harsh, inflict additional injury upon mothers, and cause them to develop feelings of self-blame and extraordinary guilt.

Disorders of somewhat less severity, however, were also routinely attributed to mothers throughout the heyday decades of psychoanalysis. In disorders from asthma (see Kanner), uncontrolled vomiting (see Sylvester), or insomnia (see Kanner, 1957), to homosexuality (see Fenichel; Bieber et al.), mothers were to blame. In discussing school phobia, for example, Kate Friedlander says, "Even the schoolteacher who had seen her only once was convinced that the boy's difficulties were entirely due to his mother's attitude," (195) while Kanner states, with respect to bedwetting, that "Lack of training often results from maternal overprotection. The child's enuresis is accepted on the basis that he is too small or delicate to be trained. Behind this rationalization there is usually the mother's desire to keep her offspring wholly dependent on her for as long as possible" (444).

A more systematic assessment of the prevalence of mother-blame, conducted by Paula J. Caplan and Ian Hall-McCorquodale in 1985, a decade, at least, after the influence of classical psychoanalysis had begun to wane, found the powerful persistence of mother-blame. In their study Caplan and Hall-McCorquodale surveyed all the main clinical journals which included substantial numbers of articles on the etiology of psychopathology in children during the years 1970, 1976, and 1982 and they assessed the frequency with which psychopathology in a child was attributed to the mother. Their review indicated unequivocally that mothers were still seen as the primary and, in most cases, the only factors contributing to difficulty in their children. Using sixty-three evaluation criteria, Caplan and Hall-McCorquodale found that on over two-thirds of the measures, mothers were perceived more negatively and more blame-worthy than fathers. More than twice as many words were used to describe mothers as fathers, and more than five times as many descriptions of family problems included examples which involved mothers as opposed to fathers. In addition, in 82 percent of the articles, the child's psychopathology was attributed, at least in part, to the mother's activity with respect to her child and this was almost twice as often as blame was attributed to the father's behavior. Finally, in no article reviewed was the mother ever described only in positive terms whereas this was the case for fathers in a number of articles. Caplan and Hall-McCorquodale also found that the process of attributing primary responsibility for psychopathology in a child to the mother was not substantially influenced by the year of publication or the sex of the author of the article. Likewise, Molly Layton, writing in the same time period, observed similar patterns and summarized the mother-blame process well by stating, "it seems that it does not matter how weak or desperate a mother really is, she is credited with dazzling powers of control, intrusiveness, and persistence" (24).

My reading of the literature on child psychopathology from the 1940s to the 1980s is the same and recent review articles continue to find mother-blame to be rampant (Cassano et al.; Phares et al.). Whatever the disorder in question, no matter the pain in the family as a unit, the mother is to blame. She is either too cold or rejecting, or too over-solicitous and overprotective; she is too intrusive or too distant, and she must change. The image is formed of a mother and child living alone in a vacuum with every aspect of the child's development being influenced solely by the mother. Even today little attention is given to other possible etiological variables, such as the temperament of the child, neonatal health, and social class and virtually none to the psychological needs of the mother herself. Shari Thurer eloquently captures this paradox when she states, "even as mother is all-powerful, she ceases to exist. She exists, bodily, of course, but her needs as a person become null and void" (335). In essence, "no one spoke with a maternal voice" (336-337). Without a voice, without an appreciation of a woman's identity as an individual as well as a mother, with little empathy for the difficulty of the tasks associated with mothering, many mothers feel profoundly isolated and guilty of failing in the most important role assigned to them—motherhood—and consequently they fall into states of anxiety and depression. Mother-blame is an oppressive process that undermines and endangers the psychological health of mothers and it is no wonder moms go *mad*.

While some of the most overtly hostile discourse on mothers in the literature considered classic within psychology abated during the 1980s, it certainly did not disappear. The work of Mary Ainsworth on attachment, for example, spawned a very rich and extensive empirical literature within psychology that continues into the present and it too placed enormous and almost exclusive attention on mother-child interactional processes in the formation of problematic adjustment patterns in children. The "mommy wars" (Peskowitz 2005), which pit "stay-at-home moms" against "working moms" in a contest about who mothers best, also play out some of the concerns derived from a popular press interpretation of the work on attachment. Beyond the "mommy wars" is what Susan Douglas and Meredith Michaels call the "new momism," which they describe as a set of images reflected in the popular media idealizing mothers and promoting a form of mothering termed "intensive mothering" which advises constant vigilance regarding the health, safety, happiness, entertainment, educational development, and social schedules of children, while also demanding a cheerful, self-less, intensely engaged relationship with the kids, and a complete mastery of the books of the popular child-care experts. While such accounts of the current expectations upon mothers may seem exaggerated at times, their impact is profound and enduring. It is hard for anyone to withstand a constant barrage of perfectionistic demands without feeling self-doubt and its unfortunate companion: shame.

THE DESTRUCTIVE IMPACT OF PERSISTENT MOTHER-BLAME

In thinking, teaching, and writing about motherhood and its multiple demands and joys, I have had numerous conversations with women about their experiences as mothers and their internalization of mother-blame, a process that they see as particularly destructive to their feelings of confidence. In trying to assess the persistence of mother-blame into the present, I spoke with three young mothers, all professionals in the field of psychology, and asked if they had ever felt pressure to be perfect mothers and/or if they felt blamed when unable to attain this perfection. I received a resounding yes to both questions! These mothers were highly educated women in stable two-parent families and all had deep and abiding relationships with their healthy and joyful children, ages two to fourteen. Yet the weight of mother-blame and the presence of perfectionistic standards were palpable in each conversation. One mother stated, "I think I feel that everyday ... I just hope that any damage is minimized but um, I would say that I daily question, question myself, question my mothering," while another mother indicated, "sometimes, sometimes I worry ... like if I'm dropping off at pre-school and I'll see other mothers volunteering to do this and I'm like, I can't do this—I can't go on the field trip or I can't do that, so I feel like, I feel like there is this permanent damage, ya know, psychologically." The third also indicated her fear of falling short by reporting through tears of sadness only minutes into the interview, "people look for where stuff comes from and a lot has to do with the raising and we think, still think, it is the mother who is at home doing the raising. I'm already crying."

One remarkable element of these conversations was that the mothers all saw the need for precision and perfection in all of their everyday exchanges with their children and, despite having healthy and happy children, nevertheless felt substantial self-doubt in contemplating what action to take in relatively uncomplicated matters. The fear of doing psychological damage imbued decisions as small as whether to change an appointment at work in order to be able to drive a child to a friend's house or whether to require a screaming two-year old to sit five minutes more at the dinner table. One mother, with considerable expertise in developmental psychology claimed, for example, that "all my research on the intergenerational transmission of everything, and especially on mother-infant interaction, um, like how important it is and how it kinda sets the stage for all social development" became an enormous burden of worry for her when she was unable to devote all of the hours she felt were needed during the infancies of her twins. She went on to say that her concerns were based on "so much thought I've put into what's important in early infancy, for life. It was just so ironic I really couldn't do what I was researching and trying to prove was really important." This lived reality led her at times to feelings of depression and personal failure. Another mother told the moving story of being at a library with her child and giving the book her daughter had been looking at to another child, not realizing her own child was not yet done with it. The event had happened years before, but nevertheless this mother still recalled it with great emotion saying, "She was crying, crying, crying all the way home, and I felt really guilty. I was trying to call up other libraries that had the book because I felt so bad that she had really wanted that book and I gave it to someone else—I didn't, like, stick up for her."

Concern over doing long-term harm to their children was especially evident when moms expressed even the smallest amounts of anger or impatience with their children. Despite the fact that caring for children almost always involves some degree of frustration, many mothers nevertheless blame themselves for their most inconsequential lapses of calm. One mother confessed, "I totally feel a little extra anxious—you know the things you are supposed to do, but you don't do them, like in the heat of the moment … you know that's not right … you just get so frustrated and then you feel guilty." And another confided that "I often project into the future, wondering if this is going to be something that my children some day are going to bring up, saying—and you did this and you did that and that's why I'm this and that's why I'm that." All of these comments are clear evidence that in at least this subset of mothers, anxiety, worry, self-doubt, and self-recrimination are pervasive dimensions of their everyday practice of mothering and that these feelings were deeply disturbing, contributing to a lack of emotional wellbeing.

There were also a number of interesting paradoxes that appeared in the conversations with these mothers, reminiscent of conversations I have had over the years with many, many other mothers. While all agreed that our culture does include many mother-blaming messages, these mothers nevertheless saw their deep anxiety about mothering to be a consequence of their unique family circumstances or of their own personal psychological limitations. One mother suggested that her anxiety and guilt are of her own making alone when she said, "I think maybe it's me and my quirkiness. I know other people go on conferences without the kids and stuff … I haven't been at a conference yet without the kids." She was genuinely surprised when I told her I had felt the same way when my kids were as young as hers and she expressed her relief by saying, "Well see, I mean, even though it's like misery loves company, it's nice to know. I always felt, like, that I was, like, this neurotic person."

These mothers also were able to comment on a second paradox, namely the fact that while they could see that the high level of anxiety they experienced while mothering was neither logical nor helpful, they nevertheless could not dispel it. Even when they observed and could laugh about the fact that their husbands, who also engaged actively in the daily care of the children in these families, did not agonize over decisions they made when in charge of the kids, still the mothers' own feelings of anxiety persisted. One commented on how she had thought a lot about how her husband was able to escape feelings of self-doubt when she could not, while another described her own process of internalizing guilt, even when her husband did not, by saying:

> *And for me, I think, emotionally, I put a lot of pressure on myself, um, so I'm defining what a good mother should be and that is almost that, is that I have no, no boundaries, no limits, ya know, emotionally, physically, I am just—whatever my kids need, whenever they need it, that's what makes a good mother. I'm not sure where that, where that comes from because again, as I would read about mothering, as I would read about being a woman, ya know, a well-adjusted, healthy person, certainly it talks about boundaries, it talks about self-care, and still I feel tremendous guilt when I put some boundaries into place, or limits.*

Another mother laughed when she explained how guilty she feels when she wakes up her kids early to get them ready so she can get to work on time, but does not feel any pangs of guilt when she has to wake them at the same time for school, when she doesn't have work. Seeing the illogic of this, she says, "If I think about it logically, probably I don't think there is any harm. But I don't think about it logically most of the time.... When I have to wake her up for school just because, ya know, she has to go to school, I don't feel that guilt, but when it's something for me, then that's when I feel that guilt." It is interesting to see that going to work for this mother is considered to be "something for me," an interesting observation in itself.

Still another paradox, reflected in the words of these mothers, has to do with their own pride in their educational accomplishments, their joy in their work, and their hopes that their daughters will also have the opportunities to pursue meaningful careers. But this pride, nevertheless, remains coupled with the enduring but competing imperative that a good mother is one who is always there for her kids. One mother talks about how important and meaningful her job is and describes it as a source of her "identity" and a way of fulfilling her "affiliation needs," but also says, "my schedule can't be a schedule ... because it really has to be able to be flexible enough, malleable enough to, to um, withstand what everybody else needs." The emotional stress evident in her words derives from the competing demands to be both an excellent worker and a "perfect" mother. But even mothers are not able to be in two places at the same time, despite the internalized expectation that somehow they should be. The attempt to do both, while understanding that such is impossible, does contribute to a feeling of being a bit insane and *mad*.

The awareness of these clear paradoxes suggests how powerful and pervasive the perfectionistic standards for mothering are and how complete the internalization of mother-blame is. These examples stand as evidence to the fact that these unachievable ideals about perfect mothering infiltrate and undermine the thinking and psychological wellbeing of even the strongest, most confident, competent, and logical women. The impression that mother-blame and its cruel legacies of self-doubt and shame are alive and well and not relics of the past, is also eloquently affirmed in the work of Thurer when she states:

> As a psychologist I cannot recall ever treating a mother who did not harbor shameful secrets about how her behavior or feelings damaged her children. Mothers do not take easy pride in their competence. Popular mother culture implies that our children are exquisitely delicate creatures, hugely vulnerable to our idiosyncrasies and deficits, who require relentless psychological attunement and approval. A sentimentalized image of the perfect mother casts a long, guilt-inducing shadow over real mothers' lives. Actual days on Planet Earth include few if any perfect moments, perfect children, perfectly cared for. (331)

It is clear that the application to the self of such unrealistic and, hence, highly oppressive standards for maternal performance continues and definitely drives mothers to the brink of madness.

One question that seems important to ask, given the prevalence of these idealized standards for mothering, is whether anything constructive results for either mothers or their children from the imposition of the cultural expectation of flawless mothering. Perhaps requiring mothers to seek perfection in their behavior toward their children is valuable for fostering a sensitive mindfulness about their mothering practices. In answering, the young mothers I spoke with felt that the internalization of these perfectionistic standards was deeply problematic and in their responses to my query about whether trying to achieve perfection might, in fact, be a good thing, expressions of guilt, anger, exhaustion, and especially depression predominated. One mother movingly said, "I probably speak for a lot of women and mothers too—I mean we, we beat ourselves up, we have self-doubt ... we're depressed, we're tired, we feel that there's no one there for us except other women." Later in the interview similar thoughts emerged as this mother claimed, "You've known me now for years. I've been depressed ... sometimes more so than others, I've been overweight and not in the best health. I've ... at times felt somewhat hopeless about, ya know, myself because there didn't seem to be much left for me. So I think it takes a great toll." While another said, "If you have any depressive tendencies, you might get immobilized ... then you're not doin' anything, ... it's so hard to mobilize yourself ... so the blaming really screws that up, it really drains your energy."

These mothers were not only able to articulate the ill-effects upon their own lives that mother-blaming exacts, but also saw themselves as poor models for their own children, especially their daughters. In this heartbreaking way they blamed themselves not only for being unable to give enough, but also, paradoxically, for whatever damage might result from giving too much. One mother summed up this impossible dilemma well when she said, "I give, give, give, I don't really care. And I thought, this is what I was doing to her, [her daughter] like teaching her this—let people step all over her and then I felt, like, guilty."

Given the worry, fear, and pain expressed by mothers whose children are doing well, one can only imagine the anguish in those who mother children in great distress. Therefore, as feminists and mothers, it is important to find the will and the ways to deconstruct the myth of the perfect mother. Given the internalization of the powerful and pervasive mandate to always put the needs of our children first, perhaps we can begin the process of liberating ourselves from mother-blame by allowing our tentative steps toward self-care to be energized initially by our well-worn adherence to the principle of doing what is best for our children. Surely, living with less guilt and self-doubt, is not only better for mothers, but for children as well. With time, however, as we fully appreciate the need to avoid burdening our own daughters with this destructive mandate, we will find the courage to actively embrace our own needs for nurturance and this, in turn, will allow us to emerge fully from the shadow of internalized mother-blame and its unkind associates: shame and depression. Only then will we move from self-doubt to self-acceptance, from anxiety to confidence, from madness to inner peace.

REFERENCES

Ainsworth, M., M. Blehar, E. Waters and S. Wall. *Patterns of Attachment: A Psychological Study of the Strange Situation*. Hillside, NJ: Lawrence Erlbaum, 1978.

Arieti, S. *Interpretation of Schizophrenia*. New York: Basic Books, 1974.

Bettelheim, B. *The Empty Fortress: Infantile Autism and the Birth of the Self*. New York: The Free Press, 1967.

Bieber, I., H. J. Dain, P. R. Dince, M. G. Drellich, H. G. Grand, R. H. Gundlach, M. W. Kremer, A. H. Rifkin, C. D. Wilbur and T. B. Bieber. *Homosexuality: A Psychoanalytic Study*. New York: Basic Books, 1962.

Caplan, P. J. *The New Don't Blame Mother: Mending the Mother-Daughter Relationship*. New York: Routledge, 2000.

Caplan, P. J. and I. Hall-McCorquodale. "Mother-blaming in Major Clinical Journals." *American Journal of Orthopsychiatry* 55 (1985): 345-353.

Caron, A., B. Weiss, V. Harris and T. Catron. "Parenting Behavior Dimensions and Child Psychopathology: Specificity, Task Dependency, and Interactive Relations." *Journal of Clinical Child and Adolescent Psychology* 35 (1) (2006): 34-45.

Cassano, M., M. Adrian, G. Veits and J. Zeman. "The Inclusion of Fathers in the Empirical Investigation of Child Psychopathology: An Update." *Journal of Clinical Child and Adolescent Psychology* 35 (4) (2006): 583-589.

Connell, A. M. and S. H. Goodman. "The Association Between Psychopathology in Fathers Versus Mothers and Children's Internalizing and Externalizing Behavior Problems: A Meta-Analysis." *Psychological Bulletin* 128 (5) (2002): 746-773.

Douglas, S. J. and M. W. Michaels. "The New Momism." *Maternal Theory: Essential Readings.* Ed. A. O'Reilly. Toronto: Demeter Press, 2007. 617-648.

Erikson, E. H. *Identity: Youth and Crisis.* New York: W. W. Norton, 1968.

Fenichel, O. *Psychoanalytic Theory of Neurosis.* New York: Norton, 1945.

Friedlander, K. "Formation of the Antisocial Character." *The Psychoanalytic Study of the Child* 1 (1945): 189-203.

Fromm-Reichmann, F. "Notes on the Development of Treatment of Schizophrenics by Psychoanalytic Psychotherapy." *Psychiatry* 11 (1948): 263-273.

James, W. *The Principles of Psychology.* Vols. 1-2. New York: Henry Holt, 1890.

Kanner, L. *Child Psychiatry.* 3rd ed. Springfield, IL: Charles C. Thomas, 1957.

Layton, M. "Tipping the Therapeutic Balance—Masculine, Feminine, or Neuter?" *The Family Therapy Networker* 8 (1984): 21-28.

Peskowitz, M. *The Truth Behind the Mommy Wars: Who Decides Who Makes a Good Mother.* Emeryville, CA: Seal Press, 2005.

Phares, V., S. Fields, D. Kamboulos, and E. Lopez. "Still Looking for Poppa." *American Psychologist* 60 (7) (2005): 735-736.

Reichard, S. and C. Tillman. "Patterns of Parent-Child Relationships in Schizophrenia." *Psychiatry* 13 (1950): 247-257.

Ruddick, S. *Maternal Thinking: Toward a Politics of Peace.* Boston: Beacon, 1989.

Searles, H. F. "Positive Feelings in the Relationship Between the Schizophrenic and His Mother." *Collected Papers on Schizophrenia and Related Subjects.* Ed. H. F. Searles. New York: International University Press, 1965. 216-253

Stone, L. J., H. T. Smith and L. B. Murphy, eds. *The Competent Infant: Research and Commentary.* New York: Basic Books, 1973.

Sylvester, E. "Analysis of Psychogenic Anorexia in a Four-Year-Old." *The Psychoanalytic Study of the Child* 1 (1945): 167-187.

Thurer, S. L. "The Myths of Motherhood." *Maternal Theory: Essential Readings.* Ed. A. O'Reilly. Toronto: Demeter Press, 2007. 331-344.

4.
Fractured Motherhood

The Insanity of Reproduction in Australia in the 1930s

ALISON WATTS

MOTHERS WHO ARE SEEN to stand outside of the narrow rules of gendered roles are often at risk of being labeled psychotic and are prone to draw a diagnosis of mental illness from psychiatrists (Matthews). This may have been true in Ada's case, a female family member, whose mothering was disrupted or fractured when she was committed to a mental institution at the age of 24 in 1936, leaving her two small children in the care of others. This is what I call "fractured motherhood" where Ada was stopped from the preservation, nurturance, and training of her children (Ruddick). With unique access to Ada's mental patient records, as a family member, I examine the fracturing of Ada's motherhood as a result of her confinement in three Australian mental institutions in the State of Victoria from 1936 to 1972. In this chapter, I use feminist methodology approaches to critically examine the sources of social power (Harding; Reinharz) Ada was subjected to and oppressed by, which ultimately fractured her motherhood. This work forms part of my ongoing research for my Ph.D. dissertation, and in what follows I firstly address the ethical issues in family research and discuss the problems of access, the limitations and nature of Ada's mental patient records. A brief historical background to Ada's life provides a crucial juxtaposition to the events represented in Ada's records that establish her fractured motherhood.

As a family member and the principal researcher, it is important to achieve balance between protecting family members from emotional distress, and gaining an understanding of the circumstances of Ada's institutionalization. Considering Ada's records are actually closed to the public, the taboo nature of mental illness, and the lack of information amongst the family concerning Ada's insanity and committal, I have removed identifiable information such as locations and replaced names with pseudonyms. The potential benefits for family members could include the experience of healing and reconciliation gained from the dissemination of this research, and over time, this may become a valuable contribution to family history. Others from the wider community have been prompted to share with me informally their experiences of their own family members' committal to mental institutions, enabling possible therapeutic benefits in the wider population, particularly for those with similar experiences. However, the benefits described above do not render the risks as invalid. The potential risks could involve exposing a family to itself, as the contents of Ada's files are contentious, alarming, and heartbreaking—so too are the family stories that sit outside the files. Assessing the potential risks and benefits in ethical family research poses significant challenges as the principal researcher and family member in this project, and for other researchers in qualitative family research (Larossa, Bennett and Gelles). Therefore pseudonyms are used in this work in order to maintain confidentiality and protect family members from exposure. The next section introduces the issues and the limitations of Ada's mental patient records.

Sourcing primary documents, as a key tool in historical methods, can prove difficult when mental patient files are closed to public access. Issues concerning closed and restricted files limit the writing of patient's lives and institutional histories (Garton 2000). However, I gained access to Ada's mental patient records as a family member, through the Freedom of Information Unit in Victoria. These records span nearly 40 years, amount to 112 pages, and are valid first-hand accounts of Ada's psychiatric history as a mental patient. Produced by Ada's attending psychiatrists in their own hand-writing, the doctors record her basic demographic details plus admission and discharge dates, and treatments prescribed across three mental institutional settings. The constraints of the limited space provided in official forms standardize these records to conform to the administrative and bureaucratic requirements in a medical context. In this way, the authorship, credibility, and authenticity of Ada's records is established, ensuring the quality and validity of these documents, essential for primary documentary sources which this research draws upon (Scott).

There is a scarcity of other primary sources; I have one letter written by Ada kept by a family member and two unsent letters written by Ada contained within the records. Ada left no diary, therefore her mental patients records are the main source of information on her life and fractured motherhood. Yet Mary Elene Wood is doubtful of patient histories that rely solely on case records. She points out that "attendants play a much larger daily role in patients' lives than doctors do" (4). Ward attendants would have greater opportunities to develop friendships and understanding through their daily involvements with patients, yet it is the psychiatrists who compile patient records, sometimes at yearly intervals only. Taking into account these limitations and nature of patient records, and the scarcity of other primary sources, I quote extensively from Ada's mental patient files in this chapter.

HISTORICAL BACKGROUND

Prior to marriage, in the early 1930s, Ada worked in Melbourne, Australia, as a comptometer operator. The comptometer machine was a mechanical, key-driven calculator, requiring speed and accuracy from the operators, who were predominantly female. Advances in office technology, such as the comptometer machine, gave single women like Ada new opportunities for both the development of new skills and the economic independence of a wage earner. Throughout World War I, the mechanization of office technology and the lack of male labor increased the demand for women's paid labor in office work (Strom). As a result, women in the 1920s enjoyed the independence and freedom that signifies the era for Western women. Yet the images of the "new woman" and "the flapper" representing freedom to women in the 1920s created hostility in some parts of society. Unemployed men hit by the economic crisis of the Great Depression of the 1930s felt working women, both single and married, were taking men's jobs. Societal attitudes deemed that working married women should devote themselves to raising their families and to housework only, and not undertake paid work as well; while attitudes towards single women saw them as filling in time by working until they were married. Whether or not Ada actually was just filling in time, or that she actually needed the income to support herself is not known; whatever the case she soon found a husband in David.

Ada met David at a dance and they married in 1932 in a Methodist church in Caulfield, a Melbourne eastern suburb. David was then aged 28 and had an established business as a carrier in the small rural Victorian town of Colac. Prior to this work, David hauled timber from local sawmills until he bought his first truck and commenced his carrier business in the early 1930s. His daily truck route from Colac to Melbourne involved collecting orders from customers along his route to the city, then delivering supplies and settling accounts on his return trip. This regular employment as the breadwinner of the family was paramount to the economic survival of the newlyweds during this era of the Great Depression. Marriage and child rearing was a desirable goal providing women like Ada the status and identity of wife and mother, the important cornerstone of femininity for women in the 1930s (Matthews). Ada was aged 21 when she took up married life with David in Colac in 1932, which meant leaving her independent life, job, and city life behind. The marriage separated Ada from her existing social networks and her paid employment to a new rural setting of her husband's domain and his family networks. Their first child was a daughter, named Hannah, born in 1934, and their second child, Graeme, born in 1936. Within two weeks of the birth of her second, Ada was diagnosed with puerperal insanity, now known as postpartum psychosis and committed to a Melbourne mental institution.

Nineteenth-century ideas of female insanity were based on the supposed vulnerability of women's reproductive organs, which were believed to affect their mental states (Coleborne; Garton 1988; Showalter). Puerperal insanity was seen to be a post-birth mental disorder triggered by giving birth. As a diagnosis, puerperal insanity rose significantly throughout the nineteenth century as the result of the rise of psychiatry as an emerging profession, and the medicalization of child-birth by insisting mothers' birth in hospitals. In Britain, by the twentieth century, puerperal insanity was in decline as a diagnosis for mothers' committal (Marland). As Australia consistently borrowed directly from the British asylum model and British medical developments, therefore it remains unclear as to why Ada was diagnosed and committed with puerperal insanity, in 1936, well into the twentieth century when it was abandoned in Britain long before.

The extended use of this diagnosis reveals the likelihood of different conditions in Australia from that of Britain. In the Australian context puerperal insanity may have been a broad term used to cover a variety of issues all related to childbirth, especially when there was no clear delineation between organic and other causes in the medical knowledge at the time. The delirium that manifests from infection may have been misunderstood as a psychiatric condition in post-birth mothers.

Home births were prominent in the nineteenth century, yet by the early twentieth century births in Sydney public hospitals had doubled between 1919 and 1933 (Lewis). This move to encourage women to birth in hospitals saw the widespread use of anaesthetics and forceps in the 1930s (Reiger). Hygienic practices such as hand washing between patients and sterilizing instruments was slow to be adopted, spreading infection between birthing mothers through doctors' hands and the instruments they used. Often it seemed that the confused states and delirium associated with fever and infection was misread as insanity or psychosis, which led suffering mothers into psychiatric care. The medicalization of childbirth through hospital labour posed serious risks to a mother's health; "in the first half of the twentieth century as many as 30 to 40 percent of cases of puerperal insanity have been attributed to toxic psychoses" (Loudon 78). Toxic psychosis means the delirium caused by infections associated with organic diseases. Ian Brockington uses the term "infective delirium" to describe delirium caused by infections, which presents clinically as "disorientation, restless disorganized behaviour, hallucinations (especially visual), transient delusions, misidentification of persons, amnesia for the illness and birth, and occasionally retrograde amnesia. But manic features like extreme loquacity and wild excitement, expansive ideas, laughter and singing are sometimes seen" (129). Upon Ada's first committal (14 days after birth), her doctor described her behavior as:

> The patient is cheerful and talkative. She is quite disorientated as regards time and place. Her answers to questions are quite irrelevant and she smiles and ...cheerfully for most of the time (casenotes, 14 December, 1936).

Ada's disorientation and cheerfulness could have been manifestations of delirium from infection, according to Brockington's clinical presentations, contracted in childbirth.

It was Ada's second birth that was seen to be the cause of Ada's insanity and there is a lack of record keeping in her files as to Ada's physical state upon committal (fever, infection), or the nature of birth she experienced (forceps, anaesthetized). The process of modernization saw an increase in medical knowledge, and it was not until the introduction of hygienic medical practice with antiseptics, the treatment of infections with sulfonamide drugs in 1935, and by 1944, that the use of penicillin finally eliminated organic causes for puerperal insanity. If Ada's puerperal insanity was actually delirium from infection, this implies grave consequences for birthing mothers committed to mental institutions as insane prior to the introduction of penicillin treatment. The progress of modernization dominated areas of women's traditional domains throughout the interwar years in Australia and is examined in the next section.

With the rise of rational and scientific knowledge, mothers were subject to many experts in the fields of domestic management and the infant and maternal welfare movements of the 1920s and 1930s. A proliferation of advice books and manuals on child rearing and mothercraft produced a governing and civilizing trend upon mothers as prescriptive ways to raise children (Kitchens). The ideology of motherhood in the 1930s placed particular emphasis on the civic duty of mothers to raise future generations of citizens, and that as wife, cook, and educator of the children, her responsibilities were highly valued and clearly defined (Summers). These strict prescriptions and yet idealized attributes of mothering ignored the power relations, social conditions, and material reality of mothering in this era.

Committed to the mental institution with puerperal insanity 14 days after birthing, Ada's maternal body would still have been in post-birth recovery mode: breasts full of milk, shrinking uterus and carrying extra body weight. The trauma of separation from her newborn son and her daughter was against her will and in spite of her body being ready to sustain her baby son's life. With the pain of not knowing about her children's safety and welfare, Ada's motherhood became fractured as she was unable to protect, nurture, and ensure the survival of both her children. Her daughter, Hannah, then aged three, was placed in a boarding school, whilst Ada's mother-in-law cared for her baby son Graeme, raised to believe that his mother was no longer alive. Over the following six years, Ada was granted a series of trial leaves to go home from the institution.

Nine months after her original committal, in September 1937, Ada was granted Trial Leave and was sent home to her husband. In March 1938, Ada was fully discharged, 14 months after her original admission, and spent the next two years at home in Colac.

During this time, Ada arranged for her son Graeme, then 21 months old, to be baptized at the local Anglican Church. A friend who attended the service recalled that Graeme as a toddler "...stacked up the kneeling (prayer) cushions while the service was going on, and everyone smiled." However, in the course of this two-year period at home, Ada became pregnant again. Knowledge of contraception appears to be limited amongst married women in the 1930s and 1940s when the advertising of contraceptives was banned in all states, except South Australia (Matthews). This suppression in advertising of abortifacients, contraceptives, and general birth control information was narrow-minded and puritanical (Summers). The institution may have failed to offer Ada any contraceptive advice in preparation for her trial leave home with her husband, or any contraceptives she did use may have failed in their effectiveness. Either way, Ada underwent both a "therapeutic abortion" and sterilization procedures in 1940. A doctor's request form and a signed consent form were required, but both were missing from Ada's files.

Abortion in Australia was unlawful at the time, unless it could be medically justified in the interests of the life and health of the mother, but doctors did not agree as to what elements constitute a threat to the mother's health. Decades later, T. N. A. Jeffcoate argues, "even a clear history of puerperal insanity on one or more occasion is not an indication for therapeutic abortion" (581). However, in Ada's case, it appears that her prior diagnosis of puerperal insanity was used to justify the decision to terminate this pregnancy, as a third child may have been deemed too risky to her mental health.

Sterilization was never legalized in Australia, but was part of the discourse of the eugenics movement in 1920s and 1930s, as a way to preserve the race from those considered unfit to reproduce, such as those committed as insane. Stephan Garton found that "voluntary sterilisation was an option explored by some NSW State Mental Hospitals, and it is likely that some operations were performed, however no figures were recorded" (1988: 164). It is likely Ada experienced grief, loss, and mourned for the lost child after it was terminated. She was also at risk of suffering emotional difficulties due the relationship problems with her husband, which later becomes more evident. Both the abortion and sterilization procedures irrevocably denied Ada any future mothering opportunities, or as Jill Matthews says, "…prevent her from ever again aspiring to the feminine status of mother" (180). Such procedures may have been at odds with her religious or philosophical values. Without a signed consent form in Ada's files, was she aware of the sort of operations performed? If so, were both procedures performed against her will? If Ada was aware of the nature of the procedures, was she coerced or able to participate in the decision-making of her reproductive future remains unclear. Whatever the circumstances, such permanent and irreversible medical interferences in the reproductive lives of women, women considered genetically inferior and mentally unfit, was unlawful in Australia. Unlike its American counterparts, who enacted compulsory sterilization laws, sterilizing more than 60,000 people without their consent (Bordo 75). Undergoing an abortion and sterilization ended her childbearing years prematurely at the age of 28, compounding further Ada's already fractured motherhood.

Following these two procedures, Ada was re-committed in May 1940 compounding her already fragile situation. Two doctors' diagnoses were required for her committal to the mental institution. The first doctor notes contained comments from Ada's husband, David, illustrating how his version of events was instrumental in her re-committal:

> Yesterday she burnt my best suit in the incinerator and also all the towels in the house. She is … complaining that the operation wound is healed on the outside but not on the inside. She never washes up the ordinary household dishes and neglects her housework (casenotes, 19 May, 1940).

The comment from David that Ada had burned his best suit and all the towels in the house are actions directed against him (and not against herself, like self-harm). Why would Ada burn specifically his best suit and the towels, but not any other item? Were the towels and suit simply just too heavy washing work for her when recovering from these two procedures? Would it be that when David returns from work, he would enjoy a shower (in need of towels) and dressed in his best suit, leave Ada at home with the children, and go out in the evenings to socialize without her? Was Ada directing her rage against him by burning the things he most needed at the end of a working day? The description that *the operation wound is healed on the outside but not on the inside*, is disturbing and may indicate either internal physical pain or the psychological pain of grief in losing a baby, compounded by the knowledge that her childbearing days were finished.

Many women will recognize the necessity for bed rest in their recovery; however, this rest possibly not afforded to Ada as her husband may have seen this as neglecting her household chores. The research of 48 women in North Carolina, who underwent tubal ligation (sterilization) found that "… the lives of many women are haunted by fear of pregnancy; and with this removed, it was not surprising to learn that sexual and marital relationships in the group had greatly improved and that individuals were much happier" (Woodside 73). Unfortunately, this was not the case for Ada. The removal of any fear of future pregnancies did not improve her marriage; in fact, their relationship was seriously at odds. Ada was possibly either unable to mourn the loss of her pregnancy or may have been preoccupied with grief, deepening her fractured motherhood, leaving her with less energy to deal with the demands of family life.

David's observation of Ada's supposed neglect of housework illustrates his construction of Ada as a failed housewife. Subject to her husband's standards and not complying with her husband's expectations of her gendered roles as wife and mother met with his punishing and coercive action to commit her. After over two years at home, Ada was re-committed and re-entered the institution again in May 1940, no longer pregnant and no longer fertile. It is clear by now that her marriage was disintegrating, and that she was continually subject to the power of her husband to send her away again whenever her behavior met with his disapproval. So Ada was sent back to the institution again, creating further disjointed family experiences with the lack of continuity in family life. In this same committal, the second doctor, noted:

> Well-oriented as regard time and space. Talks quite rationally. Says that for the last 12 months she has been hearing voices when there is no-one about; it seems as if her thoughts are being spoken aloud. Does not get on well with husband. She is the youngest of a family of six (5 brothers) (casenotes, 20 May, 1940).

Two months later, the same doctor noted:

> Little change. Is apathetic and indifferent about her fate. Reluctant to go home again. Says does not get on well with home and appears to have no love in regard to him (casenotes, 17 July, 1940).

Ada admits to not getting on with her husband and discloses she has no love in regard to him, demonstrates the marriage had disintegrated and family life was difficult. Despite the state of her marriage and Ada's reluctance to return home, ten days later Ada was released on Trial Leave and spent the following ten months at home. Upon return from Trial Leave, in May 1941, her doctor notes:

Patient is a young lady in good physical condition. She talks freely with some affectation of home. She has various delusions about her husband, thinks he is jealous of her.... In addition she says he keeps taunting her about her mental illness. They are on the verge of divorce but husband wants to claim the children. She has complained to police on many occasions mainly about her husband but she has been unable ... any satisfaction—feels that police force is corrupt (casenotes, 3 May, 1941).

It is clear from the previous three observations that her marriage is in serious trouble, as "familial conflicts and tensions were often the reasons for committal" (Garton, 1988: 143). Taunted by her husband illustrated a lack of care and empathy in the marriage, adding extra stress and anxiety, compounding an already difficult relationship. The doctor casts her complaints against her husband as delusional, privileging David's testimony over hers, which deepened Ada's powerlessness. Her complaints to police could have been based on legitimate fears of domestic violence, if her husband had battered her; nevertheless, she gained no satisfaction or protection from the police. It is likely as a mental patient on Trial Leave, the police failed to take her complaints seriously, disregarding her concerns for her safety. Teased by her husband, disbelieved by both the doctor and the police, and in constant jeopardy of being returned to the mental institution are oppressive circumstances, which would seriously affect her performance as a mother. *On the verge of divorce but husband wants to claim the children* illustrates David's need to claim the children and ensure his paternity rights. With their mother removed to the mental institution, and divorce pending, he could assume possession and control over his children and their futures.

Ada spends only two months in the institution this time and undergoes insulin treatment of daily comas for 28 days. Later the same month her doctor notes:

Marked improvement, well above treatment. Considerable gain in weight and improvements in physical condition. Mentally much improved—states she is no longer hallucinatory although remembers that she was so and seemed to have gained full insight into her ... condition. A satisfactory remission. On Trial Leave (casenotes, 26 July, 1941).

Whether the insulin treatments led to Ada's remission remains unclear. Despite being on the verge of divorce, Ada was released on Trial Leave again. This time Ada spends six months at home, then returns to the institution in January 1942. Her doctor notes:

She talks freely but in unnatural fantastic manner. She is correctly orientated and her memory is good but she obviously has no insight into her present condition. She states that Mr ... is the person who should be here as he is out of his mind. (casenotes, 14 January, 1942)

It is unknown what prompted this decline and her return to the institution at this time. Certainly undergoing the procedures of abortion, sterilization, and insulin treatments failed to assist Ada in recovery or release. Re-committed as insane again in 1942, no more Trial Leave was granted. Was this her husband exerting his influence in securing Ada's permanent institutionalization? If so, her doctor was probably unable to force her husband to accept her discharge or any further trial leave. Either way, Ada remained in institutions for the rest of her life. This form of maternal alienation illustrates a range of tactics used to "undermine and destroy relationships between mothers and their children" (Morris 416). There is no evidence to suggest they did divorce, but by placing one's wife into the mental institution would achieve the same ends, and ensured Ada's alienation and long-lasting estrangement from her children. In this way David maintained his position of father and the controlling authority of family members.

The impact of this final withdrawal to the institution stripped her of her mother role denying her the opportunity to ensure the survival, nurturance, and training of both her children. Ada's motherhood was subject to her husband's power to commit her and subject to the power of various superintendents to commit and release her at their discretion. The many entries and exits between home and institution throughout her six years of Trial Leave would have disrupted the patterns of their family life and created a fractured experience of motherhood. It is evident that Ada was in an unhappy marriage, and for some women the asylum acted as women's refuges, a safe place to go when there was nowhere else (Chesters). Despite her previous employment and independence, Ada would have lost her social networks whilst institutionalized, and unable to make alternative living arrangements for her Trial Leave periods. Throughout her six years of Trial Leave it is hard to say how much she saw her children and how her many committals affected them, but from 1942 Ada disappeared from their lives for the next twenty years.

In 1956, Ada was transferred to a large country institution in Victoria. There, the superintendent, the head of the institution, entered the diagnosis of schizophrenia with no treatment, in Ada's committal notes. This was the first time that schizophrenia appeared in her files. It is important to note that Ada was not receive treatment for this condition, when the fact that anti-psychotic drugs, such as lithium, were being administered to schizophrenic patients in other Australian mental institutions during the 1950s is well documented by both Dr. John Cade and John Cawte. At this country institution, Ada worked in the superintendent's residence (on the institutions grounds) as a housekeeper and nanny. Here, Ada had found an opportunity to explore and fulfill some mothering experiences in caring for the superintendent's children, a sad irony when denied the care of her own. Was it that Ada could settle when away from her husband, revealing irreconcilable differences in her marriage? Why is it that Ada had no more Trial Leave and denied access to her own children, whilst given the responsibility of caring for the Superintendent's children? Might it have reminded her of her own loss and her own mothering capabilities?

It seems very unusual that a schizophrenic patient could look after the superintendent's children and work in his residence. It is questionable that he would leave his children with any mental patient. Was it that her schizophrenia was mild or even non-existent, as no lithium was administered, commonly used in the treatment of schizophrenics at the time? Was it an arbitrary diagnosis, to satisfy the bureaucratic requirements, so that Ada had somewhere to live and work? Perhaps as the head of the institution, the superintendent trusted her to work in his private residence as an untreated schizophrenic, her labor easing his wife's domestic responsibilities, knowing Ada had no one else to turn to.

Aside from the schizophrenia diagnosis, the files yield very little of her confinement at this time. There is only a single entry for each year: "no change" and "as above" for a period totaling seven years. However the doctor's entry for 1962, noted:

> Does satisfactorily in … jobs. Upset by the smallest change. Refuses to be examined by anybody but the Superintendent, because she is not a patient, but a worker! (casenotes, 8 August, 1962)

The reference to being *not a patient, but a worker* provides an interesting insight into her attitude to her work. An earlier entry, prior to her transfer, notes: *Settled in Ward. Works daily in B ward which she calls going to the office* (casenotes, 10, May, 1954). Both these observations indicate that Ada took her work seriously and possibly was diligent and reliable in her duties. Identifying herself as a worker may illustrate how Ada retained the self-concept of functioning at work, and the denial of her own patient status may have been necessary for her own mental health and personal survival in the institution. The reference to *going to the office*, harks back to when Ada was working in the city, as a comptometer operator, prior to her marriage, and perhaps a wish that she has that independence again. Maintaining her self-concept as a worker provided redemptive qualities in the healing of her fractured motherhood, however vicariously through the caring of the superintendent's children.

The retirement of the superintendent in 1963, prompted Ada's transfer back to a Melbourne institution. Why she could not continue living at the country institution at this time is unclear, as other than the superintendent's retirement, the records show no further reasons for this transfer. Lacking social support or any other member of her family to meet the conditions of her probation or discharge, and unable to return home, Ada was powerless to take up living in the community. This transfer back to Melbourne fractured her mothering further in her separation from the superintendent's children, and leaving the family environment and stable routine of the superintendents' home, may have had a profound affect upon Ada.

It was around this time in the early 1960s, both Ada's children, Graeme and Hannah now adults, became aware of their mothers' existence. Under unusual circumstances, which prompted communications with their father, David confessed he had concealed Ada's existence all this time. Graeme found that their mother was living as a mental patient in Melbourne, despite being raised to believe their mother was no longer alive. David denied her existence to both her children, and by keeping her secret, rendered her invisible. Some women, who did have family contact throughout their confinement, experienced faster recovery or ways to facilitate their release (Kelm). Unfortunately this was not the case for Ada; she was alienated from her children, embedding her fractured experiences of motherhood. Graeme's discovery of Ada initiated a reunion, which marked the end of years of denial and separation. Their reunion was not as mother and baby, but as two adults with filial ties. Did they recognize any physical likenesses or resemblances or did they feel like strangers with little in common with each other? This reunion initiated a series of visits and weekend stays with her children and grandchildren, attempting to rebuild their fractured past. Would each visit remind them of their loss, reliving Ada's fractured motherhood and Graeme and Hannah's fractured mothering each time?

There may have been several factors working against Ada, including different backgrounds to that of her husband (country/city), the possibility of being from different classes and different educational backgrounds. Lacking in support and friends, lacking in familiarity in a new rural setting and possibly alienated from both family networks, all would have greatly contributed to her isolation of nursing two babies in a rural town. These issues would have produced difficulties in the marriage. Whilst their first 4 years of marriage and the birth of their first child appear uneventful, by the arrival of their second child their marriage was under stress. Subject to the strong ideologies of motherhood of the time, her responsibilities in raising her children and her role as housewife were clearly defined and socially expected. These strict prescriptions ignored the power relations within her marriage and the social conditions of her mothering. Situated within the modern patriarchal family, Ada's gendered roles as wife and mother were undermined by the power and authority of her husband as head of the family.

Throughout the interwar years, the patient populations were increasingly made up of married women (Garton 1988). For Ada, it is difficult to tell whether the institution was a refuge from an unhappy marriage and domestic strife, or an experience of further oppression. The social definition of femininity in Australia was so repressive that when women were seen to fail to live up to such expectations, they were cast aside into mental hospital confinement (Matthews). Ada's fractured motherhood occurred through many ways simultaneously. She was subordinated by the patriarchal power of the state, the medical experts, and her husband who committed her and secured her permanent removal to the institution. The medical authorities, as paternal power, failed to ensure an infection-free birth, failed to assist in recovery from her illness, denied her any future reproduction, and sided with her husband's testimony against her mothering. The police, as state power, failed to safeguard Ada from a potentially abusive husband, disregarding her need for protection.

Ada's fractured mothering occurred through the power of her husband to commit her to the mental institution, inflating his paternal power in the deception of denying her existence to her children. Her motherhood was further fractured in the institution when Ada mothered another's children, whilst alienated from her own. Her eventual reunion with her children in their adult years ended the silence and separation, however reminding them of their loss. Ada's fractured motherhood occurred as the result of the locus between motherhood, mental disorder, and patriarchal power. Mothering, in such oppressive circumstances, resulted in Ada losing her agency and control over her life, losing her identity and praxis as mother, wife, and lover.

REFERENCES

Bordo, S. *Unbearable Weight: Feminism, Western Culture, and the Body*. London: University of California, 1993.

Brockington, I. "Historical Perspective: Infective Delirium." *Archive of Women's Mental Health* 10 (3) (2007): 129–130.

Cade, J. F. J. *Mending the Mind: A Short History of Twentieth Century Psychiatry*. South Melbourne: Sun Books, 1979.

Cawte, J. *The Last of the Lunatics*. Melbourne: Melbourne University Press, 1998.

Chesters, J. "A Horror of the Asylum or of the Home: Women's Stories 1880-1910." *Madness' in Australia: Histories, Heritage and the Asylum*. Eds. C. Coleborne and D. MacKinnon. Perth: University of Queensland Press, 2003. 135-144.

Coleborne, C. *Reading Madness: Gender and Difference in the Colonial Asylum in Victoria, Australia, 1848-1888*. Perth: Network Books, 2007.

Garton, S. *Medicine and Madness: A Social History of Insanity in New South Wales, 1880-1940*. Sydney: University of New South Wales Press, 1988.

Garton, S. "Shut Off from the Source." *The Australian* 22 November 2000: 45.

Harding, S. *Feminism and Methodology: Social Science Issues*. Bloomington: Indiana University Press, 1987.

Jeffcoate, T. "Indications for Therapeutic Abortion." *British Medical Journal*, 1 (5173) (1960): 581–588.

Kelm, M. "Women, Families and the Provincial Hospital for the Insane, British Columbia, 1905-1915." *Journal of Family History* 19 (2) (1994): 177-193.

Kitchens, R. "The Informalization of the Parent-Child Relationship: An Investigation of Parenting Discourses Produced in Australia in the Inter-War Years." *Journal of Family History* 32 (4) (2007): 459-478.

Larossa, R., L. Bennett and R. Gelles. "Ethical Dilemmas in Qualitative Family Research." *Journal of Marriage and Family* 43 (2) (1981): 303-13.

Lewis, M. "Hospitalization for Childbirth in Sydney, 1870–1939: The Modern Maternity Hospital and Improvement in the Health of Women." *Journal of the Royal Australian Historical Society* 66 (3) (1980): 199-205.

Loudon, I. "Puerperal Insanity in the Nineteenth Century." *Journal of the Royal Society of Medicine* 81 (February 1988): 78-79.

Marland, H. *Dangerous Motherhood: Insanity and Childbirth in Victorian Britain*. London: Palgrave Macmillan, 2004.

Matthews, J. J. *Good and Mad Women: The Historical Construction of Femininity in Twentieth Century Australia*. Sydney: George Allen & Unwin, 1984.

Morris, A. "Gendered Dynamics of Abuse and Violence in Families: Considering the Abusive Household Gender Regime." *Child Abuse Review* 18 (6) (2009): 414-427.

Reiger, K. *The Disenchantment of the Home: Modernising the Australian Family 1880-1940*. Melbourne: Oxford University Press, 1985.

Reinharz, S. *Feminist Methods in Social Research*. New York: Oxford University Press, 1992.

Ruddick, S. *Maternal Thinking: Towards a Politics of Peace*. London: The Women's Press, 1990.

Scott, J. *A Matter of Record: Documentary Sources in Social Research*. Cambridge: Polity Press, 1990.

Showalter, E. *The Female Malady: Women, Madness and English Culture, 1830-1980*. London: Virago Press, 1985.

Strom, S. *Beyond the Typewriter: Gender, Class, and the Origins of Modern American Office Work, 1900-193*. Urbana: University of Illinois Press, 1992.

Summers, A. *Damned Whores and God's Police: The Colonization of Women in*

Australia. Melbourne: Penguin Books, 1975.

Wood, M. *The Writing on the Wall: Women's Autobiography and the Asylum*. Chicago: University of Illinois Press, 1994.

Woodside, M. "Psychological and Sexual Aspects of Sterilization in Women." Groves Conferences on Conservation of Marriage and the Family, 1947-1948 Proceedings (May, 1949). *Marriage and Family Living* 11 (2) (1949): 73.

5.
Who Decides If Mothers Are Crazy?

From Freud's Mother to Today's

PAULA J. CAPLAN

I N KEEPING WITH THE THEME of this book, this chapter is about the
fact that, given what our culture does to mothers, it is remarkable that
any mother retains her sanity and little short of miraculous that so many
mothers do the enormous amount of good that they do. As will be addressed,
the two sets of myths about mothers that pervade dominant North American
culture (and many other cultures as well) make it nearly impossible for mothers
to feel relaxed and confident that what they are doing constitutes being a good
mother or to avoid constantly feeling that they are harming their children. The
ways that many assumptions and expectations about mothers in the mental
health system are grounded in prejudice against mothers will be discussed, as
will the unrecognized fact that much of what at most has been called mother-blame in fact fits the definition of hate speech and the ways mothers have
often been mistreated in the courts.

THE MOTHER MYTHS AND HOW THEY OPERATE

Powerful myths about mothers tend to lead to the setting up of mothers and
daughters against each other, so that they are often inclined to blame themselves
and each other for the problems in their relationship with each other, as well as
for most of their family's problems and even many of the problems in the world.

As I have pointed out (Caplan 1989, 2000), the myths about mothers can be
divided into the Perfect Mother Myths and the Bad Mother Myths, which in
combination create the societally pervasive framework that leads to the blaming
of mothers for so much and to the negative labeling of potentially everything
any mother might do. I have identified at least twelve of these myths (Caplan
1989, 2000) and will here mention just some examples. The Perfect Mother
Myths set standards of perfection that are so high that no one could possibly
meet them. They include the myth that a good mother never gets angry, is
100 percent giving and nurturant 100 percent of the time, and is *by nature*

capable of knowing everything necessary to raise happy, well-adjusted children. No one, regardless of sex, could ever meet such standards, but usually fathers, unlike mothers, are not considered *bad* parents but only perhaps imperfect ones for failing to meet them. The Bad Mother Myths are used in somewhat more complicated ways; they function to encourage people to take negative, neutral, or even good things mothers do and use them as proof that mothers are deficient or harmful. These myths include that mothers cannot possibly raise happy, emotionally healthy children without a great deal of advice from experts and that mothers are bottomless pits of neediness. The first of these two myths is a portrayal of mothers as deficient, and the latter tends to be considered proof of mothers' defects and potential to cause serious harm by being too helpless, selfish, and demanding. The myth that mother-daughter closeness is sick is an example of the way that something that can be quite wonderful is instead cast as pathological. Let me describe an example of this. When *Don't Blame Mother* was first published, my mother and I were asked to appear on Phil Donahue's television show, *Donahue*. On the panel of invited guests with us were a mother and her daughter, the latter somewhere in her thirties. The daughter had moved back to her mother's home to try to save money while starting a business. Donahue asked which of them was doing the laundry, and when the mother said she was, some audience members laughed and rolled their eyes, reacting as though there were something wrong with this – perhaps that the mother was still treating the daughter as though she were a young child. When Donahue asked which of them was doing the cooking, and the daughter said she was, because if she did not, her mother would not eat well, again some audience members responded as though something were wrong with this – perhaps this time that this was a role reversal, with daughter taking care of mother? I pointed out that these reactions were cause for concern: If we had simply reported that two adults were sharing living space with each other, that one was doing the laundry, and that the other was doing the cooking, everyone would have said, "Good. Makes sense. That's called sharing." However, I noted, as in this example, as soon as you introduce a mother into virtually any scenario, you can be sure that people will begin to read pathology into it, to mock the behavior of mother, offspring, or both. Cumulatively, the myths about mothers lead nearly every mother to monitor her own behavior constantly, terrified that she is doing too much or not enough, being too loving or too unloving (Caplan 1989, 2000).

In the examples of myths I have mentioned, you may have noticed that some are mutually exclusive. For instance, one cannot simultaneously *naturally* know everything necessary to raising happy, healthy children *and* need copious advice from experts in order to achieve this aim. Similarly, one cannot simultaneously (if only on sheer physics principles about forces and vectors) be constantly, totally giving (nurturant) and constantly, totally demanding (needy), simulta-neously producing a total outgoing force and generating a total incoming one. How, we might ask, can such mutually exclusive myths not only co-exist in our society but also be strong and pervasive? I have suggested (Caplan 1989, 2000) that this mutual exclusivity serves an important function. In societies characterized by dramatically unequal distributions of power, like ours, those with more power tend to want to retain that power, and a primary method for achieving that retention is finding and maintaining certain individuals or groups as scapegoats. That way, if anything goes wrong, and those with less power move for greater spreading of the power (and/or wealth), those with more power can say, "The current power distribution is not causing the problem. What's causing the problem is Person X or Group Y," the scapegoated person or group. Mothers have long constituted an easily scapegoated group, for they have tended to have very little power or wealth, and they have been subjected to tremendous pressures to raise happy, even perfect children, so they have not been in positions to organize to protect and defend themselves or to get their group out of a scapegoated position. Furthermore, since society assigns to mothers almost total responsibility for how their children turn out and for their daily care, mothers have had little or no time and energy left over to consider how to move out of the role of scapegoat. Precisely because mothers are given so much responsibility, it has been dead easy to blame them for virtually anything that goes wrong with their offspring, including rudeness, psychological and behavioral problems, and criminal conduct (Caplan and Hall-McCorquodale, 1985a, 1985b). And because one of the Bad Mother Myths is that mothers are dangerous when they are powerful, mothers who have asserted themselves even slightly have been blamed for their husbands' sexual impotence, for men's failure to obtain employment, and for family members' drug and alcohol abuse and eating problems. Indeed, it is hard to think of anything that is not blamed on mothers. Returning, then, to the question of the function of mutually exclusive myths about mothers, we see that in order to maintain mothers as scapegoats and thus to maintain the current distribution of societal power, it is dangerous to those with the most power if mothers are seen to do anything admirable, because that makes it harder to keep them scapegoated. Thus, a myth for every occasion is needed, a myth that enables one to take anything a mother does and use it to "prove" that mothers are bad.

THE MENTAL HEALTH ESTABLISHMENT PATHOLOGIZES
AND BLAMES MOTHERS

The mental health establishment, since the time of Sigmund Freud if not before, has played a powerful role in pathologizing mothers. The use of psychiatric diagnoses—which are nearly always appallingly lacking in scientific foundation—has promoted the crazymaking ways mothers are treated. For instance, some of the authors of the third revised edition of the psychiatric diagnostic manual, *The Diagnostic and Statistical Manual of Mental Disorders III-R* (APA) thought up the idea, when that edition was in the planning stages, of creating a category they first called Masochistic Personality Disorder, later called Self-defeating Personality Disorder (see Caplan, 1995 for the history of creation and insertion of this category into the *DSM* and its later removal). This category was used, among other things, to treat as a mental illness the placing of other people's needs ahead of one's own. Since mothers are expected to do precisely that with their own needs, they were in a Catch-22 situation, being damned for being bad mothers if they failed to behave in selfless ways but being labeled as mentally ill if they did behave in selfless ways (Caplan 1995). Although political considerations led to removal of that category from the *DSM*, many therapists still label as "self-defeating" or "masochistic" unhappy mothers who legitimately wonder if they are appreciated, given the invisibility of so much that mothers do. A mother who experiences a loss of a loved one and is still grieving two months later is at high risk for being diagnosed with Major Depressive Disorder rather than as experiencing normal grief, because that category appears in the diagnostic manual. A mother who becomes understandably irritated with her partner or children or who becomes anxious or angry at them is at high risk of being diagnosed with Premenstrual Dysphoric Disorder, another *DSM* category created by some of the manual's authors (Caplan 1995). And as research has revealed, if just about any psychiatric label is applied to a child or adult, that person's mother is highly likely to be blamed by those in the mental health system. Ian Hall-McCorquodale and I read 125 articles in nine major mental health journals and categorized each article according to 63 different measures of mother-blame (Caplan and Hall-McCorquodale 1985a, 1985b). We found that in the 125 articles, mothers were blamed for 72 different kinds of psychological problems. Two examples will illustrate how far the authors of these articles sometimes had to reach in order to blame the mothers. In one article about men who had been prisoners of war, the authors said that they had found that the children of former POWs were more likely than other children to have emotional problems, and they attributed this to the fact that the fathers remained deeply disturbed by their POW experiences and that this upset their wives, whose upset then harmed the children. The fathers' upset was not named as a cause of the children's problems. In another article, a little boy whose parents were farmers was described as having school phobia. Who was blamed for this? Only his mother. For instance, she was described as having allowed him to stay up late watching television, but his

82

father was not mentioned as someone who might also have allowed that or who might have tried to put a stop to it if indeed the mother was the one allowing it (see Caplan and Hall-McCorquodale 1985a, 1985b for more detailed descriptions).

MOTHER-BLAME OFTEN IS HATE SPEECH

Deeply troubled by the persistence of mother-blame, I had spent many years writing and lecturing on the topic when it suddenly struck me how often mother-blame fits the description of hate speech. I spoke about this at a Massachusetts conference about mental health and human rights, and I was encouraged to keep talking and writing about it. I think that one reflection of the low esteem in which mothers are held—although perhaps it was just that the quality of my writing was poor (you can judge for yourself)—is that when I wrote a piece about mother-blame often taking the form of hate speech, it was rejected by, among others, *The New York Times, The Washington Post, The Los Angeles Times, The Boston Globe, San Francisco Chronicle,* and *Atlanta Journal Constitution.* I believe that still more rejected it, but I stopped keeping track. Ultimately, the piece was printed online at <rejectedletterstotheeditor.com>, a site specializing in the publication of letters to editors and other pieces that editors have declined to use. It is called "Mocking Mom: Joke or hate speech?" and here it is:

Imagine: a stand-up comedian says, "I've gotta tell you about this Black guy," and people in the audience roll their eyes and guffaw ... just because the comedian said, "Black guy." We would recognize this as racism. But when a comedian says, "I've gotta tell you about my mother," and people roll their eyes and guffaw, we don't usually recognize this as "momism," prejudice against mothers. Despite increased awareness of the damage done by nasty comments about women in general, those who make such comments about women who are mothers do so with impunity. The mocking and blaming of mothers are committed by many who would not dream of telling a generally sexist "joke" and would protest if someone else did so. But replace the word "women" with the word "mothers," and anything goes. Mothers—and stepmothers and mothers-in-law—are considered legitimate scapegoats, and when anyone objects, as I regularly do, I hear, "Oh, but you don't know my mother!" Often, the nasty things said to and about mothers sink to the level of hate speech. That is, it is speech that is intended to or has the effect on its targets of silencing, shaming, intimidating, and rendering them powerless, helpless, and hopeless.

If that stand-up comedian says, "I've gotta tell you about my father!" the audience waits to hear what's funny. Simply being a father does not put one in an easily scapegoated group; simply being a mother does. Why is the bumper sticker that reads "Mother-in-law in trunk" considered hilarious, and if it's so funny, where is the "Father-in-law in trunk" sticker? Why do audiences laugh uproariously when I observe, "No one ever says, 'Thanks, Mom, for the week's worth of nourishing and tasty meals and the great job of dusting the furniture',", but wait silently for what comes next when I say, "Does anyone ever say, 'Thanks, Dad, for the great work you did on the lawn'?" Except on Mother's Day and greeting cards, the thought of praising women for mothering work strikes us as funny. Why? Because it is unimaginable in a way that praising men for being good fathers is not. After 20 years of doing research, clinical work, teaching, and writing about mothers, it recently struck me: Mother-blame is often hate speech. So is the mockery of mothers. That sounds melodramatic; we realize we put mothers down but don't consider ourselves frankly hateful. Hate speech, though, is vilification of a person because of their membership in a demeaned group and is aimed to shame, silence, intimidate, and otherwise control its targets. Here is one common example: A major television network producer called me last week, because she was doing a "light, funny" piece about "meddling mothers." Mothers are expected to love and protect their children nonstop, but caring, conscientious mothers are often labeled as meddling, intrusive, and controlling or are simply ignored. So of course they feel ashamed, silenced, intimidated. The most extreme and terrifying consequence of the hatred of mothers is that the leading cause of death of pregnant women in America is murder, usually by their male partners.

I worked in a clinic where no therapist described any mother as good: They described mothers as either intrusive, smothering, and overly emotional or cold, rejecting and—if the child was male—castrating. How do demeaning, blaming, and name-calling affect mothers? The same way they affect anyone: Mockery causes shame, fear, and a sense of powerlessness. And because mothers are blamed for anything that ever goes wrong with their children, other effects include intense fear, anxiety, self-monitoring, and exertion to the point of chronic exhaustion, because a mother's worst nightmare is her child being harmed. For more than two decades, nearly every mother I meet has acknowledged constantly judging herself, wondering whether she is intrusive and smothering or cold and rejecting. It is virtually impossible to locate the narrow band of behavior that seems acceptable for mothers.

How did it come to this? For centuries, mothers have been expected to meet impossibly high standards and to do so without expressions of appreciation and without credit for success, although they have usually been the only ones blamed when anything bad happens to their children. Empirical studies of therapists' articles in clinical journals have shown how far clinicians, regardless of their sex, often reach in order to blame mothers. Even the kinds of information they provide about patients' fathers often differs from what they provide about mothers: One professional reported that the patient's father was 36 and a bricklayer, while the mother was 34 and "nervous." And as a prominent radio host once said on-air just before interviewing me when, as a misbehaving young boy, he was taken to a psychiatrist, who asked what was wrong. He told the psychiatrist that his father beat him; but soon, said the host, the psychiatrist had him blaming his mother rather than his father.

Not long ago, mothers were expected to teach their daughters to be sweet, passive, and selfless and to support their sons' striving for independence, assertiveness, and achievement. They were also expected to be perfect role models for their daughters, showing how to be unfailingly good wives, mothers, and housekeepers. With the women's movement's Second Wave, the entry of increasing numbers of women into the paid workforce, and the rise of Martha Stewart, expectations for mothers have only increased: Now, they also have to teach their daughters to be assertive and achievement-oriented and nevertheless avoid being threatening to men who have traditional ideas about women. Mothers are expected to execute flawlessly the tasks of wives, mothers, and housekeepers while also holding down a paid job...and do it all with ease and calm. Mothers who protest these superhuman standards are likely to be called selfish, ungrateful, whiny, or strident.

Myths about mothers pervade our culture, some casting mothers in a negative light (Bad Mother myths) and some setting impossibly high standards, so that mothers look bad because they fail to meet them (Perfect Mother myths). It is fascinating that some myths are mutually exclusive, such as the Perfect Mother myth that "Mothers naturally know everything about raising happy, healthy children" and the Bad Mother myth that "Mothers cannot raise happy, healthy children without lots of help from experts." Such mutually exclusive myths serve the function of keeping mothers scapegoated: With a myth for every occasion, everything mothers do can be used to support the claim that they are deficient.

All of this happens in a social and political culture that has limited high-quality, affordable daycare; underpays women relative to men; and penalizes parents of both sexes when they leave work to care for ill children: Women are "not truly committed to their job," and "What kind of man takes time off work to care for a kid?" Furthermore, despite the spate of books on "The New Man," the average father living with wife and children still does less than one-third of the child- and household-related chores, and many of those are the more visible, less daily and monotonous kind (getting the car repaired, changing light bulbs). Compounding mothers' difficulties is the myth that women have achieved equality in all respects and the only reason men don't do half the housework is that women are too controlling to "let" them. This makes the contemporary mother, who tends to believe that she is failing everyone—her children, partner, parents, employer, workmates, friends—feel as crazy and inept as Betty Friedan's unhappy housewives of the 1970s: What's wrong with me, that I am so unhappy, frustrated, and absolutely exhausted?

In a society that truly values mothers, mockery and vilification of them would not be considered acceptable and certainly not funny. In such a society, the myths of motherhood would be recognized as unfair, crazy-making obstacles to the essential work of raising daughters and sons.

—Paula J. Caplan, Ph.D., is a clinical and researcher psychologist and the author of ten books, including *The New Don't Blame Mother: Mending the Mother-Daughter Relationship.* She will teach "Myths of Motherhood" at Harvard University this fall. [that was in 2007]

EDITOR'S NOTE [from the editor of <rejectedletterstotheeditor.com>]: *One of the interesting aspects of Paula J. Caplan's Op-Ed piece is that in its original usage—coined by writer Philip Wylie in Generation of Vipers (1942)—"momism" connoted a mother's overbearing smothering of a child, and the excessive attachment of a child to a mother, according to the Wordsmith website. The online Thinkmap Visual Thesaurus offers "overshielding" and "overprotection" as synonyms for "momism." Caplan's reappropriation of the term points to the momism within Wylie and subsequent authors' definition of "momism."* (Published online at <http://www. rejectedletterstotheeditor.com/culture4.html> May 15, 2007)

FREUD'S MOTHER SPEAKS

Many of the things I have said about blaming of mothers and the use of hate speech about mothers are in various ways embodied in the character I wrote into my play, *Call Me Crazy*, which is about the dangers and the absurdity of psychiatric diagnosis. From the beginning of the play, an old woman dressed in early twentieth-century clothing silently watches the proceedings as late twentieth-century therapists discuss their patients, often without understanding them very much, and as four actors in hospital gowns portray "mental patients" who use various comedic and satirical performances to try to break through the wall of ignorance that separates the therapists from them. About two-thirds of the way into the play, the old woman comes downstage and speaks to the audience as follows:

(AMALIA FREUD enters, dancing, to "The Blue Danube," then speaks to the audience)

AMALIA: Thank you for coming. I'm Amalia Freud. Amalia Nathanson Freud. I lived to be 95 years old. I wanted people to know my son was the great psychoanalyst, winner of the Goethe Prize for literature. But behind their polite smiles I saw the thought, "This is the mother whose son discovered that all little boys want to have sex with their mothers." *Discovered*. Hah!

And about girls and their mothers what did he "discover"? That our daughters resent us for not having had the courtesy to provide them a penis. I had five daughters. How do you think his words made me feel? I love my Sigmund, but this is too much.

He told people he felt all his life like a conqueror because he was my "indisputable favorite." Hah! So he thought. The truth is I adored all of my children. How could I not? Sigmund was my first-born. I loved my daughters also but kept having to have more—five in all—until Jacob got one more son.

Most of the time Sigmund was growing up, his father and all the other children and I shared three bedrooms, but he had his own. He needed to study. He complained that his sister Anna's piano lessons were noisy when he was trying to study. We got rid of the piano. Anna and I were sad but not angry. We understood. Maybe he had too much. And he decided who was normal.

You know, he threw up his hands and said, "What do women want?" What's not to understand? Is it healthy to take a mother's love or a wife's love and make it seem so complicated?

Normal, shmormal. Oh, I realize some people have to be put away—they can hurt themselves, or someone else. But it's a tough problem. You start putting people away, and somebody's going to decide *who* gets put away, somebody's going to choose the rules. Is what these guys decide any better than what my son decided? Thinking about it makes my head hurt.

But I'll tell you what I *have* noticed. Who decides is who has the power. And somehow, they seem to decide the people most like them are the normal ones, the good, the healthy, the deserving. It's the others who are derided, called dangerous ... sent away. My five daughters—one went to New York, three were gassed in Auschwitz, and the last one starved to death in the camp at Theresienstadt.

Thank you for listening.

(AMALIA turns and walks off, as "The Blue Danube" plays) (excerpted from Caplan, 1996 © 1996 Paula J. Caplan)

BIAS AGAINST MOTHERS IN THE COURTS

In the courts, as we know in no small measure from the brilliant Phyllis Chesler, what happens to many mothers involved in child custody cases is alarming and shameful, especially when the child's father is sexually abusing the child. In fact, when child sexual abuse by the father is raised by the mother, the court is much more likely than otherwise to switch custody from the nonoffending mother to the father (Caplan 2005). How can this happen? It often happens through the father's lawyer's use of either the specific term Parental Alienation Syndrome (which currently does not appear in the *DSM* but the inclusion of which in the forthcoming *DSM-5* is the subject of intense lobbying: See Ancis) or the more general "alienation" to pathologize and damn a mother who has good reason to believe that her child is being molested by the child's father. These labels are used to argue that the problem is not that the father has indeed been abusive but that the mother is a sick and/or vengeful woman who for no good reason is trying to turn the child against its father. Sometimes the diagnostic category of Munchausen's Syndrome by Proxy is used to argue, similarly, that the father has done no wrong and that the primary problem is that the mother has a sick need to draw attention to herself by falsely claiming that her child is being harmed. Whichever label is used, the effect is to take attention away from the father's criminal, abusive conduct and instead to focus on the mother as the allegedly evil one who forces her child to lie. Underlying these arguments is the assumption that fathers do not sexually abuse their children, and indeed, many people's (and judges') antipathy to acknowledging such horrific behavior by fathers helps make it easier to have the pathologizing of the mother accepted. Today, it is estimated that at least 58,000 children are being molested in these situations, according to Leadership Council on Child Abuse and Interpersonal Violence (leadershipcouncil. org). In an attempt to stop these abuses and persuade the courts to handle the cases in ways that lead to protection of molested children and cessation of the unwarranted, knee-jerk blaming of their mothers, some people are forming the Family Court Reform Coalition that includes the National Organization for Women, Justice for Children, and many other groups. They are aiming for legislation by the United States Congress that would change what happens in regions that receive funding from the federal *Child Abuse Prevention and Treatment Act* (CAPTA); that is, since too often the criminal nature of child sexual abuse is ignored, and cases of molestation within the family are heard in family courts and treated as though they were simply family matters and mental health matters, it would be good to change legislation so that regions failing to treat these as criminal cases would not receive CAPTA funding. I believe that it would be important to hold Congressional hearings about these cases, but approaches I have made with Eileen King from Justice for Children, to staff working with Senator Patrick Leahy's Senate Judiciary Committee and to Senator Ted Kennedy's Health, Education, Labor and Pensions Committee have borne no fruit beyond their expression of concern that such things happen. It has been clear that the suffering of these tens of thousands of children is not a priority. As one aide said, "We have big things to think about, like the detainees at Guantanamo." It got us nowhere to point out that even though human rights abuses of several hundred adults at Guantanamo are appalling and should be stopped. What we are also asking them to deal with involves vastly more individuals, all of whom are children.

Feeling sad and horrified by what I have seen happen in so many of these child sexual abuse cases when they go to court, how powerless are so many of the mothers, and how they and the children suffer from a court system that contains so many misogynist (or at best, uninformed) judges, I wrote a play called *What Mommy Told Me*. It is based on one particular case with which I am familiar but is also typical of these cases in nearly every respect. The play was commissioned by Manhattan Theatre Source's "Estrogenius" Festival for women playwrights and premiered at that festival. At the Mamapalooza conference in New York in 2009, it was read by Nichole Donjé Allison, who also directed it, and by Laurence Cantor, Evelyn Holley, and Noura Joust Boustany. One excerpt from the script illustrates the tendency of many judges to assume that mothers are either mentally ill or pathological liars or both and the way this keeps them from learning the truth, in this instance in a case in which the child had disclosed that her father had molested her. This excerpt is one key to the title of the play, because the mother had told her child to speak the truth to the judge, and the truth is that the father did molest her, but the judge's assumption that what the mother told the child was to claim falsely that her father molested her is what the judge takes from his interview with the child:

(Lights up on JUDGE, seated in his chambers, wearing his judicial robes)

JUDGE: Bring in the child.

(CHILD takes two steps toward JUDGE, holding a stuffed animal, a bunny.)

JUDGE: *(gently)* Don't be afraid. Come here.

(CHILD steps toward him.)

JUDGE: It's okay. No one is going to hurt you.

CHILD: Mommy said you will help me.

JUDGE: Yes, my child.

CHILD: Where's Daddy?
JUDGE: You'll see him later. I want you to tell me the truth.

CHILD: Okay.

JUDGE: You told your teacher that your Daddy does bad things to you.

CHILD: That he puts his hand in—

JUDGE: You don't have to tell me. I know what you told the teacher.

CHILD: He shows these movies to me and his girlfriend. The ladies dance around these poles—

JUDGE: It's all right, you don't have to say any more. I just want to ask you a few questions about today.

CHILD: *(relieved)* Okay.

JUDGE: You live with your Mommy?

CHILD: Yes.

JUDGE: Does your Mommy like your Daddy?

CHILD: Mommy told me that she wants him to be nice to me.

JUDGE: Your Mommy knew you were coming to talk to me. Did she tell you what to say?

CHILD: She told me to tell—

JUDGE: To say your Daddy does bad things?

CHILD: *(beat)* Yes, because he—

JUDGE: All right, my dear. You've done very well. You can go now.

(CHILD exits from chambers.)

JUDGE: Full custody of the minor child to the father.

FINAL NOTE

Those who claim that we now live in a post-feminist world, meaning that women now have rights and benefits that equal those of men, have failed to look at the world of mothers, where far too often the still-pervasive, influential myths about mothers, the general societal condoning of mother-blame to the point that even hate speech about mothers tends to remain invisible, and where the traditional mental health system and the courts too often perpetuate the casting of mothers as inadequate, damaging, and even mad.

Speech from Moms Gone Mad Conference, 2009, revised and reprinted.

REFERENCES

American Psychiatric Association (APA). *The Diagnostic and Statistical Manual of Mental Disorders III-R.* Washington, DC: American Psychiatric Association, 1987.

Ancis, J. "Parental Alienation Syndrome." 2009. Web. <http://www.rejectedletterstotheeditor.com/culture4.html>.

Caplan, P. J. CALL ME CRAZY (A comedy-drama with music). 1996. DVD available from <paulacaplan@gmail.com>.

Caplan, P. J. *Don't Blame Mother: Mending the Mother-Daughter Relationship.* New York: Harper and Row, 1989.

Caplan, P. J. "Mocking Mom: Joke or Hate Speech?" Web. <http://www.rejectedletterstotheeditor.com/culture4.html>. May 15, 2007.

Caplan, P. J. *THE NEW Don't Blame Mother: Mending the Mother-Daughter Relationship.* New York: Routledge, 2000.

Caplan, P. J. *They Say You're Crazy: How the World's Most Powerful Psychiatrists*

Decide Who's Normal. Reading, MA: Addison-Wesley, 1995.

Caplan, P. J. "Sex Bias in Psychiatric Diagnosis and the Courts." *Women, Mental Disorder, and the Law: A Feminist Reader.* Eds. Wendy Chan, Dorothy Chunn and Robert Menzies. London: GlassHouse 2005. 115-26.

Caplan, P. J. WHAT MOMMY TOLD ME. (theatre script) 2008. Available from <paulacaplan@gmail.com>.

Caplan, P. J. and I. Hall-McCorquodale. "Mother-Blaming in Major Clinical Journals." *American Journal of Orthopsychiatry* 55 (1985a): 345-353.

Caplan, P. J. and I. Hall-McCorquodale. "The Scapegoating of Mothers: A Call for Change." *American Journal of Orthopsychiatry* 55 (1985b): 610-613.

Chesler, P. *Mothers on Trial: The Battle for Children and Custody.* New York: McGraw-Hill, 1986.

II. MOTHERHOOD:
RESISTANCE AND EMPOWERMENT

6.
Matroreform

Toward Collapsing the Mother's Panopticon

GINA WONG

ATROREFORM (Wong-Wylie 2006, 2010) is a transformative maternal practice and is "an act, desire, and process of claiming motherhood power ... a progressive movement to mothering that attempts to institute new mothering rules and practices apart from one's motherline" (Wong-Wylie 2006: 739). In original writings, I describe matroreform as a psychological, spiritual, and emotional reformation of mothering from within that includes removal and elimination of obstacles to self-determination and self-agency as a mother and woman. Indeed, a maternal revolution can and is being achieved through the twenty-first century motherhood movement. Furthermore, matroreform is required in order to gain asylum from the mother's panopticon (see below). As such, it is important to clearly delineate matroreform, which captures the process by which this can happen.

In the introduction to this volume, I write about the mother's panopticon and the ubiquitous "observational gaze" that mothers are conscripted into by virtue of gender and fertility. The panopticon (Foucault 1979, 1989) is a figurative embodiment of the imprisonment that keeps mothers under malevolent, omnipresent surveillance. This metaphor captures that an observer (opticon) sees all (pan) prisoners without prisoners knowing whether and when they are being watched (see also Chapter 2). Imprisonment in the mother's panopticon is a result of oppressive ideologies and discourses that regulate mothers' lives (e.g., the *good mother* ideology; *intensive* and *sacrificial mothering* expectations). Depression, anxiety, self-doubt, low esteem, as well as competition and comparisons, judgment, and regulation of other mothers as well as herself are natural reactions to imprisonment in a panopticon. Mothers revolting from the hegemonic forces occur through the process of matroreform. As such, matroreform—as our way towards collapsing the mother's panopticon—requires further conceptualization and substantiation which are the aims of this chapter.

The purpose of this chapter is to further elucidate matroreform. Herein, I explore this transformative process that represents mothers coming into their own power apart from individual and societal constraints. I suggest matricentric feminism (O'Reilly 2011) and the social ecological perspective to inform and undergird the developing concept of matroreform. As well, the qualitative research method of Institutional Ethnography (IE) will be explored and described as an appropriate method of studying matroreform. Future as well as current explorations and conceptualizations of matroreform are needed and thus underscored in this chapter.

HISTORY OF MATROREFORM

Matroreform, which I explored at the *Moms Gone Mad* conference, was derived from the term *matrophobia* first introduced by poet Lynn Sukenick. The concept was more fully developed by Adrienne Rich, who describes how matrophobia occurs when girls and women eclipse any part of themselves that wants to become mothers. This is evoked out of fear and is described as a desire to purge themselves of their mothers' bondage, to become individuated and free from expectations of self-sacrifice and pressures to be a perfect domestic housewife (Wong-Wylie 2010). Renowned French feminist and author Elizabeth Badinter articulates the continued constraints of marriage and motherhood in her best-selling and controversial book entitled: *The Conflict: How Modern Motherhood Undermines the Status of Women*. She writes:

> ...married life has always come at a social and cultural cost to women, not only in terms of the unequal division of household work and child rearing, but also in its detrimental effect on their career and salary prospects. Today, it is not so much marriage itself that takes its toll on women (marriage no longer being a necessity), but sharing a household and especially after the birth of a child. Sharing a household, which is now widespread, has not brought an end to domestic inequality, even if surveys show that it is more favorable to women than marriage ... [i]t is the arrival of a child that dramatically increases the amount of time women spend on domestic chores.... (16)

Ever present today as it was when Rich described the oppressive constraints of motherhood, Badinter expresses the continued toll on women. Bearing ideologies such as the *good* woman and *sacrificial* mother in mind and recognizing their influence on mother's roles and in our inherited roles from previous generations, Rich describes:

> Matrophobia is the fear not of one's mother or of motherhood but of *becoming one's mother*. Thousands of daughters see their mothers as

having taught a compromise and self-hatred they are struggling to win free of, the one through whom the restrictions and degradations of a female existence were perforce transmitted. Easier by far to hate and reject a mother outright than to see beyond her to the forces acting upon her. But where a mother is hated to the point of Matrophobia there may also be a deep underlying pull toward her, a dread that if one relaxes one's guard one will identify with her completely. (193)

This fear of becoming one's mother and experiencing the oppressive bonds of conventional motherhood in matrophobia pushes daughters to deny and denigrate any part of themselves that are similar to those of their mothers in any way. The daughter may enact life choices and create standards of living that are in contrast to what her mother represented in an effort to perform "radical surgery" as Rich depicted (194). There exists a push and pull to her mother nevertheless. In much the same way, a woman in a tenuous and dying marriage may avoid a newly separated or divorced woman, the fear of assimilation and over-identification with that which is most dreaded and feared when one is at the precipice—in a paradoxical push and pull—is what Rich attempts to capture in the concept of matrophobia.

Rich believes that matrophobia is a result of a daughterhood fraught with witnessing the self-sacrificing, capitulating, and self-denial of mother as she attempts to live out the good, sacrificial mother expectations. These daughters experiencing matrophobia attempt to extricate themselves from anything remotely close to their mother, to do everything possible to avoid the same trap. From a feminist analysis, daughters deconstructing (consciously or sub-consciously) their mothers' oppression and the trap of the good and sacrificial mother ideologies, exemplifies empowerment and agency. Nevertheless, the original concept of matrophobia is not derived from feminist approaches, but about the experience of daughters having unrealistic and unfounded fears and thus desiring to project themselves out of the motherline (Wong-Wylie 2010).

When I first introduced the original concept of matrophobia and translated it to matroreform (Wong-Wylie 2006) I used reflective understandings and narrative recounts of journal entries to my daughters. I included seven pho-tographic images to describe my relationship with my mother, layered with first generation Canadian born-Chinese cultural differences between myself and her. I connected reflections and understandings of my relationship as a daughter to my mother and shared how I actively worked to forge a different kind of bond with my two daughters. By engaging in this process, I deployed and enacted the active practice of matroreform.

I argue that Rich's conceptualization of matrophobia inadequately and inac-curately captures the full experience behind the fear of becoming one's mother.

I criticize Rich's use of the term *phobia*, which is defined as an intense and unrealistic fear. Instead, I advance that the concept of phobia fails to capture the real and common experience of feminist girls, woman, and mothers and their refusal "to reproduce or [remain] trapped in the oppressive bonds of conventional motherhood" (Wong-Wylie 2006: 142) or the mother's panopticon. Such a process, I argue, is necessary and certainly not borne out of unrealistic fears. In the place of matrophobia, I propose instead *matroreform*—as 'reform' aptly represents an essential feminist model of practice and an empowering process toward claiming motherhood power.

More specifically, I translate the experience into one that has the potential to be a transformative maternal practice. In this sense, "matroreform is an act, desire, and process of claiming motherhood power" (142). Legitimizing matroreform, Canadian feminist maternal scholar Fiona Joy Green identifies it as a central process in her longitudinal and intergenerational study of feminist motherlines. Through this research and her article *Matroreform: Feminist Mothers and Their Daughters Creating Feminist Motherlines* and book *Practicing Feminist Mothering*, Green confirms matroreform as a process that "is not only reforming and reaffirming (but also) a feminist act of voicing up and out of invisibility and silence" (Wong-Wylie 2006: 136). Greene illustrates how a small group of feminist mothers and their daughters dismantle the patriarchal script and reform their own stories of motherhood and daughterhood. She describes how feminist daughters with feminist mothers can perpetuate an enduring feminist motherline and argues that matroreform is central to this process.

Matroreform is further supported by Andrea O'Reilly in her writing "Feminist Mothering as Maternal Practice: Maternal Authority and Social Acceptability of Children" (2009). O'Reilly explores Ruddick's concept of *maternal practice* and sheds light on a contradiction for feminist mothers. That is, Ruddick's definition of *maternal practice* includes mothers raising daughters to be socially responsible and to have an identity and belonging within the culture. O'Reilly cogently presents the conflict that "as a feminist mother I view this demand as interfering with, and negating the overarching aim of my feminist maternal politic and practice; namely to raise my children apart and against the culture of patriarchy" (217). O'Reilly poignantly articulates the paradox of feminist mothering and maternal practice and conceives matroreform to be among the processes that feminist mothers engage in that remains consistent with Ruddick's concept of maternal practice. She maintains that as a community of feminist mothers, we do have a responsibility to raising our daughters to be socially responsible and to have an identity and belonging with the culture (of feminist mothers). Matroreform thus contributes to developing an ethic of maternal practice still in line with Ruddick's concept as feminist mothering and our community grows and connects motherline generations. Indeed, matroreform is as an empowering process out of oppression toward reformation of mothering through individual and collective resistance.

THEORETICAL UNDERPINNINGS OF MATROREFORM

Several theoretical underpinnings substantiate the concept of matroreform. A specific mother-centred feminist approach coined as *matricentric feminism* (O'Reilly 2011) paves the way to fuller deconstruction of the mother's panopticon and aids in formulating matroreform. Furthermore, a *social ecological model* as well as *institutional ethnography* (IE) provide foundational basis for systematic understanding of matroreform. Institutional ethnography is a qualitative method of research that is appropriately suited to delineate ways in which matroreformic change occurs. Each of these approaches is delineated below followed by advancement of a current research study I am conducting on matroreform. Also, I describe an upcoming international conference hosted by the *Motherhood Initiative for Research and Community Involvement* (MIRCI) in October 2013 that is dedicated to the theme of matroreform.

MATRICENTRIC FEMINISM

Revisiting my earlier discussion in the introduction of the book, without feminist analysis and critique, we cannot fully come to know the entrapment of the mother's panopticon. The mandate and objectives to revolutionalize motherhood are distinct and need recognition and legitimacy in their own right. O'Reilly explains:

> I use the term matricentric to denote a mother-centred standpoint and to emphasize and designate it as a particular, long overdue, and urgently needed mode of feminism. This is not to suggest that a matricentric feminism should replace traditional feminist thought; rather, it is to remind and emphasize that the category of mother is distinct from the category of woman, and that many of the problems mothers face—socially, economically, politically, culturally, psychologically and so forth—are specific to women's role and identity as mothers. (2011: 25)

Through matricentric feminism, matroreform can be fully activated and fully realized as an empowering process that can reform motherhood outside the prison of the mother's panopticon. That is, in order to release mothers, matricentric feminism is imperative to deconstruct ideologies and discourses.

Feminist strategies to shred damaging ideologies that buttress the mother's panopticon can be explored once the contours of the prison are understood and realized. The dominant discourses are so prevalent, ubiquitous, and automatically promulgated that they are ostensibly invisible. Through the rigor of matricentric feminist analysis, we can see, deconstruct, and critique the deeply ingrained and endemic ideologies. At this stage, awakening to the observational gaze and mother's panopticon, and generating meta-understandings to what drives how we feel and what we do as mothers, are the first steps.

MATERNAL DEVELOPMENT: THE SOCIAL ECOLOGICAL MODEL

Social ecology is the study of people in the context of their social environments (Hawley). Kurt Lewin was one of the first to assert that behavior is determined by an interaction between the individual and her or his environments. The Social Ecological Model (SEM) is an effective and appropriate framework to understand people in their individual, community, social, and global contexts; as well as the theory and politic of their lives. The human ecological model (Bronfenbrenner) parallels the SEM in that they are both holistic conceptualizations underscoring the development of a person within her or his environment. However, SEM more specifically focuses on the social ecology of women. As such, this approach captures the bidirectional influence between the multiple levels of ecosystems ranging from the microsphere (individual mother) to the macrosphere (global issues). Matroreformic change ideally occurs at all levels in the ecology of mothering. Nevertheless, from SEM perspectives, a shift on one level influences and affects change on other levels.

The SEM applied to maternal development fosters awareness of the multiple levels of environmental and institutional contexts that impact mothers. It also provides a lens to deconstruct the ways in which mothers' lives and circumstances are circumscribed. Maternal praxis, identity, politic, theory, and ideologies examined from a social ecological approach captures the complexity involved in reforming the institution of motherhood. That is, SEM fosters systematic deconstruction to compel deeper understanding of mothers' madness, oppression, resistance, and empowerment. Regarding mother's development vis-à-vis social ecological contexts involves the following parameters.

The innermost sphere or level is the *microsystem* which consists of the individual mother: psychological factors, roles, genetics, behaviors, identities, personal history, and the many components that make up who she is. The microsphere is where many mothers exclusively locate and attribute their mothering identity. Motherhood, as an unexamined institution, engenders a sense that mothering is a deeply personal, intimate, and unregulated enterprise (neoliberal perspectives). Indeed, mothering is deeply personal and an intimate relationship; but it is much more ... and is most certainly regulated. Viewing maternal development through the lens of SEM calls forth such recognition and awareness. The next level in conceptualizing maternal development is the *mesosystem*, which is where interpersonal interchanges and relationships (e.g., mother-child) in the family and within close small groups occur. Here we find the influence of schools, teachers, local community groups, friends, and small-scale organizations that impact the mother and vice-versa.

Next is the *exosphere* which is a broader scale level of influence including social codes for women and mothers, larger organizational ideologies, institutional practices, medical and psychiatric discourses on women/mother's mental health, and ethics of a culture to name a few. It also can include political affiliation and in effect, "any setting which affects the individual although the individual is not required to be an active participant" (Bronfenbrenner 43). Existing at the level of the exosphere are the discourses and ideologies such as the *good, sacrificial, perfect* mother that impacts everyday experiences for the mother at all levels. The mother's panopticon takes more shape and texture when we examine it from influences specifically at the level of the exosphere. For example, depression, anxiety, guilt, shame, and self-recrimination are often experienced by mothers when they feel they are not living up to being the mothers they envisioned themselves to be. Rather than seeing our entrapment in the panopticon, mothers may firmly believe that the pressures and ideals of how she hoped to mother are her own self-made standards (analysis exclusively from the level of micro/mesosphere). Critique from matricentric feminism and a social ecological perspective reveals broader level influences (exo and macrosphere) and transforms our understanding of self-denigration and culpability.

A profound example of this is conveyed by Donna F. Johnson and Helen Levine in Chapter 11. They share the ways in which five mothers they worked with were gripped and overcome by internalized blame and self-loathe when their own child died by suicide. The support mothers received from each other, along with the feminist analysis provided by Levine, enabled the mothers to see that there exists a socially constructed ideal of the perfect mother that blames mothers for all ills of their children. They were then able to disentangle and understand their feelings from this promulgated ideology that provided some release. Well exemplified by this, a feminist analysis extending to broader levels of influence was paramount to engendering deeper awareness and deconstruction of how sociocultural discourses of motherhood shape mothers' legitimacy, personal identity, and socio-emotionality.

Lastly, the *macrosphere* includes many ideologies that may or may not be directly related to mothering (e.g., disease, war, Christianity, ethos, political discourses, and so forth). These external realities affect mothering to varying degrees. Many greatly impact mothering and motherhood identity, agency, and development. They involve aspects such as cross-cultural representations and experiences of mothers across the globe (e.g., Gusii's preference for sons and definition of "childlessness" to mean "sonlessness" as discussed in Chapter 7). Practices, policies, and ideologies around the globe can impact the role and status of mothers at individual, community, and social spheres. Transference of global understandings occurs through transnationalism, globalization (for example) and media. Practices and policies, for example, involved in overseas adoptions can greatly affect women, mothers, families, and local communities. On a broad scale, macro-level happenings influence the everyday lives of mothers although perhaps more distally than the other levels. A mother's panopticon deconstructed at the level of macrosphere under social ecological principles identifies the broader ideological contexts and overarching interactions between the mother within the greater social and institutional landscape.

INSTITUTIONAL ETHNOGRAPHY: RESEARCH METHOD TO STUDY MATROREFORM

Institutional ethnography (IE) is a qualitative method of research developed by Canadian sociologist Dorothy Smith (Devault; Taber; Walby) whereby people's everyday experiences and lives are understood from the context of social and institutional relations. Institutional ethnography goes hand in hand with the theoretical framework of social ecology. Institutional ethnography furthermore is grounded in symbolic interactionism, ethnomethodology, phenomenology, Marxism, and feminism (Campbell). Fundamental to IE research is the understanding that people do not exist independently from the social ideologies that are imbedded in the culture and the influences from all levels of their environment (micro, meso, exo, and macrosystem). This approach to studying individuals within the context of their lives can include an array of data gathering methods: mapping, text-analysis, participant observation, and interviews (Devault; Walby).

Institutional ethnography has been successfully applied in mothering research. Marj Devault provides a detailed account of how Smith's initial concepts of IE were used to study single mothers working to manage their children's schooling. Devault furthers Smith's argument by showing that IE as a research method can not only determine social and economic inequities for single mothers, but can identify solutions for amending the organization of schooling. Institutional ethnography fosters understanding of issues from holistic perspectives and can locate broader institutional ideologies and practices that thwart maternal growth and identity.

CURRENT ENDEAVORS IN MATROREFORM
AN EVOLUTION OF MOTHERING: RESEARCH ON MATROREFORM

A program of research is underway and at this stage involves a funded study on matroreform conducted through the auspices of Athabasca University in Alberta, Canada entitled: *An Evolution of Mothering: Understanding the Experience of Matroreform*. The main impetus for this research study is to gain understanding into the process of matroreform and how it is evolving the institution of mothering. To date, matroreform has been conceptualized mainly from theoretical perspectives. While a growing body of literature is developing in the area of matroreform, conceptualizations informed by the lived experiences of mothers themselves are needed. This investigation will contribute overall to the development and understanding of matroreform and the revolution of mothering with a point of entry in the microsphere (the mother herself) and exosphere (perspectives and interpersonal relationships specifically with her own mother as well as with her own children). This study will generate understanding of how those levels are impacted by the mesosphere (ideologies, maternal discourses) and macrosphere (global policies and institutional practices).

The purpose of the study is to explore the lived experiences of matroreform from mothers who self-identify as having made the intentional choice to mother her children in fundamentally different ways than how she was mothered. The goal of this research is to gain insight and in-depth understanding into the phenomenon and process of matroreform. Implications for further maternal scholarship in the area, for best counselling practices, and for research directions will be highlighted at the end of the study. This study is in line with matricentric feminism and underscores maternal development from a social ecological lens and utilizes IE to investigate matroreform.

Mary E. Bhave demonstrates through her research involving twenty-first century mothers that they shape their own narrative of motherhood in reference to their experience of being mothered. Bhave states that, "these 21st century moms engage in a dynamic, intentional selection process of components to develop how they see themselves as a modern mother" (188). The current study on matroreform will shed light on *how* they do this; *why* they choose to mother differently than their own mothers; *what* components, if any, do they maintain; *what* occurs in the moment-to-moment interactions that are different from the way they were mothered; and on a larger scale, *what* affects and fosters women to engage in matroreformic change. These insights will generate greater understanding into how mothers, from micro to macrosphere, engage in an empowering process to reformulate mothering. The findings will be related to the institution of motherhood and specifically elucidate the process, development, and understanding of matroreform.

MATROREFORM AND MOTHERLINES: INTERNATIONAL CONFERENCE

In January, 2011, the following conference call for papers was disseminated: (http://www.motherhoodinitiative.org/MatroreformCFP.pdf). The international conference will be held in Toronto, Ontario on October 18-20, 2013. It will be the first of its kind across the globe that brings together maternal activists, scholars, and mothers to inform our understanding on all levels of matroreform and motherlines.

CALL FOR PAPERS (REPRINTED)

Matroreform, a feminist term coined by Canadian psychologist Dr. Gina Wong, is a psychological, spiritual, cognitive, and emotional reformation of mothering at an intra- and interpersonal level, a process by which mothers reproduce a new way of mothering apart from her motherline; and it represents an holistic, sociocultural revolution of motherhood at a global level. As a transformative maternal practice of claiming motherhood power, this progressive movement to mothering includes new and empowering motherhood ethos, ideologies, rules, views, and practices apart from one's motherline and apart from dominant and normative discourses of the sacrificial and good mother. Adrienne Rich describes matrophobia as the result of a daughterhood fraught with witnessing the self-sacrificing, capitulating, and self-denial of the mother who is trapped in the oppressive bonds of conventional motherhood. These daughters attempt to extricate themselves from anything remotely close to their mother, which often includes a fear of becoming mothers themselves. Instead, through a process of matroreform, these daughters become mothers and instigate mothering practices and ideas that are right for them; thereby entering new possibilities of what it means to mother. *Motherlines*: Award-winning poet, author, and Jungian analyst Naomi Ruth Lowinski notes that our mothers are the first world we know, the source of our lives and stories, and embody the mysteries of origin that tie us to the great web of kin and generation. Motherlines acknowledge the embodied experiences and knowledge/s of mother/child relationships and the responsibilities, challenges, and labour involved in motherwork. Motherline stories contain invaluable lessons and memories of mothering, as well as support for mothers.

This conference will examine the experiences and counter-experiences of matroreform and motherlines that are enduring, severed, or threadbare. We will explore the feminist, political, social/cultural, economic, historical, religious, spiritual, and psychological dimensions of these topics. We welcome submissions from scholars, academics, students, artists, mothers, daughters, and others with experience and knowledge in the areas of matroreform and motherlines.

Narratives of experiences as well as cross-cultural and comparative works are encouraged. We also encourage a variety of submissions including scholarly papers from all disciplines, creative submissions, and reflective pieces such as poetry, narratives, artwork, and performance art.

CONCLUSION AND FUTURE DIRECTIONS IN MATROREFORM

Matroreform is a concept that requires further emphasis and research in order to fully understand how it aligns and contributes to the twenty-first century motherhood movement. It is an empowering process of maternal revolution from oppression to empowerment at various levels. This chapter outlined endeavors currently underway to gain greater understanding of matroreform. Matricentric feminist perspectives, social ecological theory, and IE as a suitable research method were described to substantiate and undergird the construct of matroreform. Further maternal scholarship in the area and research endeavors are needed to understand the ways in which we can counter hegemonic forces and collapse the mother's panopticon.

Research that examines matroreform at each and all levels of influence is needed. For example, investigating oppressive ideologies reified by local community groups and the ways in which mothers resist those forces would further illuminate the process of matroreform at this level of ecological influence (exosphere). Likewise, studying how an organization like MIRCI (York University) or Demeter Press (focused specifically on publishing motherhood scholarship) collectively revolutionizes mothering at the micro, meso, exo, and macrosphere is also worthwhile investigation of matroreform. Employing other research methods, for example, a narrative inquiry (Clandinin) into the stories or a phenomenological investigation (van Manen) into the essence of the experience of matroreform from, for example, lesbian mothers' perspectives, is also encouraged. Our resistance and empowerment is enhanced as we document and more fully grasp how matroreformic change occurs and contributes to the twenty-first century motherhood movement and the collapse of the mother's panopticon.

Author's Note: Inquiries about the conference or program of study on matroreform, please contact Gina Wong <ginaw@athabascau.ca>.

REFERENCES

Badinter, E. *The Conflict: How Modern Motherhood Undermines the Status of Women.* Toronto: HarperCollins Publishers, 2011.

Bhave, M. E. "Burning the Apron Strings: How 21st Century Women Conceptualize Their Mothering in Comparison to That of Their Own Mothers." Eds. M. Walks and N. McPherson. *An Anthropology of Mothering.* Eds. M. Walks and N. McPherson. Bradford, ON : Demeter Press, 2011. 83-101.

Bronfenbrenner, U. *The Ecology of Human Development: Experiments by Nature and Design.* Cambridge, MA: Harvard University Press, 1979.

Campbell, M. (2003). "Dorothy Smith and Knowing the World We Live in." *Journal of Sociology and Social Welfare* 30 (1) 3-22.

Clandinin, J. D. (2007). *Handbook of Narrative Inquiry: Mapping a Methodology.* Newbury Park, CA: Sage Press, 2007.

Devault, M. L. "Introduction: What is an Institutional Ethnography?" *Social Problems, 53* (3) (2006): 294-298.

Foucault, M. *Discipline and Punish: The Birth of the Prison.* Harmondsworth, UK: Penguin, 1979.

Foucault, M. *Madness and Civilization: A History of Insanity in the Age of Reason.* New York: Vintage Books, 1989.

Green, F. J. "Matroreform: Feminist Mothers and Their Daughters Creating Feminist Motherlines." *Journal of the Association for Research on Mothering* 10 (2) (2008): 11-21.

Green, F. J. *Practicing Feminist Mothering.* Winnipeg, Manitoba: Arbeiter Ring, 2011.

Hawley, A. H. *Human Ecology: A Theory of Community Structure.* New York: Ronald Press, 1950.

Lewin, K. *A Dynamic Theory of Personality.* New York: McGraw-Hill, 1935.

Lowinski, N. R. *The Motherline: Every Woman's Journey To Find her Female Roots.* Carmel, CA: Fisher King Press, 2009.

O'Reilly, A. "Feminist Mothering as Maternal Practice: Maternal Authority and Social Acceptability of Children." *Maternal Thinking: Philosophy, Politics, Practice.* Ed. A. O'Reilly. Bradford, ON: Demeter Press, 2009. 217-229.

O'Reilly, A. *The 21st Century Motherhood Movement: Mothers Speak Out on Why We Need To Change the World and How To Do It.* Bradford, ON: Demeter Press, 2011.

Rich, A. *Of Woman Born: Motherhood as Experience and Institution.* New York: W. W. Norton & Company, 1976.

Taber, N. "Institutional Ethnography, Autoethnography and Narrative: An Argument for Incorporating Multiple Methodologies." *Qualitative Research* 10 (1) (2010): 5-25.

van Manen, M. "Phenomenology of Practice." *Phenomenology and Practice* 1 (2007): 11-30.

Walby, K. "On the Social Relations of Research: A Critical Assessment of

Institutional Ethnography." *Qualitative Inquiry* 13 (7) (2007): 1008-1030.

Wong-Wylie, G. "Images and Echoes in Matroreform: A Cultural Feminist Perspective." *Journal of the Association for Research on Mothering* 8 (1,2) (2006): 35-146.

Wong-Wylie, G. "Matro-phobia and Mothering." *Encyclopedia of Motherhood.* Ed. A. O'Reilly. Newbury Park, CA: Sage Publications, 2010. 722-725.

7.
Cultural Representation of Childlessness

Stories of Motherhood Resistance

GRACE BOSIBORI NYAMONGO

I N THE GUSII SOCIETY childlessness has two definitions, natural and socio-cultural. Natural childlessness is the inability to bear children as a result of sterility or old age, also referred to as involuntary childlessness (Dyer et al.). Socio-cultural childlessness is the definition of gender imbalance in the African perspective. Accordingly, in some African patrilineal societies childlessness is a situation when couples have children of the same sex, partic- ularly girls. This is considered as gender imbalance in regard to childbearing. However, having boys only is not considered childlessness. This condition is more problematic when children are girls only. It is more critical in patrilineal societies such as the Gusii where sons as opposed to daughters are considered the main determinants of a lineage. Within this context, childlessness does not always mean barrenness, but instead, it may literally mean lack of male children. Therefore, among the societies that value male children, infertility and sonlessness are offhandedly looked upon as childlessness. At the same time there is a hatred for childlessness (Ahanotu). Hence, the boundary between infertility and childlessness is indiscernible. Moreover, the socio-cultural and psychological consequences of such a situation have the same impacts (such as unhappiness, humiliation, stigma, and social isolation) on the 'childless' woman.

This chapter explores the predicament of women in some African traditional societies like the Gusii, who must act "madly" in order to cope with the societal perception of cultural and natural childlessness. In this chapter, childlessness denotes the social cultural definition of sonlessness as opposed to barrenness. In fact, the amount of resistance experienced by the so called childless women among the Gusii and other societies where male children are a valuable asset is a clear demonstration of cultural madness entrenched in society's perception about sonlessness. The cultural inclination towards male children, also referred to as male-child preference syndrome is responsible for gender inequality and discrimination against women at all levels in contemporary society. Thus the chauvinistic madness caused by various discriminatory practices against women in society is ingrained in societal perspective about male-child preference. Thus, society is "mad" due to the belief that a woman is worthless without a son or a child.

Several studies have focused on barrenness in third world and developing countries, but a few studies have critically examined the cultural experience of childlessness in Kenya and fewer still have explored the overwhelming aspect of male child preference in the Gusii society. The purpose of this chapter is to analyze the concept of childlessness, and in particular sonlessness among the Gusii from a cultural perspective so as to bring to light the Gusii women's perspectives and experiences of socio-cultural childlessness, and the 'gendering' of children that has brought to the fore the value of male children in African societies especially the Gusii. This chapter thus re-interprets childlessness by exploring the concept of male-child preference syndrome and the 'madness' strategies that the Gusii women employ so as to cope with the situation of childlessness.

My decision to explore childlessness among the Gusii women stems from my personal connection with the Gusii society. I was born and socialized among the Gusii, where male children were and still are favoured over females. In particular, my choice to study childlessness among the Gusii has been strongly inspired by Uma Narayan and Chandra Talpade Mohanty, Ann Russo, and Lourdes Torres who have emphasized the importance of analyzing women within a specific cultural context so as to avoid generalizing women's experiences and concerns. The aim of this chapter is to contribute to an underexplored cultural aspect in African society so as to provide answers to the following questions: How does male-child preference syndrome affect Gusii sonless women? What is the attitude of men and women towards sonless women? How does the society treat sonless women? What are the remedies of negative attitudes towards sonlessness? In an attempt to answer these questions, I hope to contribute to new knowledge about the socio-cultural definition of childlessness from the African context. I will also contribute by helping society find strategies to change negative attitudes towards sonlessness and childlessness.

This chapter employs the Women, Culture and Development (WCD) framework to discuss childlessness from a cultural perspective. The WCD does not only help us to understand culture as a representation of people's lived experiences, but as ideas, norms, values and practices that shape perceptions of society in regard to socio-cultural and development issues. "Drawing on culture as a lived experience, a WCD lens brings women's agency to the foreground as a means for understanding how inequalities are challenged and reproduced" within a specific cultural context (Bhavnani, Foran and Kurian). Therefore, this chapter uses the WCD framework to theorize the cultural construction of childlessness among the Gusii and how it shapes women's lives in contemporary society.

Culture is an integral factor as it influences women's social status of childlessness (Bhavnani et al. 7-21). Researchers focusing on the WCD framework including Bhavnani et al. consider culture as a crucial aspect of society through which we can understand peoples' experiences, beliefs, and practices. Therefore, WCD is significant in exploring the Gusii society's attitude towards childlessness as it enables us to understand Gusii women's experiences and how they articulate their socio-cultural conditions as a result of childlessness. While on the one hand researchers have shown that infertility among women in some developing countries can cause social isolation and stigmatization (Van Balen), on the other, before the promulgation of the Kenyan constitution in August 2010, sonlessness among the Gusii and other Kenyan communities has been found to be a customary reason for women in patrilineal societies to be denied access to and control over ancestral land on the basis of gender (Ellis et al.; Kenya Land Alliance; Kevane; Mackenzie; Maloba; Neil; Nyamongo 2009; Verma). Even after the promulgation of the Kenyan constitution in August 2010, nothing has changed. The majority of the girls and the Gusii in general do not seem to understand what the new constitution entails especially in regard to women and girls' rights.

Since these traditional practices and beliefs are deeply entrenched in people's minds, it becomes problematic and critical to question the cultural beliefs and practices that discriminate against women. Accordingly, in many African cultures, traditions are significant as they influence people's attitudes and beliefs. For instance, the works of Austin Ahanotu, Ayuen Majok and C. W. Schwabe, and Bethwell Ogot confirm that societies consider children as an important aspect in marriage institutions across African cultures and the belief in children to provide continuity to a lineage. Therefore, children bear a significant landmark in marriages in the African societies.

An examination of the situation of childlessness from a cultural perspective is pertinent as it provides insight into some customary practices such as patrilineal inheritance and male child preference syndrome that are usually responsible for discrimination against the Gusii women. Customary practices and beliefs hinder women from questioning practices that disparage them, such as gender discriminative rights to land, the practice of polygyny, unequal gender relations, and decision making at all levels in society. On the whole, childlessness prevents most African women from inheriting ancestral land or making decisions on key issues. It thus helps us to understand why and how women and girls are marginalized in the African society (Ellis et al.; Mackenzie; Maloba; Nyamu-Musembi). As Kum-kum Bhavnani and colleagues note, drawing on culture as a lived experience enables us to examine the "socio-cultural, political, and economic domains in order to understand how inequalities can be challenged and reproduced" (8) by society and women themselves. At the same time, Grace Nyamongo (2009) points out that most Gusii people continue to hold the cultural belief that daughters can not inherit ancestral land because of cultural prohibition against this practice and that this perception is a clear depiction of the cultural influence on people. It thus shows the extent to which Gusii cultural beliefs have been ingrained in the Gusii people's minds. The following section provides a brief background within which the cultural madness of the male-child preference is reinforced and promulgated among Gusii.

THE GUSII CULTURAL AND HISTORICAL BACKGROUND

The Gusii people live mainly in three districts of Western Kenya namely: Nyamira, Kisii, and Gucha. The Gusii are the second largest ethnic group in Nyanza Province after the Luo. They are concentrated in several subdivisions (Girango, Gitutu, Machoge, Nyaribari, Bassi, and Bonchari). The Gusii people speak *Ekegusii*; one of the Bantu languages. According to Isaac Nyamongo (1998) the Gusii share common customs, traditions and history, and trace a common ancestry from *Mogusii* whom they claim to be their founding father. For this reason, they refer to themselves as *Omogusii/Abagusii* (singular/plural). The Gusii, a short form of *Abagusii* are patrilineal and trace their descent on the male lineage. Lineage and clanism form a significant aspect of the Gusii kinship system (Uchendu and Kenneth). This is reflected in the emphasis placed on patrilineal rights to land inheritance and in traditional obligations bestowed on men/sons as future heirs and protectors of the community, especially during confrontations with violent neighbours (Ogot).

Historians suggest that the name Gusii or Kisii originates from Gwassi, a place on the shores of Lake Victoria where these Gusii settled prior to their present settlement in the Gusii highlands. After a terrible drought and famine in the sixteenth century, the Gusii people migrated from Kisumu and settled in the Kano plains near the shores of Lake Victoria. The Gusii lived in the Kano plains for five to seven generations. Throughout this period, the Gusii engaged in various activities such as hunting, grazing, gathering wild fruits, and producing grains especially finger millet. Nevertheless, because of the Luo expansion, cattle raids, and attacks against the Gusii during their stay in the Kano plains, they moved to Kabianga area in Kericho District.[1] At the Kabianga area, rinderpest (a cattle disease) and bad climate did not favour the rearing of livestock and cultivation of crops by the Gusii. This situation forced the Gusii to relocate to the current Gusiiland (Bogonko; LeVine and LeVine; Maxon; Ng'ang'a; Ochieng).

According to Sorobea Bogonko and William Ochieng the Gusii encountered various attacks from their neighbours, the Kipsigis, Maasai, and the Luo, before and after settling in Gusiiland. For instance, during the battle of Saosao in the late 1880s, the Gusii collaborated with their Luo neighbours in a successful war against the Kipsigis who had entered Gusiiland for cattle raids. The hostility experienced by the Gusii from their neighbours may have influenced the wide-spread practice of polygyny among the Gusii men in order to produce more children, especially sons who could protect their community against ethnic conflicts over boundaries and cattle raids by neighbouring communities. Such protection could only be achieved through the community's physical security which was anchored on men. As is reflected by Ogot in a Padhola song: "*Eee one child is not enough, One child is inadequate, Eee, when the war drum sounds 'tindi! Tindi!' Who will come to your rescue—one child?*" (99).

Men's role of protecting the society from violent encroachment is one of the reasons for male-child preference among the Gusii. In retrospect, it is also a justification for the widespread practice of polygyny among the Gusii. Within this context, the Gusii believed that having more sons was a source of future security. It is worth noting here that a polygamous Gusii men household acquired social status by having several wives and children especially sons. Traditionally, the practice of polygamy mainly benefited men as it promoted their social status. It also symbolized wealth and leadership.[2] On the contrary, for the Gusii, women's social status could and can still be achieved through their sons. Such lopsided cultural practices and beliefs threaten the position of sonless women in society as without sons/heirs, it means that that they cannot have social recognition or access to the most significant resource for subsistence farming and socio-economic well-being, particularly land (Ellis et al.; Nyamu-Musembi; Wanyeki). Meanwhile, a recent study of the Nyamira women tea producers revealed that male children were, and still are, preferred to girls because they are considered future heirs and individual household's mainstay (Nyamongo 2009). This has driven Gusii women *mad*.

REASONS FOR MALE CHILD PREFERENCE

In African societies, children are the primary reason for marriage (Ahanotu; Majok and Schwabe). Children are a significant resource to many couples as they provide companionship and a promising socio-economic environment to the lonely parents, in particular the aging and the sickly. Although having children is considered a blessing to those who need them, some researchers have shown that barrenness as a source of childlessness is a serious problem among couples and has been recognized as a major cause for divorce and abandonment of wives throughout many African cultures (Larsen; Walraven et al.). In many Kenyan patriarchal societies lack of boy child is also considered childlessness. For example, among the Gusii, a woman who has daughters only suffers similar consequences as a barren woman. As such, a barren or sonless woman is unlikely to win societal recognition and respect in the Gusii society. Therefore, while on the one hand a barren woman may be expected to keep trying until she conceives, on the other, a sonless woman is required to continue having children until a male child is born. Yet, such practice is most likely to be detrimental to a woman's health. Staff van Bergstrome and Mario Samucidine argue that because of the consequences of childlessness, women risk their health to correct the situation as seen in some of the mechanism used for responding to childlessness such as illegitimate marital relationships. Given the prevalence of HIV/AIDS the *madness* of striving to conceive the "right sex" (albeit understanding) may be fatal to the woman, her child, perhaps her husband. Nonetheless, women are conditionally forced to respond to the madness caused by societal stigma.

Another factor that reinforces the value of male children is the widespread belief that a sonless parent will not receive a decent burial (Denga). The Gusii, like other societies where ancestral worship is strongly upheld, continue to believe that sonless couples will be forgotten as soon as they die due lack of lineage (Pashigian). Hence, the common question in favor of male child preference is "who will bury me when I die?" Traditionally, neither women, daughters, nor granddaughters can take part in funeral rites in the Gusii society let alone making decisions concerning burial issues. Therefore, the way the Gusii approach life and death shape their attitude toward male children. Completely entrenched, such cultural practices encourage couples to have several sons and great grandsons to ensure a proper burial and to ensure continuation of their lineage.

Besides lineage, another factor that encourages male child preference over females is men's traditional connection to ancestral land. Among the Gusii, having daughters is problematic when it comes to inheriting ancestral land. Sonless women are concerned that their land and property will be taken away by their male kinsmen upon their death, so they need sons to inherit their ancestral land. Like other African patriarchal societies where patrilineal inheritance is commonly practiced, the Gusii customs prohibit women from inheriting ancestral land in their homes because male children are the only designated heirs (Maloba; Nyamongo 2009; Nyamu-Musembi). Moreover, under some customary practices across African cultures, sonless women only have usufruct[3] rights to land and very little rights to inherit their spouses' property (Ellis et al.; Sundby). The assumption is that once women are married, their husbands will allocate them land. However, even those limited use rights are precarious because of the socio-cultural conditions attached to land use. Researchers concur that some women are likely to lose the usufruct rights upon the death of a husband or divorce of a spouse (Cliggett; Ellis et al.; Gordon; Kevane;

Wanyeki). According to Price Neil, if "a man dies with no sons, his eldest brother inherits his property and authority. A woman who is widowed without sons … is likely to be evicted from her deceased husband's land…" (416). The same applies to many widows in some parts of Uganda and Tanzania (Bondo).

Taking this all into account, I argue that as a result of cultural "childlessness," women commonly experience unhappiness and humiliation. As a Gusii woman, I reflect on how the madness of male-child preference affects sonless women. The oppression experienced by sonless women is so intense that it causes not only social isolation but also emotional madness. The consequences of son-lessness are profoundly felt when such women are jilted by their spouses or discriminated against in terms of ancestral land inheritance. Some researchers concur that the practice of allocating land to sons in many patriarchal societies has forced women to bestow their loyalty upon their male kin, particularly husband and sons (Garson; see also Kevane; Maloba; Wanyeki). This practice underlines women's dependence on the male kin. It further contributes to the marginalization of women and girls by reinforcing the propensity of giving sons more value and recognition in society.

According to Lisa Cliggett, Majok and Schwabe and Ritu Verma women in many cultures believe that sons will provide economic and social security for their parents at old age. Likewise, such women consider their sons as a 'pension plan' as well as economic security in old age. As a result, there is a tendency to invest in their sons for future reciprocity. But among the Gusii, Nyamongo (2009) argues that in the past girls were considered significant assets for labor and wealth in terms of dowry. In the contemporary society, there appears to be a slight change of attitude towards girls. Currently, some Gusii people believe that highly educated women will marry rich husbands who will pay huge amount of dowry in the form of cattle or money to their parents, while others think that educating girls enables them to be socially and economically independent. A few Gusii people think that girls are better assets than boys as they tend to be more supportive to their parents compared to the sons.

TRADITIONAL REMEDIES FOR CHILDLESSNESS

Researchers focusing on childlessness in many parts of Africa argue that child-less (barren) women are stigmatized and socially isolated (Dyer et al.; Gerrits). Moreover, these women live with the fear of being abandoned by their spouses. Additionally, they are under pressure to prove their 'productivity' all the while experiencing frequent humiliation and ridicule (Dyer et al.; Nyamongo 2009). Therefore, childless women, that is, both barren and sonless have to make all attempts to solve their problem of childlessness.

Among the Gusii, having daughters only is not sufficient. Hence, like sonless women, men without sons are usually mocked by their age-mates for inability to prove their "manhood." Consequently, some sonless men may be forced to marry another wife(s) with the assumption that the new wife will bear a son(s) not only to elevate his social status but also to prevent "the extinction of his name" and lineage (Ahanotu 47).

A sonless husband may keep on marrying wives until a son (s) is born. However, a sonless or barren wife is not allowed to oppose her husband's decision as she is blamed for inability to bear the 'right children' or future heirs. She also cannot take another husband for the same purpose. While this practice is one of the justifications for polygyny among most African men, the humiliation and insecurity experienced by sonless women is more severe if they are uneducated and economically dependent on their husbands. Couples, and especially women, have devised mechanisms of coping with challenges of both cultural and natural childlessness.

Women who are infertile may seek modern and traditional treatment. Individuals usually rely on traditional treatment before turning to modern treatment. According to Ivan Van Sertima, African healers had a solid understanding of human anatomy and symptoms of a variety of diseases were capable of healing a wide range of ailments. In support of traditional healers, William Barnnet points out that "African healers followed pragmatic steps in which they would examine patients, reach a diagnosis, and prescribe treatment based on their experience with curing the patient's problem" (204).

Like other African societies, the Gusii believe in explanations to the cause of a problem before seeking treatment. Traditionally, the Gusii people associate infertility with witchcraft and other superstitions. For example, the Gusii believe that if a young woman met a bear or found a mound of stars on the ground at night then it could cause barrenness if not reported for immediate ritual cleansing. Similarly, if an unmarried girl visited a house where a "circumcised" initiate lived and it turned out that the traditional fire in that house (commonly known as the initiates' fire or *omorero bw' omware*)[4] had accidently gone off, then, the girl and the initiate would face future consequences particularly barrenness. Such encounters were believed to find a cure in traditional explanations. Yet, hardly any traditional explanations have been found to be the cause of sonlessness. As a result, many sonless Gusii women have to rummage around for remedies to put right the predicament of sonlessness by devising various mechanisms including embracing polygyny, woman to woman marriage, child adoption, child "purchase," secret maneuvers-illicit sex, or traditional medicine. In this process, I point out that sonless women use different approaches according to their circumstances as not all approaches are conducive to all women.

As already discussed in this volume, polygyny has been a common customary practice across many African cultures including the Gusii. Traditionally, there were and still are various reasons for polygyny. Among the Gusii men, it is a status symbol for leadership, wealth, prestige, and sexual indulgence. Lineage is a significant aspect in many patrilineal African societies. Hence, sonlessness is often a good reason for a man to practice polygyny. This practice is based on the assumption that if the first wife has no sons, the second or third wife would bear sons. Traditionally and practically, women are blamed for being sonless or barren. Although women are generally not allowed to challenge polygyny, for a sonless or barren woman it is more acute. Such woman may only address the situation by devising methods to cope with childlessness and sonlessness.

While acquisition of many wives and children was considered a source of labor or status symbol for men, according to Toyin Falola and [FIRST NAME?] Hakinsson, women in traditional agrarian societies often embraced polygyny for companionship and sharing of strenuous farm labor and domestic activities. However, contemporary societies which are experiencing overwhelming socio-economic challenges, women bear the brunt of polygyny such as sharing scarce resources amid widespread poverty. Moreover, due to the fact that women in polygynous marriages have little authority over their sexual rights, they may be at greater risk of contracting HIV/AIDS and other sexually transmitted diseases (STDs). This is because in polygamous relationships men are likely to engage in unprotected sexual relationships with multiple women (wives), contributing to women's medical and mental "madness." Women are aware that men's decision to be polygynous does not solve the problem of childlessness as polygyny could result into further social isolation should the new wife bear son(s). Due to this possible disparagement, a childless or sonless woman may look for coping strategies to resist cultural "madness."

Woman to woman marriage is a practice whereby a sonless widow/woman, barren woman contracts a form of marriage by paying dowry for another woman for the purpose of representation and inheritance (Ahonatu; Neil). Also known as "female husbands"[5] (Mackenzie; Amadiume) among some African ethnic communities, it is intended for the sonless or infertile woman to guarantee and increase her husband's lineage by acquiring a woman who already has children, particularly sons. Usually dowry is paid by the childless woman to the would-be "wife's" parents. The dowry serves as security for the children of the woman-to-woman union. The dowry also guarantees the children the right to inherit the sonless woman's property including land. Woman to woman marriage is acceptable on condition that the woman getting married already has children and specifically sons. Such woman may have more children with a man of her own choice or the husband wife chooses a husband for her. The practice is only intended to compensate the sonless woman's loss of social status and to ensure continuity of the lineage.

Another form of resistance that women employ to solve the madness of childlessness is a situation whereby an elderly woman confidentially advises the childless wife to have a sexual relationship with a man from her (the wife's) husband's clan in order to bear sons that will appear to be genetically alike. This is a very discreet, surreptitious practice as it is done without the husband's knowledge. It is mainly done if a husband's potency regarding child bearing is in question. In view of this, I argue that this strategy is an oppressed women's covert mechanism because of the confidentiality that is involved. Should a spouse suspect his wife, the elders typically defend her; if not defended she will be divorced or abandoned for being adulterous.

Child adoption is another form of resistance and a strategy for solving the problem of oppression against childless women. This usually involves following legal procedures of adopting children. However this strategy is only accessible to couples who are able to go through all the legal procedures of adoption. Because of the bureaucracies involved, some women opt for the traditional child adoption which is referred to as *okogora omwana*, or literally 'buying a child,' in the local language. In child "buying," a childless woman or her friends identify a fatherless son regardless of age. His kin are approached and a negotiation between the boy's foster parents and the childless woman takes place. Then after payment is made in the form of money or a cow, the boy is released to go to a new home. Such transactions are a significant bond between the two families. Hereafter, the boy enjoys all the social and economic privileges without any reservation.

The other mechanism of addressing the problem of childlessness or barrenness is through traditional medicine. Among the Gusii, there are women who are believed to cure childlessness women by administering traditional herbs.[6] The approach to traditional medicine varies depending on each healer's expertise. Sometimes, a woman may seek remedy without her spouse's knowledge, especially if he is not cooperative. In other cases, both husband and wife may together agree to visit a traditional healer. In such situations, the procedure is more open and once a son is born, the healer is paid for her/his job in terms of a goat(s) and she/he is also allowed to shave the child's hair.[7] This is a popular method of responding to cultural oppression against childlessness among the Gusii community of Kenya. Interestingly, having witnessed some sonless women who were cured by a medicine woman known to me, it is certain that the traditional medicine worked for some women and so far no harm has been reported by those who had used it at that time.

In the recent past, incidents of child theft at hospitals, schools, or homes in many parts of Kenya have been associated with child trafficking and childlessness. In the case of the latter, a childless woman may fake pregnancy and decide to steal a baby through a network of friends.[8] This method is usually futile as many people have been apprehended for stealing infants. Instead of causing agony to another woman by stealing her child, I propose that it is necessary for a childless/sonless woman to employ legitimate methods for coping with the madness of childlessness including woman-to-woman marriage or child adoption.

More specifically, I argue that some of the approaches for solving the problem of childlessness may contribute to the risk of acquiring STDs or HIV/AIDS. For instance, the audacious practice of engaging in extramarital sex, or having several wives as a solution to childlessness, is a great risk to all parties given the fact that no cure has been found for HIV/AIDS. Because of the risks and the audacity that is involved in "curing" childlessness, Bergstrome and Samucidine, believe that people fear childlessness more than STD or HIV/AIDS. However, nowadays, educated women have been empowered with knowledge of human rights. Hence, they are able to strive and thrive in the midst of cultural discriminative practices. Such women have resisted the stigma of childlessness by moving out of the matrimonial home and ensuring that they educate their daughters to become economically independent. In some isolated cases, women have ensured that daughters inherit their late father's property in spite of frown by relatives. Such resistance is a good example for the rest of the womenfolk.

CONCLUSION

In this chapter, I have re-interpreted the concept of childlessness from a Gusii African standpoint and have argued that in the Gusii African patrilineal society childlessness refers to barrenness as well as the lack of a male child. For the Gusii, the lack of a male child may result into a form of social cultural childlessness that greatly reduces a woman's social and economic standing. Children are an important aspect in all African cultures as they are not only the main purpose for marriage, but they determine a woman's social status. Childlessness has negative implications on individual childless women. Hence, those affected have to devise possible means of coping with the problem.

The chapter explored cultural childlessness, also referred to as sonlessness, and has outlined some of the factors that contribute to male preference over females and how this affects the Gusii women. Some of the effects of sonlessness include social isolation, stigma, and ridicule by relatives, the imminent abandonment by spouse or loss of land upon the death of a 'childless' or sonless woman's spouse, and presumed loss of lineage after the death of a childless couple. I have attempted to demonstrate how childless women actively search for solutions to childlessness through various strategies including embracing polygamy, woman to woman marriage, child adoption, and child "buying" among others. The application of these innovative strategies is in response to the issue of cultural childlessness. It is also a means of compensating women for the loss of privileges such as biological motherhood and socio-economic status in a patrilineal society. Through these methods some Gusii women believe that there is always a solution to childlessness.

There is need for further research on African women's perspectives about cultural childlessness and how to recognize traditional expertise in solving women's problems. There is also a need for society to reassess beliefs and practices which are harmful to women's health in their mad response to childlessness. In this vein, awareness raising campaigns need to be conducted to change society's attitude about male-child preference in relation to the current socio-economic situation. For instance, given that the Gusii occupy the most overpopulated districts in Kenya, there is hardly any reasonable land left for future heirs. Hence, the issue of male child preference in relation to land inheritance should not be a pertinent issue. But still, there is need for a holistic approach in relation to African culture within the context of community, individual women, and close relatives. This involves a community's commitment to providing women with adequate resources as well as a good environment to support women's development and their role in sustaining themselves and their dependents. Through this writing, I hope to deconstruct cultural childlessness to recommend to the society to treat all children equally regardless of sex and to make cultural childlessness no longer a neglected issue, but instead, embrace it as a social concern that is common in many societies. Hence, childlessness should not be a hindrance to women and girls' empowerment.

[1]*Kabianga* is a Gusii word that literally means "refusal." Thus, it was the belief that things refused to work in favour of the Gusii. Apparently, following the Gusii encounters at Kabianga. The term Kabianga also symbolically explains that the area was inhabitable to the Gusii (Ng'ang'a 52-55; see also Nyamongo 1998; Ochieng 90-96).

[2]In many African societies a polygynous marriage is an ultimate symbol of male leadership, authority, political domination, security, prestige, wealth, or social status (Gordon).

[3]Usufruct rights refer to temporary access to resources. This is common in most agrarian societies where women have only access to the major agricultural resources such as land. Moreover, women are only custodians of their sons' land.

[4]Circumcision is one of the rites of passage that was and still is performed by some ethnic communities across Africa including the Gusii. Among the Gusii the initiates lived in a hut where they continued to learn and observe community's customs. During the entire period (i.e one month) fire was not expected to go off. It was regarded as a sacred fire. It was called the initiates' fire because it was lit for that purpose and was keenly protected not to go off as

this would be a bad omen to the initiates and those who coincidentally visited the initiates at that time.

[5]In Africa the concept of woman-to-woman or female husbands does not imply that a childless woman would practically marry and have sexual relations with the new woman. Instead, the madness in this kind of relationship is that it allows such woman to bring forth more children with a man or men of her choice in order to "correct" the problem of childlessness.

[6]There are different categories of traditional healers, those who generally heal women from sterility. Hence, the choice of a child's sex does not arise. The second category consists of healers with expertise in a child sex whereby a healer is either known for helping women have sons or daughters. Rarely do such healers do both.

[7]When I was about 15 years old, I learned from my maternal grandmother (one of the healers) how she cured her patients. I noticed that both man and wife were involved in the healing process right from the beginning. The husbands of my grandmother's patients were expected to cooperate.

[8]Many cases of child theft have either been associated with childlessness as seen in the case of Reverend Deya's miracle baby scandal that dominated the Kenyan newsrooms in the past few years.

REFERENCES

Ahanotu, A. M. "Social Institutions." *African Cultures and Societies Before 1885*, Africa Vol. 2. Ed. T. Falola. Durham, NC: Carolina Academic Press, 2000. 35-58.

Amadiume, I. *Daughters, Female Husbands: Gender and Sex in an African Society.* London: Zed, 1987.

Barnnet, W. C. "Medicine, Science and Technology." *African Cultures and Societies Before 1885*, Africa Vol. 2. Ed. T. Falola. Durham, NC: Carolina Academic Press, 2000. 189-215.

Bergstrome, S., and Samucidine, M. "Vulnerability of Childless Women to Sexually Transmitted Infections." *Social Science Research on Childlessness in Global Perspective*. Eds. F. Van Balen, T. Gerrits and M. Inhorn: Amsterdam: University of Amsterdam, SCO-Kohnstamm Publishers, 2000. 160-165.

Bhavnani, K., F. Foran and P. A. Kurian. "An Introduction to Women, Culture and Development." *Feminist Futures: Re-imagining Women, Culture and Development.* Eds. K. Bhavnani, F. John and P. A. Kurian. London, New York: Zed Books, 2003. 1-21.

Bogonko, S. "History." *Kisii District Sociological Profile.* Eds. G. Were and D. Nyamwaya. Ministry of Economic Planning and National Development and

Institute of African Studies, Nairobi: University of Nairobi Press, 1986. 12-27.

Bondo, J. "Women's Rights Within the Family." *Voices of African Women: Women's Rights in Ghana, Uganda and Tanzania.* Ed. J. Bond. Durham, NC: Carolina Academic Press, 2005. 75-82.

Cliggett, L. "'Male Wealth' and 'Claims to Motherhood' Gender Resource Access and Intergenerational Relations in the Gwembe Valley, Zambia." *Gender at Work in Economic Life.* Ed. G. Clark. Walnut Creek, NY: Rowman and Littlefield, 2003. 207-223.

Denga, D. L. "Childlessness and Marital Adjustment in Northern Nigeria." *Journal of Marriage and Family* (44) (1982): 779-80

Dyer, S. J., N. Abrahams, M. Hoffman and Z. M. Van der Spuy. "Men Leave Me as I Cannot Have Children: Women's Experiences with Involuntary Childlessness." *Human Reproduction* 17 (6) (2002): 1663-1668.

Ellis, A., J. Cutura, N. Dione, I. Gillson, C. Manuel and J. Thongori. *Gender and Economic Growth in Kenya: Unleashing the Power of Women.* Washington, DC: World Bank, 2007.

Falola, T. *The Power of African Cultures.* Rochester, NY: University of Rochester Press, 2003.

Garson, K. "Understanding Work and Family through A Gender Lens." *Community, Work and Family* 7 (2) (2004): 163-178.

Gerrits, T. "Infertility and Matrilineality: The Exceptional Case of Macua." *Infertility Around the Globe: New Thinking on Childlessness, Gender and Reproductive Technologies.* Eds. M. C. Inhorn and F. V. Balen. Berkeley: University of California Los Angeles Press, 2002. 233-246.

Gordon, A. A. "Women and Development." *Understanding Contemporary Africa.* 4th ed. Eds. A. A. Gordon and D. L. Gordon. Boulder, CO: Lynne Reinne, 2007. 293-316.

Hakinsson, T. *Bride Wealth, Women and Land: Social Change Among the Gusii of Kenya.* Uppsala, Stockholm: Almquist and Wiksell, 1988.

Kenya Land Alliance and Nzioki Akinyi. "Land, Environment and Natural Resources." Submission to the Constitutional of Kenya Review Commission. Nairobi: Kenya, 2002.

Kevane, M. *Women and Development in Africa: How Gender Works.* Boulder, CO: Lynne Reinner, 2004.

Larsen, U. "Primary and Secondary Infertility in Sub-Saharan Africa." *International Journal of Epidemiology* 29 (2000): 285-291.

LeVine, R. A. and B. B. LeVine. *Nyansongo: A Gusii Community in Kenya.* New York: Wiley, 1966.

Mackenzie, F. Gender and Land Rights in Murang'a District (pp.). In *Journal of Peasant Studies,* 17 (4) (1990): 609-43.

Majok, A. and C. W. Schwabe. *Development Among Africa's Migratory Pasto-*

ralists. Westport, CT: Bergin and Garvey, 1996.

Maloba, W. O. *African Women in Revolution.* Asmara, Eritrea: African World Press, 2007.

Maxon, R. M. *Going Their Separate Ways: Agrarian Transformation in Kenya, 1930-1950.* Madison, NJ: Farleigh Dickinson University Press, 2003.

Mohanty, C. T., Ann Russo and T. Lourdes, eds. *Third World Women and the Politics of Feminism.* Bloomington: Indiana University Press, 1991.

Narayan, U. "The Project of Feminist Epistemology: Perspectives from a Non-western Feminist." *Feminist Theory Reader: Local and Global Perspectives.* Eds. Carole R. McCann and Seung-Kyung Kim. London: Routledge, 2003. 308-317.

Neil, P. "The Changing Value of Children Among the Kikuyu of Central Province, Kenya." *Africa: Journal of the International African Institute* 66 (3) (1996): 411-436.

Ng'ang'a, W. *Kenya's Ethnic Communities: Foundation of the Nation.* Nairobi: Gatundu Publishers, 2006.

Nyamongo, G. B. *Gusii Women and Small-Scale Family Tea Farming in Kenya.* Unpublished Ph.D. dissertation. York University, Toronto, 2009.

Nyamongo, I. K. *Lay People's Responses to Illness: An Ethnographic Study of Anti-Malaria Behavior Among the Abagusii of Southwestern Kenya.* Unpublished Ph.D. dissertation, University of Florida, 1998.

Nyamu-Musembi, C. "Addressing Formal and Substantive Citizenship." *Gender Justice Citizenship and Development.* Eds. M. Maitrayee and S. Navsharan. Ottawa. International Development Research Centre, 2007. 171-232.

Ochieng, W. *A Pre-Colonial History of the Gusii of Western Kenya from C.AD. 1500 to 1914.* Kampala: East Africa Literature Bureau, 1974.

Ogot, B. *History of Southern Luo.* Vo.1. Nairobi: East Africa Publishing House, 1967.

Pashigian, M. J. "Concerning the Happy Family, Infertility and Marital Policies in Northern Vietnam." *Infertility Around the Globe: New Thinking on Childlessness, Gender and Reproductive Technologies.* Eds. M. C. Inhorn and F. Van Balen. Berkeley: University of California Los Angeles Press, 2002. 134-151.

Sundby, J. "Infertility in Gambia Traditional and Modern Health Care." *Patient Education and Counselling* 31 (1) (1997): 29-37.

Uchendu, C. V. and A. R. M. Kenneth. *Agricultural Change in Kisii District, Kenya: A Study of Economic, Cultural, and Technical Determinants of Agricultural Change in Tropical Africa.* Nairobi: East African Literature Bureau, 1975.

Van Balen, F. "Involuntary Childlessness: a Neglected Problem in Poor-Resources Areas." *Oxford Journals: Human Reproduction* 1 (2008): 25-28.

Van Sertima, I. ed. *Blacks in Science: Ancient and Modern.* London: Transaction Books, 1983.

Verma, R. *Gender, Land and Livelihoods in East Africa: Through the Farmers' Eyes*. Ottawa: International Development Research Centre, 2001.

Walraven, G., C. Scerf, B. West, G. Ekpo, K. Paine, R. Coleman, R. Bailey and L. Morison, eds. "The Burden of Reproductive-Organ Disease in Rural Women in the Gambia, West Africa." *Lancet* 357 (2001): 1161-1167.

Wanyeki, M. L. *Women and Land in Africa: Culture, Religion and Realizing Women's Rights*. London: Zed Books, 2003.

8.
The Space Between

Mothering in the Context of Contradiction

JOANNE MINAKER

I wonder what it feels like to die? (my youngest son, then three years old, Taryk, ponders). His five year old brother Ayden responds: "There are lots of theories, but no one knows for sure until they do it."

MOTHERING IS LIKE THAT TOO—"no one knows for sure until they do it." Perhaps death is an odd beginning to a paper about mothering because it is so often associated with the giving of life and nurturing of children. The death/life binary is, however, salient here given how becoming a mother figuratively can represent both birth (of a new identity) and death (of a pre-maternal self). Rebecca, a woman in the research study described herein, reveals how becoming a new mother is an infinitely complicated process. Her daughter's birth was all too quickly eclipsed by her death.

> *I had lost my daughter when she was only two days old due to doctor/midwives and hospital error. So with Larissa I feel honoured to have known her for the short period of time that I did, but still, almost ten years later, I face enormous trauma over losing her. I think of her every day and losing her haunts me.*

Rebecca's encounters of stark life and death are perhaps far more extreme than "the highest of highs, the lowest of lows" that many women experience as mothers. The acute divide between high and low is a contrast that obscures the space within which mothering takes place. The beautiful/ugly truth about mothering is that so much of maternal existence is neither wholly oppressive nor altogether empowering. In the following pages, I demonstrate how the theme of contradiction permeates mothers' lives. This chapter is based on a qualitative and quantitative research project I conducted (2009-2011) where I examined the interplay between the various spheres, roles, and activities women encounter outside of motherhood and both their material practices and maternal identities. Using convenience and purposive sampling, I obtained a sample of 180 participants, each of whom completed an anonymous, on-line survey including open and closed ended questions about their experiences of being a mother. I also did in-depth (in person or telephone) interviews with 20 mothers. This group represents diversity in terms of age, socio-economic status, and mothering circumstances. The purpose of the study was to understand how mothering frames women's lives and the ways in which the contexts of women's lives (i.e., emotional, social, cultural, political, and economic relations) condition/constrain/create their experiences of motherhood. In this chapter, I explore a sample of twelve mothers' narratives, focusing on their roles, responsibilities, and relationships vis-à-vis their mothering experiences. I chose these stories because they represented the common themes within the larger project.[1]

These richly textured mothers' accounts reveal how women mother *in the context of contradiction*. Each narrative tells a partial story of a journey full of contradictions—between simplicity/complexity; joy/sorrow; constraint/choice; weakness/strength, opening/closure. Hidden within the two extremes (these seemingly polar opposites) is a *space between* wherein mothers subjectively experience mothering practices and actively create maternal identities; one fraught with tensions, opportunities, and a myriad of challenges. Examining this *space between the contradictions* allows us to appreciate how mothering is not entirely a site of resistance, nor one of oppression. Rather, it is a context through which mothers resist and are oppressed. Put another way, mothering represents both closing *and* opening of possibilities (Driver-McBride).

In recent years we have seen a rise in maternal activism, the proliferation of mothers' groups, an explosion of "mommy lit" and the advent of "Mommy Blogs." While these trends may be indicative of some advance in the status of women (and mothers), maternally inclined knowledge claims are up against anti-feminist backlash. Like Adrienne Rich, I am concerned with *mothering* as a process. This view stands in stark contrast to the traditionally male-defined, patriarchal conception of motherhood. The former is female-defined, potentially empowering to women, and allows women to, as Judih Arcana puts it, "mother against motherhood." In *Of Woman Born,* Rich encouraged feminist scholars to think critically about motherhood as site of power and resistance, rather than simply a patriarchal bastion of male domination and oppression. More recently authors, such as Sara Ruddick, Andrea O'Reilly, and Susan Hays, have argued that the dominant trope of motherhood is constraining, limiting, and oppressive, referring to it as sacrificial motherhood and intensive mothering. My work can be located as an effort to produce "counter narratives of mothering, in particular woman-centred and feminist meanings and experiences of mothering" (O'Reilly 2006: 12).

My research examines the reciprocal connections between how mothering frames women's lives and the ways in which women's mothering experiences get filtered through the sites upon which they encounter motherhood.[2] I refer to the diverse relational, emotional, social, economic, and political circumstances in which women mother as "mothering contexts." I explore the spaces and places through which women locate their lives, actions, interactions, and identities *in* and *outside* of motherhood. While women mother in different circumstances (e.g., as lone parents and/or living in poverty etc.), mothering contexts are not objective social positions, but are rather socially constructed, subjectively perceived, and lived out in different ways. Mothering contexts, then, are personal *and* political, individual *and* collective.

There is not *one* way to conceive a child, to give birth, to raise a child or otherwise mother or be mothered. However, a powerful and pervasive discourse of the "full-time mother" shapes the way women talk about how they do mothering (Ranson). Counter-discourses that challenge, resist, or deconstruct how motherhood is imagined represent an alternative to the normative 30-something, white, middle-class, able-bodied, married, and heterosexual mother situated in a nuclear family, preferably as a stay-at-home or full-time mother.

A rich and burgeoning motherhood literature (on topics ranging from infant feeding to domestic violence, family/life balance to postpartum depression) fosters an opening to engage with the *situatedness* of mothering. Both maternal identity and maternal practice must exist somewhere; that is, mothering is situated in particular social locations, one contextualized in relation to specific other actors, and within prescribed limits of possibility. Motherhood, as with all of our experiences, occurs within the context of a larger social order; that is characterized by structural inequalities and power imbalances of gender, race, ethnicity, nationality, age, sexuality, and (dis)ability. Further, any practice of mothering, from breastfeeding to potty training or seeing a young adult off to university or watching one leave for prison, is a social relation that women actively negotiate.

Dominant, normative discourses of "good motherhood" permeate the lives of all mothers. Yet, the myth of the good mother and the official definition of motherhood tend to delegitimize and marginalize *other* experiences of mothering, including but not limited to those of working class mothers, non-white or racialized mothers, teen mothers, poor mothers, older mothers, non-custodial mothers, single mothers. If mothering is practiced in diverse conditions of (in)equality and marginalization/privilege, then women have varying degrees of choice/constraint and agency with which to access resources or support. Mothering, then, intersects with women's other identities, such as those of race/ethnicity, class, gender, age, nationality, (dis)ability and sexuality. I am concerned with the intricate and nuanced ways in which women navigate the tensions, challenges, and opportunities they encounter as mothers. To what extent do women mother *around*, *against*, *by*, and/or *through* the various circumstances of their lives; conditions of which are not necessarily of their own choosing? Andrea O'Reilly argues "the study of the oppressive and the empowering aspects of maternity, and the complex relationship between the two" is the "central issue in motherhood studies today" (2006: 9). Through the conceptual lens of choice, context, and contraction I examine the extent to which oppression/resistance is a useful point of departure.

THEORIZING CONTRADICTION

Contradiction tends to imply opposites, antagonisms, and struggles. I am not here concerned with identifying simply how motherhood is experienced as *either/or*, but rather how *both* sides of the binary—oppression and resistance—are intrinsic to maternal experience. According to Valerie Renegar and Stacey Sowards, contradiction "functions as a transcendent term that includes a myriad of other strategies such as ambiguity, paradox, multiplicity, complexity, anti-orthodoxy, opposition, and inconsistency" (5). Theorizing contradiction must move beyond a limiting concept and toward a more fluid and elastic one. Consider the baby in utero; s/he is separate yet distinct from the mother in whose womb s/he is carried. The question, "where does one begin and one end?" is futile. Perhaps they do not, but instead the mother and growing baby is at the same time mutually exclusive *and* independent.

Contradiction(s) work as tensions rather than a struggle of opposing forces. Contradiction as tension is a more nuanced concept. Renegar and Sowards argue that contradiction is a strategy third wave feminists employ "to foster agency in social, political, and collaborative contexts" (2). If contradiction is understood not as something to be derided or avoided, but as something that can be embraced, then it becomes possible to appreciate how mothers' narratives reveal choice in the context of contradiction. While it first appears contradictory that within oppressive social relations, whereby mothers' lives are constrained by systemic factors beyond their control (e.g. gendered violence, patriarchal ideologies, employment inequities, racism etc.), women simultaneously exercise agency, develop strength and build capacities to resist, narratives of mothers' lives reveal how oppression co-exists with resistance within the same social spaces.

Mothers' agency is shaped by and produced within wider socio-cultural contexts and political circumstances. Mothering is a rich experience—you get *all* of this—despite the fact that much popular discourse continues to position one side of the binary against the other and to encourage us to think of mothers' lives in terms of one (i.e., mothering is empowering) or the other (i.e., mothering is oppressive). Mothers' narratives reveal that rather than standing in opposition to one another, oppression and resistance blend.

This intertwining begins with the pregnant woman. Mothering is an inside/outside experience where so much is going on inside (i.e., fetal development) and becomes manifest on the outside, visible as a belly expands, feet swell, and breasts engorge. Rather than inevitable contradictions that women must work against, mothering is a negotiation of tensions in the spaces between oppressive constraint and empowering possibility. Conceived in this way motherhood is recognized as a blending of the two sides of each of the traditional binaries or divides through which women mother—public/private, family/work, child(ren)/mother, self/society, and personal/political. As the following discussion will illustrate, the oppression/resistance dichotomy, then, obscures the tensions at work within and across these divides.

THE SOCIAL ARRANGEMENTS OF MOTHERING

[T]o be a mother is to learn a particular state of being because of the way in which society organizes mothering, that the social arrangements of mothering dictate, in large part, a woman's experience of mothering. (Langan 27)

The mothers in this study demonstrate the ways women act, think, and feel *as mothers*, which reveals how mothering is both connected to, and separated from, other aspects of who or what women are in the world. Feminist writing on mothering accords women a selfhood outside and beyond motherhood, which recognizes the multidimensionality of a mother's identity and expands childrearing beyond the care of the biological mother. Emily Jeremiah argues: "To posit a utopian space outside patriarchy, and thereby suggest a potential untarnished maternal subjectivity is to ignore the complex psychological interaction between subject and ideology" (60). This interaction is evident in Michelle's story. She illustrates how the Western cultural tendency to narrowly define mothers as self-sacrificing and consumed with the lives of their children is at odds with her lived experience:

I think mothers are too often placed into the category of "mother" instead of viewing mothering as another aspect of our identities rather than the singular aspect from which other parts of our lives "fit" in.

Michelle explains how integrated she views her maternal self from other aspects of who she is when she states:

I like to think of being a mother as being part of who I am as a person, not who I am.... When I became a mother and made the decision to quit my full-time job, I suddenly realized the 'mother' label was more powerful than any previous identities and this made me realize the magnitude of the word "mother" in North American society and all its associated meanings.

While the "magnitude of the word mother" was not lost on Michelle, we cannot assume that her own mothering follows a narrow script that is typified in the "stay-at-home mom" stereotype. She is keenly aware of both the parallels and contradictions between her experience of mothering as only one aspect of her identity and the ways motherhood is constructed in contemporary Western culture as all encompassing. Becoming a mother launches another self, yet not one necessarily fixed and stagnant in an external, socio-cultural script. Given her ability to rely on her male partner's economic contributions to the household, Michelle chose to leave paid employment in the public sphere.

The interplay of identity and practice across spheres (family, work, community, recreation, etc.) can be messy or disorganized, and at the same time, fluid. In effect, the diversity of roles and identities coinciding with being a mom brings with it conflicts and competing demands. Raina, a thirty-something mother of one, puts this poignantly when she explains: "I think often despite the appearance of multiple choice, we often have no choices at all." She is attending to the widely held belief that mothers can *have it all*—a rewarding career, adoring children, a loving and involved parenting partner. A list of options (e.g., in-home care, nannies, and grandmothers, daycare centres, privatized childcare, Montessori pre-schools, and before and after school programs, and private and licensed day homes) obscures the context in which a woman makes child care arrangements. Without socialized daycare (i.e., a national day care policy) and with costs for formal day care ranging between $650-$1200 per month for full-time care for children under five years, mothers like Raina (many of whom made less than their male partners in their jobs) decide to leave the paid labour force to assume primary responsibility for their young children. It is not simply the extent of the supports available (or quantity of child care spaces), but the nature of the arrangement (or quality of child care) that matters. In other cases, in the absence of additional income mothers may stay home with their children and reply on state assistance.

There are obstacles constraining mothers' ability to make meaningful choices. As Stefanie illustrates:

What choices do we have as mothers? We have a choice in pretty much everything with the exception of who is the primary caregiver. I'd like to think that the world has evolved enough that men could take on this role but somehow, it seems to continue to fall to us mothers. And that is not a bad thing ... it's just something that several of my friends have struggled with.

Mothers face many dilemmas with decision-making, not the least of which is the so-called plethora of choices available. However, obscured here are the external and internalized pressures to view particular options most desirable. On the one hand, dominant discourse glorifies motherhood but, on the other, Western culture largely devalues mothers. Women's lives are situated within race, class, age, and other power relations where women find themselves with differential access to supports and resources, giving some more autonomy to exercise meaningful choices than others. Stefanie's statement, particularly "that is not a bad thing," also reveals the tensions at work in mothers' own acceptance/rejection of the assumption that women are to be primary caregivers.

Cara, who describes herself as a feminist mother, is a thirty-something mother of a three year old. She posits:

> Daycare costs, individual realities, and emotion all factor into the concept of "choice," making the word "choice" itself irrelevant. And the societal concept of choice only makes the reality of this fallacy all the worse. Even the idea of "choosing" motherhood is a contentious one.

Cara goes on to explain:

> I certainly do not agree that the choice to become a mother means we must give up other areas of our lives. It really comes down to what works for the individual. Just like everything else, we come into mothering with different personalities and perspectives, so how we view mothering depends on our own subjectivities, which is why the concept of "mother" is so limiting because it is based on too many essentialized presuppositions.

"Essentialized presuppositions" widely circulate in medical discourse, parenting literature, children's literature, in the media etc. Such tropes are presented with rigid 'good' or 'bad' characterizations that reinforce and entrench the myth mothers are either in control or out-of-control. The result, however, is that the context and complexity that characterizes maternal identity and practice gets eschewed.

BEING A MOM IS ... LOVE, AMAZING AND REWARDING

Mothers have both similar and different experiences of mothering. One that is shared is evident the phrase "being a mom is ... love, amazing and rewarding." These three descriptors were the most commonly used. Also pervasive in the mothers' accounts was their use of terms like fascinating, wonderful, enriching, life altering, inspirational, and monumental to capture mothering. Karen is in her mid- 30s with a modest income. A new mom whose infant was only eight days old at the time of the interview, Karen referred to motherhood as "exciting, fulfilling, and awe-inspiring."

Nina, a Metis teenager, is a young mom, whose two children now live in foster care. While she is not currently responsible for the primary care/control of her children, she describes how "nothing could be better" than being a mother. Nina puts it this way:

> *Learning how to be a good mother—the challenge is the most rewarding thing I've done in my young life. I want to show them how wonderful life can be and hope they can call on me for anything. I'll always be here. Nobody will ever love them more and giving birth is certainly a gift in itself, to have had them in me and to have seen them breathe for the first time—nothing could be better.*

We see here how mothering for women, even within constrained circumstances, can be perceived as a positive experience.

Dawn is a new mom, living in a much more affluent environment than mothers like Nina. With a Masters degree and an income over $200,000 at first blush her world seems a dramatic departure from that of Nina, who is on social assistance, struggling to get her children out of state care. However, the monumental impact of becoming a mother is shared between the two. Dawn reveals:

> *My role as mother is my most important role right at this time because Oliver is so young and, he is still breastfeeding. I go nowhere without him and I love it that way! Eventually though, my relationship with my husband will have to become as important... This I'm sure will be a challenge because I feel a physical need to focus on Oliver first.*

Unlike Nina, who is unemployed and did not have a high school diploma, Dawn's "most important role" is cast alongside another goal of pursuing graduate studies. She explains:

> *My career though will most likely take a back seat for a while. I'm currently working on my doctorate and have decided to put a hold on that for now. I may change my mind about restarting it later but right now, it's just not important. And I can't manage it at this point in time. I don't want to spend any time away from Oliver right now—even to take a class.*

While Dawn can "change her mind" about re-entering her profession, Nina's economic and social marginalization are more circumscribed. We can anticipate she will experience more obstacles.

Brianna is a professional mother in her forties, whose experience of motherhood takes place in a blended family with her husband. There are four children (two teens and two young adults). Her comments demonstrate the openness of the role of mother. Even though a woman's choices on if, how, when, and where to mother are not hers alone, there is considerable space which offers all women some latitude within which to express her own style of mothering.

> *Undeniably our choices have an impact on our children. But I see there as being many opportunities to expand and challenge ourselves within the context of our role as mother. It is about taking risks, being creative, choosing not to see ourselves as sacrificing martyrs. There is enormous comfort and inspiration to be found in the community of mothers around us.*

She is reflective on the experience, after 16 years of mothering her opinion is that:

> *I do not think we can stand back and say choosing motherhood means giving anything up. It is about finding what we need within the experience; it is about not judging other mothers for the choices they make but supporting them along the way.*

Supporting all mothers is only possible when we resist the tendency to view motherhood in dichotomous ways as either/or—oppressive/empowering. When we challenge the assumption that maternal practices are good/bad we can appreciate the multi-dimensionality and complexity of maternal identities.

BEING A MOM IS … EXHAUSTING AND CHALLENGING

Mothers are keenly aware that mothering contexts, while they often provide unparalleled rewards and moments of pride, can also be thankless, stressful, and difficult. Being a mom, several women explained, is crazy, harried, draining, and overwhelming. *Challenging* and *exhausting* were the two most commonly used words! Diane, now in her 60s, is a grandmother and divorced mother of three thirty-something adults. Her experience exemplifies the difficulties associated with mothering in a context with limited support. She shares how being raised by what she describes as a "strong mother figure" and an "absent father (alcoholism)" has influenced her mothering.

> *I carried this same mothering into my life. I chose absent partners—work, other women, alcohol, not involved. I loved my children but found the task*

difficult, as I was virtually alone in the parenting department. Today, I realize that this is a two-person job, if possible. I never encouraged my children to have a relationship with their father (nor discouraged) and today I see them as adults and they all suffer the effects of an absent father—as I do too.

Choice, as Diane's experience suggests, is not synonymous with empowerment. Diane laments that she spent years feeling guilty that she "wasn't a better parent." Looking back she admits: "Now I understand that I did the best I could with what I had and there is no going back, I have forgiven me."

Ginger, who described herself as a white woman in her thirties, is a mature student, raising her eight-year-old son on her own with minimal financial or family support. Ginger's circumstances, while unique from Diane's, present similar obstacles. This made life "extremely challenging." She explains:

Advocating for a child with extra needs can be a full-time job. Trust me. I have always intended to have a career and never would I have imagined myself in such a vulnerable position. Sole-parenting a child with so many extra needs and minimal support is extremely challenging but I am trying, despite my constrained choices available to me, to have a foundation (my education) that will one day make me financially independent and make my son proud! He sees me going to school and knows that that is a feasible option for him. I am so proud of myself for being able to be that kind of a role model for him.

Being a role model who demonstrates what agency looks like was important to many of the women.

Another negative aspect the women associated with motherhood was judgments. Ginger was no exception. Illuminating the contradictory site in which so many women find themselves as their mothering is read through a binary lens of good/bad mother, she continues:

When I did work in the paid labour force, I do remember feeling very judged as a working mom. I have also felt judged as a stay at home mom. I have come to the conclusion that you can't win in this respect. You are either a "bad-mom" for working or "lazy" for not. As a mother, someone is always going to have something to say and you have to do ultimately what is right for you.

However, doing "what is right" in each woman's case is not always feasible, as Dakota—who also combined the student and mother role—explains the tensions involved in simultaneously combining education, employment, and motherhood. Dakota is an Aboriginal mother in her twenties raising her one year old son with her fiancée.

> *I am currently in post-secondary full-time, working 30 hours a week and I feel guilty feeling like I am not spending enough time with my son. From maternity leave, being full-time with my son, to sometimes only seeing him two and a half hours a day. It is a hard adjustment, but I want to have a career, bring in a great income, be a mentor and be able to academically stimulate my son. I am doing my sociology degree and initially had wanted to go to law-school, but as I am in school right now, I realize and understand that it is not practical and that I have a different view on what is important to me.*

Dakota has (at least for the time being) successfully negotiated this contradiction between her career goals and her motherhood role, though she admits to "hitting a glass-ceiling in terms of being a mother." It seems she is referring to a threshold contained within her mother role that allows only so much outside motherhood to penetrate her life and identity. She elaborates:

> *In a male-dominated career, I would not be able to, nor would I want to, put in the hours required to succeed. My focus is my son and my fiancée. I guess it is like hitting a glass-ceiling in terms of being a mother, but it's what makes me happy. My family will make me the happiest—they are my love and my joy.*

She appears to have accepted that mothers "give up other areas of our lives for our family, but I don't look at it as a negative choice, but that my priority is different." For Dakota, like many mothers, her "goals and aspirations changed dramatically" when she found out she was pregnant. She rationalizes her decision as follows: "It's almost as if I am choosing the more practical, safe way to have an income and an enjoyable career, rather than aiming to be a lawyer which is not practical—it is actually impossible."

At least for now, she places stronger emphasis on what she believes to be her child's needs than on her own career aspirations. On the surface, this choice can be read as sacrificial motherhood. Yet, this assertion fails to appreciate the complex negotiation and agency inherent in Dakota's decision to prioritize her family. It is disingenuous to criticize mothers for having chosen their kids as "their love and joy." Positing empowered mothering in opposition to intensive/sacrificial motherhood does not allow for a blending, nor an in between space where mothers like Dakota practice both elements traditionally associated with patriarchal motherhood (i.e., putting kids needs first, choosing home and family over career), while at the same time contest other aspects of social life which constrain their ability to mother on their own terms.

> *For my child, I want him to have the resources, the opportunity, basic needs, LOVE, support, encouragement, options—all of these mean more to me than a "career" for myself. If I can make amazing money doing something, I would do it so that I could provide for my son and allow for him to have a good and happy life. ...*
>
> *As a mother I am working hard towards a career so that I can provide for my family and also have time, the most priceless aspect to mothering, to spend with my family. Law school may not be an option to me, but it has not decreased my happiness by any amount and I am excited to see where my life takes me and the exciting times ahead. I know I will work towards a career that challenges me and makes me feel like I'm making a difference, but also allows for me to be a mother.*

Narrowly categorizing Dakota's choice to prioritize her son's needs over her goal of law school ignores her desire to be a mother as one of her life goals; thereby perpetuating the devaluation of mothers.

THE SPACE(S) BETWEEN THE CONTRADICTIONS

Our choices are limited by our social context. (Mary)

Although choice is constrained by the social circumstances of our lives, mothers do exercise considerable agency. Women's experiences are multifaceted and blur the boundaries between the favourable and unfavourable aspects of being a mom. In what follows, I share the stories of Carmen and Mary, whose accounts reveal the tensions between a woman's maternal self and the wider socio-cultural landscape in which mothering takes place. Their narratives also illustrate several of the key themes to emerge from the research—*context, choice,* and *contradiction.*

Carmen, a mother in her early thirties, is raising two boys in a multi-racial family with a low income. She shares how motherhood has brought her unconditional love, purpose, and the opportunity to see sons' joy. For Carmen, teen and single motherhood, social exclusion, and detrimental systems (court and child welfare) represented huge obstacles. "Our choices are limited by our social context," Carmen echoes a central concern of the study. Her narrative emphasizes how social relations and social systems inform, but do not dictate, mothering experiences. Carmen argues:

For a mother who has a lot of social support—where the people in her lives support her and her decisions through their time, money, etc.,—she can have a lot of freedom of choice in many areas. For a mother like me who has had to rely on systems and/or unsupportive persons, there is limited choice, relatively speaking (relative to what this society defines as "normal" mothers).

Carmen goes on to explain that her children's abusive father was able to get the courts, through an access order, to force her to stop breastfeeding. Because of this she felt compelled to stop attachment-parenting in ways that felt right to her. Carman continues:

Even though accumulating financial resources is a form of mothering, the cost of this type of mothering may not outweigh the benefits for a particular family. A poor mother cannot choose how best energy and time is spent to fulfill her family's potential because family actualization is cast aside due to basic survival needs. Food and shelter take precedent over achieving wholeness and wellness.

Within this context Carmen persevered in her attempts to find what she refers to as "wholeness and wellness." She articulates the multi-dimensionality of the women's lives as mothers beautifully when she states:

I believe that motherhood cannot be compartmentalized. A mother who tends to multiple areas of her life tends to them as a mother. This is how she is "doing" motherhood. If she's doing what's she believes is best for her/her family then she's doing what she is "supposed" to be doing in having chosen motherhood. If a mother decides to let go of certain areas of her life in favour of more direct and hands-on child-caring, great—if that's what she feels is best. If she does it because society or someone else has pressured her decision, then this mother is not living freely or authentically and that is a tragedy. [emphasis added]

It is remarkable that Carmen uses the word "authentically," which is one of the criteria Andrea O'Reilly (2004) uses to evaluate the extent to which women engage in empowered mothering or to do "what she feels is best." Unlike Carmen, Mary shared her journey through motherhood with a partner. Mary describes her life purpose as "making a difference to women with children who are struggling in life due to life circumstances;" women like Carmen.

Mary is an Eastern European mother who is now in her 40s, married with two teenage kids. Her desire to support other mothers is intimately connected to her own experiences of motherhood, parenting four children with her husband. Mary recalls:

> When I first became a mother, I felt that I was in my own separate universe with my daughter. The times with her were so precious to me. I was the "good wife" and the "good mother." I took care of my daughter, our new puppy, and the household. I had dinner on the table every night when my husband came home from work. It was after about three months when I started to die inside. I struggled with myself and wanting to go back to work. I called to find out whether they had any jobs in the evening available, and then I justified this plan to myself because I felt that at least my daughter would be with her father in the evening and me during the day. She wouldn't have to go to daycare.

Here Mary was struggling with the conflict so many women face when they leave the workforce to care for their infants—the internal tension not simply between motherhood and employment, but missing "a piece of the world that was my own." Mary went back to work during the evenings until her second child was born. She goes on to explain:

> I stayed home only two weeks after having him. People thought I was crazy. And honestly, we needed the money anyway, so I told people I had to work, but I was so grateful to have a piece of the world that was my own, that I was in control of, and that kept my mind alive. For a long time I felt guilty about how I put my needs above the needs of my children. I wondered why I wanted to "get out of the house" so much.

Mary remembers feeling guilty about making the choice to work. Reflecting back she states that she realized in making this choice she was demonstrating many things to her children, especially her daughter. Mary argues, so poignantly, that "women can have their own lives along with being a mother. They can be strong and independent, and still make their children a priority." Our culture tends to hold the two as mutually exclusive (a woman's independence and a mother's responsibility to her children). Mary discusses how she reconciled the two.

> I never missed a Christmas concert, or a soccer game, and I'm still playing chauffer and hostess to my children and their friends. And I love that! I have worked days since both my children were in school. I have never cared too much about what other people thought of me, and now I don't care at all. But I do know that in order to be a good mother to someone, you have to be good to yourself, too.

Mary is challenging the myth that good mothers always put their children's needs ahead of their own. It appears that she, unlike some mothers, pays little attention to societal expectations or judgments of others about her parenting decisions. She explains:

> *Life is about choices, and about balance and prioritizing. Sometimes choices for one person are not the same as for another. Each person is different. For me it's so important for me to know I am not perfect, but I am willing to do what works for me and my children and that I will learn from experiences both good and bad along this journey of life. This helps with the choices I make.*

For Mary this journey now involves new challenges, like finishing a degree she began before she got married at twenty-one. Mary's "bigger aspirations" include finishing her Bachelor of Arts. She is taking part-time courses and thinking about graduate studies and volunteering in her community. Below Mary shares how much her identity has changed.

> *I don't know whether it is because of being a mother, or because I have just evolved as a person, but I have bigger aspirations for myself. I have a good job, but I want more out of my life now.... But we have a nice home, food and shelter, and most importantly, the love of each other to keep us going...*

While custodial mothering (parenting children with whom one resides) is temporal, Mary realizes the impact her imprint will make on her kids later on, but also how important the *now* of everyday is. As she puts it: "my children and I are sharing this life journey, but the time will come when we will not be so closely tied." She believes that has learned as much about living from her children as she has taught them. The relationships she develops with her kids matter, as she makes clear here:

> *My kids will not be in my house forever, and I want to enjoy them and teach them and mentor them as long as I have them, so they have a good foundation in their own lives. I want them to know themselves as much as they can before they go on to the adult world and create their own experiences all on their own. I want them to be the best they can be AND follow their passions in life. I want them to know that being an adult doesn't mean you're finally there!*
> *...It's not always easy; I've had many feelings of failure, but I think seeing them now as young adults, and how they look at the world, and how they*

react to people, situations, and experiences tells me that I have influenced them in a positive way, and that makes me very proud of them.

LESSONS FROM MOTHERS' NARRATIVES: ROPE OR RUBBER BAND?

I think that being a mother has informed so many other areas of my life. I feel like as they've grown, so have I, and it is these things I take out into the world with me.... I want them to know that I am also learning as I go, and life is a series of lessons in which we never stop learning and growing. I will never stop being a mother, either, so as I learn, I will share with them, and keep the conversations going.... (Mary)

So why does all this matter? Returning to the question posed in the title of this paper—do women mother in the context of contradiction? Yes and No. Mothers' stories complicate the established binaries and suggest a closed conception of contradiction as either/or masks the tensions at work in women's mothering. In so far as women are confronted with contradictory cultural and social contexts in which they practice mothering, there are active agents navigating *both* unappealing choices *and* exciting possibilities. One of the most important lessons to learn from this may be from Mary who argued that if a mother believes what she is doing is best, "she's doing what she is 'supposed' to be doing in having chosen motherhood."

Like Mary, being a mother has informed the other aspects of my life, including my scholarship. At all times I am both a mom and an academic. On my way to take my son to school I stopped at a light and pulled a pen out of my bag. Along with it came a small, thin rubber band. Coincidentally, I was searching for the pen in order to make myself a quick note: CONCLUSION: ROPE OR RUBBER BAND? I wanted to remind myself when I got to work that I should think about which analogy worked best to make sense of mothering. It is fascinating how either/or thinking is so deeply entrenched! Despite being immersed in this chapter attempting to challenge binaries, there I was falling into the trap of choosing one or the other. Maybe mothering is *both* like a rubber band, elastic, flexible, and easy to bend *and* like a rope, tightly wound, and strongly bound.

Contesting the constraining aspects of mothering, resistance against oppression, and working toward mothers' empowerment demands that we "keep the conversations going." Given how women forge maternal identities and practices in the open spaces between contexts that condition our complex lives, it is imperative that as academics, as activists, and as mothers, and citizens of the world that we collectively continue to push the limits of possibility to make mothering more like a rubber band when we need it and strong like a rope when it suits us. This will involve challenging the contexts that hinder our ability to make choices that empower us, and our children. Mothering lives not at the far extremes of maternal bliss, or discord. Instead, within the *space between the contradictions* there are challenges and tensions through which we can find opportunities to mother on our own terms.

[1]Sociologists define context as the space and place within which we locate our lives, our actions, our interactions, and our identities. As a researcher and a mother, I am committed to giving voice to mothers' stories.
[2]While I recognize that mothering may not in our lived experience *happen* outside of other aspects of our lives, I would argue that how we act/be/think/feel "as mothers" reflects the extent to which our mothering is/is not connected to other aspects of who and what we are.

REFERENCES

Arcana, J. *Our Mother's Daughters*. Berkeley, CA: Shameless Hussy Press, 1979.

Driver-McBride, K. " 'No, I'm Not Catholic, and Yes, They're All Mine.'" *Feminist Mothering*. Ed. A. O'Reilly. Albany, NY: State University of New York Press, 2008. 45-60.

Hays, S. *The Cultural Contradictions of Motherhood*. New Haven, CT: Yale University Press, 1996.

Jeremiah, E. "Murderous Mothers: Adrienne Rich's *Of Woman Born* and Toni Morrison's *Beloved*." *From Motherhood to Mothering: The Legacy Adrienne Rich's "Of Woman Born."* Ed. A. O'Reilly. Toronto: Women's Press 2004. 59-71.

Langan, D. "Using Mothering at Work: Embracing the Contradictions in Pedagogy and Praxis." *Journal of the Association for Research on Mothering* 6 (2) (2004): 27-35.

O'Reilly. A. *Mother Outlaws: Theories and Practices of Empowered Mothering*. Toronto: Women's Press 2004.

O'Reilly. A. *Rocking the Cradle: Thoughts on Motherhood, Feminism and the Possibility of Empowered Mothering*. Toronto: Demeter Press, 2006.

Ranson, G. "Paid Work, Family Work, and the Discourse of the Full-Time Mother." *Mother Matters: Motherhood as Discourse and Practice*. Ed. A. O'Reilly. Toronto: Association for Research on Mothering, 2004. 87-97.

Renegar, V. R. and S. K. Sowards. "Contradiction as Agency: Self-Determination, Transcendence, and Counter-Imagination in Third-Wave Feminism." *Hypatia* 24 (2) (2009): 1-18.

Rich, A. *Of Woman Born: Motherhood as Experience and Institution*. London: Virago Press, 1986. [1977].

9.
Reconceiving and Reconceptualizing Postpartum Depression

GINA WONG AND KATHRYN BELL

EW EXPERIENCES IN A WOMAN'S LIFE parallel the adjustment required in transitioning to motherhood, a time that is culturally celebrated and expected to be joyful despite substantial 24-hour demands on a new mother (O'Hara). Postpartum depression (PPD) is the psychiatric label associated with depression in early motherhood provided in the *Diagnostic and Statistical Manual of Mental Disorders* (APA 2000). However, such a label fails to capture or take into account a mother's familial, relational, and sociocultural experiences (Jacobs and Cohen). While some women find the psychiatric diagnosis of PPD comforting and normalizing because it provides understanding to her suffering, Paula J. Caplan emphasizes in her play *They Say You're Crazy* (1995) and in her contribution to *Moms Gone Mad* (Chapter 5) that psychiatric labels oppress women. Instead, listening to what a mother tells about her own suffering and what she experiences is an empowered approach that is necessary. Likewise, David Jacobs and David Cohen emphasize how a pathology framework and diagnostic label favor mood disorder as a rationale for depression and deem irrelevant the individual's circumstance and life context. They note:

> By separating feelings, thoughts, and behavior from the context *for* the person in question, the *DSM* defines how a person should not be *regardless of circumstances* (e.g., the person should not be in a depressed mood most of the day, every day, for two weeks). This can only be characterized as a moral position masquerading as a medical diagnosis. (325)

In this chapter, we acknowledge that there are both empowering and disempowering aspects of being diagnosed with PPD and by no means intend to further oppress women but aim to validate mother's experience as well as reconceive and reconceptualize PPD.

RISK FACTORS

Prevalence estimates for depression, both antenatal (during pregnancy) and postpartum, range from 12 to 21 percent (Leigh and Milgrom; Wylie, Hollins, Marland, Martin, and Rankin), similar to the prevalence of depression in the general population. Given that there is a stigma associated with PPD and that the symptoms themselves can preclude a mother from seeking help, diagnosis, and treatment, it is reasonable to suggest that the prevalence is greater and that many more mothers experience symptoms associated with PPD than the statistics show.

In reconceiving and reconceptualizing PPD, an appreciation of the risk factors associated with PPD is paramount to enhancing awareness of mechanisms and forces by which mothers become depressed, in contributing to strategies for prevention, and in furthering empowered and efficient treatment for PPD. Although precise etiology of PPD has not been elucidated, many investigators posit a multifactorial etiology, including biological factors and psychosocial stressors as potential triggers (Letourneau et al.; Miles; Miller; O'Hara). While mainstream researchers explore risk factors in women such as hormones, genetic vulnerability, poor social support, and ruminative coping styles, feminist researchers such as Stoppard (1999, 2010) have staunchly criticized this research, asserting that this discourse serves to medicalize and pathologize women's experiences. Instead, feminists advocate for approaches that take into account gender-driven, social, and cultural factors that underlie emotional suffering occurring in early motherhood.

Approaching PPD from sociocultural perspectives has been largely negated in North American patriarchal reification of PPD. Sociocultural forces are far more difficult to validate through research and, in this understanding, are marginalised or disregarded as justifiable risk factors. This dichotomous/polarized debate in the literature of medical *dis-ease* in woman *or* cultural forces underlying PPD fuels confusion surrounding the development and maintenance of PPD. As such, from a holistic perspective, the purpose of this chapter is to address: (1) biological, (2) psychosocial, and (3) sociocultural risk factors contributing to the development of PPD. Although we discuss categories of risk factors as discrete, in fact, they are interconnected and aspects of some are directly related to others. Our intent is not to elevate one category over other categories of risk factors in the development of PPD; rather, we acknowledge a confluence of factors. We propose a theoretical "pie chart" model of PPD, as Faulkner Fox describes, including a multitude of aspects which factor into each mother's individual experience of PPD and is in flux over time. In this chapter focused on reconceptualizing and reconceiving PPD, we will describe details as to this organizing schema of PPD, discuss implications of sociocultural factors in PPD, and examine ideologies such as the *good woman* and *good mother* (and resultant pressures on women) in light of PPD.

Within a holistic framework of risk factors associated with PPD, our underlying belief is that stress, anxiety, and stressful events/forces, which increase levels of cortisol in women, increase risk of developing PPD (Ching-Yu and Pickler; Groer, Davis, and Hemphill; Smyth et al.). Indeed, recent research is showing "that inflammation is involved in the pathogenesis of depression. And stress triggers this process" (Kendall-Tackett 2010: 7). From this perspective, biological, psychosocial, and sociocultural risk factors of PPD operate by heightening stress experienced by women, thereby increasing their risk to develop PPD. By no means are we purporting that these risk factors cause PPD nor that stress, anxiety, and stressful events/forces themselves always result in PPD.

BIOLOGICAL RISK FACTORS

Researchers have examined the relationship between biology and mood disorders and have identified a number of biological risk factors in developing PPD. In this section, we briefly describe nine biological risk factors determined from extant literature on PPD.

1. *Psychiatric history.* A family or personal history of depression or other mental disorders (e.g., bipolar disorder, anxiety disorders, posttraumatic stress disorder) has been found to increase risk of developing PPD (APA n.d.; Lanes, Kuk and Tamim; O'Hara; O'Hara and Swain). In a study of new mothers, elevated PPD symptom levels were significantly related to elevated postpartum posttraumatic stress symptom levels (Beck, Gable, Sakala, and Declercq), suggesting postpartum mood and anxiety disorders may also occur comorbid with PPD. Women with a personal history of severe stress or depression are more at risk of developing PPD partially because of how their bodies are primed to react to stress in general, with a more rapid inflammatory response to current stressors (Kendall-Tackett 2007). Researchers have found a previous history of depression and current emotional problems, rather than single mother status, predicts antenatal depression (Bilszta et al.) and likely PPD as well, as antenatal depression is a risk factor for PPD (Leigh and Milgrom; also see discussion below on antenatal depression).

2. *Antenatal depression.* Anxiety and stress during pregnancy (Saisto, Salmela-Aro, Nurmi, and Halmesmaki) including a history of abuse and/or domestic violence (Austin et al.), and immigration (Zelkowitz et al.) have been found to contribute to the development of depression during pregnancy (antenatal depression). These are important to consider as antenatal depression is a risk factor for a mother to develop PPD. That is, women who have developed major depressive disorder during pregnancy are more at risk of developing

PPD (Leigh and Milgrom; Rapkin, Mikacich, Moatakef-Imani, and Rasgon; Seimyr, Edhborg, Lundh, and Sjogren).

3. *Postpartum blues.* Reports regarding the association between postpartum blues and PPD have been mixed due to variations in diagnostic measures and methodological problems (Henshaw, Foreman, and Cox). Nevertheless, C. Henshaw and colleagues found that women who suffer from severe postpartum blues are at a higher risk of developing PPD. More recently, although in a small sample, researchers found a high score for postpartum blues to be a strong predictor of PPD (Watanabe et al.). In addition, Scandinavian researchers found that stress and stressful events were risk factors in developing postpartum blues at 1-week postpartum (Dennis, Janssen, and Singer).

4. *Hormonal changes postpartum.* After delivery, rapid changes in hormone levels such as estrogen, progesterone, and thyroid hormones have a strong effect on mood (APA n.d.). Although findings across studies are inconsistent with regard to hormonal etiology of PPD, largely due to differing methodologies employed, they suggest reproductive hormone measures (thyroid, cortisol, prolactin, and melatonin) differed between depressed mothers and control groups (Parry et al.). Explanations for these differences have included differences in biological rhythms and interruptions on hormonal production with greater sensitivity to reproductive hormone changes for women experiencing PPD (Bloch, Schmidt, and Danaceau). Conversely, one study determined biological risk factors (progesterone concentrations, genetic risk) had no direct effect on prenatal depressive symptoms, but rather, had indirect effects mediated through both psychosocial stressors and symptoms of anxiety (Ross, Sellers, Gilbert, Evans, and Romach). These findings support our assertion that stress, anxiety, and stressful events and forces contribute to the development and maintenance of PPD; an assertion further supported by recent research on inflammation. The risk of PPD is increased when stress is added to the normal increase in inflammation during the final trimester and postpartum (Kendall-Tackett 2007, 2010).

5. *Physiological stressors.* Certain physiological components may put mothers at a greater risk of developing PPD. For example, early postpartum anemia is related to reduced cognitive performance, emotional instability, and an increased risk for PPD (Corwin, Murray-Kolb, and Beard; Milman). Anemia is associated with physiological stressors such as increased fatigue, breathlessness, palpitations, and infections (Milman). Furthermore, there are a variety of physical stressors (e.g., breastfeeding complications, fatigue, hemorrhoids, poor appetite, constipation, illness days, respiratory symptoms, sexual concerns, pain, etc.) that a mother may experience postpartum (Groer et al.). Although not every woman with multiple or severe physical postpartum complaints develops PPD, such physical complications are likely associated with functional impairments, emotional distress and PPD (Webb et al.). Additionally, because breastfeeding,

when going well, may lower cortisol and act as a protective factor against PPD (Kendall-Tackett 2007), when mothers bottle-feed or experience significant breastfeeding complications or pain, they may lose the protective factor.

6. *Complications in pregnancy.* A high incidence of antenatal maternal health problems such as pregnancy-induced hypertension, hyperemesis (severe nausea and vomiting in pregnancy), pre-eclampsia, and premature contractions, have been shown to put new mothers at higher risk of developing PPD (Blom, et al.; Dennis et al.; Josefsson et al.). Pregnancy-induced hypertension may be considerably stressful for the mother as management includes frequent monitoring and, in some cases, hospitalization (Dennis et al.). While not all cases of pregnancy-induced hypertension lead to the management of pre-eclampsia, Swedish researchers have found that the experience of high intervention may be very stressful and consequently contribute to the development of PPD (Josefsson et al.).

7. *Pregnancy loss.* Odette Bernazzani and Antonia Bifulco found a relationship between pregnancy loss and PPD. In this respect, 20 to 30 percent of women who experience the loss of a child (stillbirth or neonatal death) suffered depressive symptoms up to 30 months after the loss. Other research shows that pregnant women with a history of stillbirth have higher prevalence of depression than pregnant women with no history of stillbirth (Golbasi, Kelleci, Kisacik, and Cetin). Bernazzani and Bifulco suggested that pregnancy loss in itself is a very stressful event and while others have submitted an association between grief and depression, they proposed that these are two different concepts and two distinct ways of coping with loss of a child (Wijngaards-de Meij et al.).

8. *Delivery.* Results as to the delivery experience itself as a risk factor of PPD have been mixed (Hiltunen, Raudaskoski, Ebeling, and Moilanen; Koo, Lynch, and Cooper; Patel, Murphy, and Peters; Saisto et al.). Nevertheless, Vincent Koo and associates found that women who had an emergency delivery were twice as likely to develop PPD at six weeks postpartum. Instrumental (e.g., vacuum suction, forceps) and surgical deliveries negatively impact maternal emotions and have been associated with PPD (Rowe-Murray and Fisher). Furthermore, PPD has been related to experiencing posttraumatic stress disorder after childbirth (Beck et al.). Mothers with posttraumatic stress after delivery often had had a high level of obstetric intervention, including caesarean or instrumental deliveries (Beck et al.).

In contrast, a small study by Paulina Hiltunen et al. and a larger study (Patel et al.), indicated that delivery by emergency caesarean was not associated with PPD development. Explanation for mixed findings may be due to lack of research that takes into account a mother's expectation and perception of her delivery experience and her emotional response to the dissonance or discrepancy between the two. For example, Terhi Saisto and associates showed the more satisfied a woman was with her delivery, the less depression she reported postpartum.

9. *Infertility*. Mothers who experienced difficulty in conceiving and in maintaining pregnancies have also been found to be more susceptible to developing PPD (Olshansky). Stress, in terms of the invasive aspects of infertility treatment (Kulkarni), and the stress of several months or sometimes years of unsuccessful pregnancies, or no pregnancies, has been implicated in development of PPD. It appears that research in this area is lacking and further studies are required to understand the association and relationship between infertility and PPD, although it seems clear that a link does exist.

PSYCHOSOCIAL RISK FACTORS

Many researchers have investigated psychosocial factors related to the development of PPD and are finding "many postpartum depressions seem to arise in the same psychosocial contexts as do depressions that develop at other times in a woman's life" (O'Hara 1261). Below, we describe 12 psychosocial risk factors derived from the extant literature.

1. *Coping styles*. Researchers have suggested that women with certain personality styles, characterized by worrying about interpersonal relationships, anxiety, and lack of assertiveness, were at risk of developing PPD (Boyce; Seimyr et al.). Carolina McBride and R. Michael Bagby , in particular, discussed rumination (responding to depressed symptoms with repetitive thoughts about meaning and consequences of symptoms) and interpersonal dependency (excessive investment in relationships) as risk factors for depression in women. Ruminating interferes with problem solving, and is linked with negative self perceptions, with feeling less in control, and with hopelessness about the future (Lyubomirsky and Nolen-Hoeksema) and is associated with increased severity of depression (Nolen-Hoeksema, Parke and Larson). Dana Jack (1999a) conceptualizes this rumination as an intense inner focus on how to balance aggressiveness (what many would refer to as *appropriate* self-assertion) with a wish to be *good* and maintain relationships. Nevertheless, self-reflective aspects of ruminating, which involves adaptive problem solving to reduce symptoms, versus the brooding aspects of ruminating, was associated with less depression over time (Treynor, Gonzales, and Nolen-Hoeksema).

Notably, McBride and Bagby pointed out how early on "girls are socialized to invest in collectivism and positive interpersonal relationships" (187) and that "early socialization and inequities in social power might contribute to the tendency for women to ruminate" (186). Likewise, Jelena Spasojevic and Lauren Alloy found that a history of emotional and sexual abuse is associated with the ruminating (brooding) cognitive style in adulthood. This shows there is much more to women's individual coping style as direct risk factors of PPD.

2. *Interpersonal stress and partner conflict.* The multiplicity and overlapping of roles for new mothers can provoke conflict, stress, and dissatisfaction with one's intimate relationship following birth (Groer et al.). Mothers experiencing difficulties with friends, family, or a partner are particularly vulnerable to developing PPD (Flores and Hendrick; Pajulo, Savonlahti, Sourander, Helenius and Piha). When compared with unpartnered mothers, women in a partnered relationship with poor partner-derived support are at greater risk for antenatal depressive symptoms (Bilszta et al.), and the same is likely true for the postpartum period, as antenatal depression is a risk factor for PPD (Leigh and Milgrom).

3. *Lack of support.* Stress and interpersonal conflict affect a mother's support system. A lack of social support is a risk factor for developing PPD (Dennis et al.; Lanes et al.). A supportive environment acts as a buffer against stressful events or situations, and a high level of support from family and friends is associated with lower symptoms of PPD (Leahy-Warren, McCarthy and Corcoran). A number of studies have indicated it is not the actual support system but rather, when support is important to her, a mother's perception of low available support is a risk factor for PPD (Dennis et al.; Dennis and Ross 2006; Pajulo et al.). According to recent research, mothers who had high levels of informational support, instrumental support, emotional support and/or appraisal support were less likely to experience symptoms of PPD (Leahy-Warren et al.).

4. *Experience of abuse.* Experience of abuse is a risk factor linked to PPD, and women who experience the most cumulative exposure to violence and abuse are also more likely to report symptoms of PPD (Garabedian et al.). In one study, mothers described how past abuse experiences affected their thoughts and views of labour, delivery, and postpartum experiences (Mason, Rice, and Records). The mothers reported that combined recall of trauma events and labour and delivery experiences provided the foundation for their development of PPD (Mason et al., 2005). Consistent with this perspective, women who experienced past sexual trauma were 12 times more likely to experience childbirth as stressful and traumatic (Soet et al.). Women who have experienced abuse are more likely to have a personal history of depression (Kulkarni; Randolph and Reddy) and research shows evidence of an independent relationship between experiencing abuse prior to pregnancy and the development of PPD symptomology (Silverman and Loudon).

5. *Socioeconomic (SES) factors.* While symptoms of PPD have been correlated with low SES (Flores and Hendrick; Lanes et al.), the literature presents conflicting evidence for the relationship between SES and PPD (Goyal, Gay and Lee). Women living in families with low-income are more likely to be exposed to high-stress living conditions such as overcrowding, noise, and violent communities (Dearing, Taylor, and McCartney). Although Eric Dearing and colleagues found "income gains resulted in the alleviation of depressive symp-

toms, especially when these gains were substantial enough to lift families out of poverty" (1376), the association between gain of income, employment, and depression was directly influenced by mother's perception of the consequences of working. For example, the belief that work has negative consequences to her child limited the ameliorative effects of income gains on PPD (Dearing et al.). Deepika Goyal and colleagues found increased depressive symptoms for women with low-income in the third trimester and at two and three months postpartum, but similar rates of PPD symptoms for the two groups at 1 month, a finding that may explain some of the discrepancy in the literature. Overall, first-time mothers with SES risk factors for depression (including low monthly income, less than a college education, unmarried, unemployed) were almost eleven times more likely to develop PPD than those without such risk factors, and the risk was compounded with multiple SES risk factors present (Goyal et al.).

6. *Low self-esteem and self-compassion.* Researchers conducted a meta-analysis study and found that self-esteem emerged not only as a significant predictor of PPD but as one of the strongest predictors (Beck). Self-esteem, with its emphasis on feelings of self worth, buffers negative effects of stressful life events (Bovier, Chamot, and Perneger). Nathaniel Branden (e.g., 1994, 2001) discussed the central role of self-esteem and its relation to everyday experiences and its connection to depression. Mothers with high levels of self-esteem have the ability to withstand stressors that may jeopardize positive self worth. Feelings of "low competency may even be a greater concern for adolescent mothers" (Birkeland, Thompson, and Phares 293) who are often criticized about their parenting skills.

Self-compassion, originating from Buddhist tradition, is a burgeoning field of psychological study. Kristin Neff and Pittman McGehee defined self-compassion as compassion turned inward, or the ability to hold one's feelings of suffering with warmth, understanding, concern, and connection. Neff (2003a) examined self-esteem and self-compassion together and found they are positively correlated, and that self-compassion fills in where self-esteem is lacking. That is, when self-esteem is low due to negative life events, people often feel anxious and depressed and seek external validation. In contrast, when individuals with self-compassion experience difficult times they are anchored without a feeling of decline in self-worth because they can be kind and compassionate to themselves (Neff and Vonk). In fact, researchers are finding that self-compassion is a buffer against depression and anxiety (Neff 2003a; Van Dam, Sheppard, Forsyth and Earleywine), rumination (Neff 2003b; Raes), self-criticism (Gilbert and Proctor; Neff 2003a), and shame (Gilbert and Procter).

Though the concept of self-compassion is relatively new and has yet to be explored directly in relation to PPD, it represents an area that is rich in potential and insight regarding the importance of self-acceptance for psychological well-being (Maloney and Wong). While self-compassion has been shown to increase psychological well-being in general, the gendered and highly competitive nature of Western society still presents barriers to the cultivation of self-compassion in the lives of women and mothers.

7. *Mother's age.* A number of researchers have found mother's age as a risk factor in developing PPD (Birkeland, et al.; Boyce; Hiltunen et al.; Lanes et al.). That is, women aged 19 or younger were significantly more likely to experience PPD. Teenage motherhood has also been linked with poorer health, poorer educational attainment, poorer employment prospects, and SES deprivation which are psychosocial stressors (Bradley, Cupples and Irvine). Whether it is the risk factor of age or the stress associated with young motherhood or multiple role integration that contributes to PPD continues to be a question.

8. *Immigration.* Recent immigrant status has also been found to be a significant predictor of PPD (Dennis et al.; Lanes et al.) as well as a predictor of antenatal depression (Zelkowitz et al.). The immigration process brings about a number of stressors such as concerns about finances, social alienation, isolation from family, not understanding medical practices, and potential difficulty accessing resources in the community. As well, a language barrier may further impede access to social and health services. Researchers have suggested lack of support experienced by immigrant women, rather than immigrant status per se is related to higher levels of reported stress (Zelkowitz et al., 2004). However, the relationship is more complex and might be influenced by the disparity between the country of origin and the new country of residence as well as the situation that prompted immigration (Dennis et al.). Consistent with this perspective, Nancy Arthur and Noorfarah Merali proposed that the greater the disparity between the two cultures, the greater the difficulties encountered by the immigrant to adapt and Andrea Lanes and colleagues suggest the time since immigration may moderate the risk, accounting for effects of acculturation.

9. *Cultural differences.* Researchers have suggested that postpartum cultural rituals such as the Chinese ritual of "Zuo Yue" or the Mexican ritual of "La Cuarentena" may protect against PPD (Flores and Hendrick). These rituals usually incorporate a rest and seclusion period (one month to approximately 40 days, depending on the culture) where a mother is confined to the home, is relieved of or partially relieved of chores and housework, eats special foods, and may be attended to by a female in the family (Kulkarni). Even though it has been hypothesized that the absence of these rituals may be an important contributor to PPD in Western society, it has not been supported by some studies (Huang and Mathers 2001, 2010; Posmontier and Horowitz) or literature reviews (Bina; Grigoriadis et al.; Miles). It may be, rather, that the mother's perception of the ritual is a mitigating factor (Bina) and that various contextual factors, such as whether support is solicited or imposed, the relationship

between the mother and support person, whether the ritual is carried out fully or partially, and whether the new mother is in her country or is an immigrant (Grigoriadis et al.; Miles) come into effect.

10. *Mother's fatigue and infant temperament.* Mothering infants with health problems, who are colicky, or are perceived and experienced as temperamentally difficult (Beck; Dennis et al.) has been linked to PPD. Canadian researchers, Cindy-Lee Dennis and Lori Ross (2005) found that maternal report of frequent infant crying was one of the strongest predictors of their depressive symptoms and mothers who reported that their infant cried frequently were also more likely to indicate their infant slept poorly and that they often felt fatigued. However, a number of studies have found that colicky infants do not suffer from sleep disorders even when parents perceived this to be the case (Kirjavainen et al.). Wendy Mason and colleagues found mothers implicated their own inability to sleep or rest postpartum as a major contributor to PPD. Even though mothers with PPD retrospectively reported less subjective sleep than non-depressed mothers, when measured objectively and prospectively, mothers with PPD did have impaired sleep efficiency , but no worse than those without PPD (Dørheim, Bondevik, Eberhard-Gran, and Bjorvatn). Such findings suggest the stress of having a child who suffers from colic or medical problems may be a risk factor for PPD due to lack of maternal rest (Dennis and Ross 2005), but, furthermore, that the mother's perception of her own and her infant's lack of sleep may influence that risk.

11. *Short interpregnancy interval.* A short time interval between pregnancies may also be associated with PPD (Dennis et al.). Subsequent pregnancies within 24 months were an indicator of poorer mental health and of trauma experiences among adolescent mothers, when compared to adolescent mothers who did not become pregnant again in such a short time (Patchen, Caruso and Lanzi). Danish researchers found that short interpregnancy interval was more often due to unplanned pregnancies (Kaharuza, Sabroe, and Basso), which is also known to be a risk factor for PPD (Beck). Whether the stress is psychological or physical, short interpregnancy interval also brings its own stressors in terms of mothering and draws once more the link between stress and PPD.

12. *Post-adoption depression.* Similar to biological mothers, adoptive mothers experience the stress, sleep deprivation, and physical work that accompanies having a new baby or child, along with stresses that may be unique to adoption, such as infertility, financial issues, and evaluation for parental fitness (Payne, Fields, Meuchel, Jaffe, and Jha). Research pertaining to post adoption depression is sparse, but post-adoption depression does seem to be fairly common, although not as common as PPD (Payne et al.; McKay, Ross, and Goldberg). Research emerging in this area indicates post-adoption depression is linked with several variables already implicated in PPD (Payne et al.; McKay et al.).

Adoptive and biological mothers are exposed to many of the same environmental changes, although adoptive mothers do not experience the same level of hormonal changes and may experience other stressors that biological mothers do not (Payne et al.). This area of research speaks to the importance of considering more than the biological risk factors in PPD, that risk factors shared between PPD and post-adoption depression, such as psychosocial and sociocultural risk factors, might help to paint a clearer picture of depression after the transition to motherhood.

SOCIOCULTURAL RISK FACTORS

Sociocultural factors influencing PPD are rooted externally to mothers and located within the social and cultural landscape. From this perspective, forces interact with women at the individual level to construct depressive or *mad* experiences. A holistic understanding of these experiences, including, for example, the social rules, norms, expectations, social locations (such as ethnicity and SES), and social structural conditions (such as status of women, violence against women, poverty, and abuse) elucidates justifiable reasons a mother might feel she has gone *mad*. Indeed, women's own accounts of depression often include, at their core, the economic and social conditions of their lives (McMullen and Stoppard).

The dominant North American cultural messages women receive about how to behave in intimate relationships play an important role in depression. According to Dana Jack's (1991, 1999a, 2011) *silencing the self* theory of depression, women must stifle their expression of true feelings; self-silencing "refers to removing critical aspects of self from dialogue for specific relational purposes" (Jack 1999a: 225). Women can become alienated from their wants, desires, feelings, and very selves in an effort to nurture, please, and look after others, leading them to abandon care of themselves or perceive self-care as selfish (Jack 1999b). Care for others often goes unreciprocated, leaving women feeling disconnected, unsupported, and angry. Although these feelings would seem normal in such circumstances, women shut these *bad* feelings out of awareness through the internalization of cultural scripts related to goodness.

DISCOURSE AND CULTURAL IMPERATIVE OF THE *GOOD WOMAN*

Andrea O'Reilly and Adrienne Rich deconstructed ideologies of how women *must* and *should* mother. Betty Friedan criticized the promulgation of the *good woman* by deconstructing how societal values and definitions of what it means to be a woman can lead to depression and other psychological issues. Even as women reclaimed their identity apart from domesticity, social control is maintained by the age-old ideology of feminine beauty (Wolf). Lisa Held and Alexandra Rutherford, in a review of popular magazines and advice books through the late twentieth Century, revealed an intense and enduring cultural ambivalence "toward situating motherhood as a cause of emotional distress and a persistent prescription to distressed mothers to fix themselves so that they can be good mothers" (2). They put forward that, even still, the complicated experiences of motherhood are overshadowed with the cultural insistence that *good* mothers are happy mothers, at all costs.

Feminist researchers (e.g., Mauthner) have found that many women with depression have internalized social messages and struggle with behaving in a way that adheres to rigid social norms. "Society constructs a basic conflict for women: it demands women's selfless nurturance in relationships yet requires assertion for self-development and achievement" (Jack 2011: 523). Women may lose themselves in an effort to achieve unrealistic standards of goodness in their roles as wives and mothers and compare themselves to other women as well to a fictitious *perfect* mother/wife to gauge their own progress in achieving this impossible goal. Researchers, including Jack (1991, 1999a, 1999b, 2011), Deanna Gammel and Janet Stoppard, Natasha Mauthner, Linda McMullen and Rita Schreiber, have found that women with depression consistently use moral language such as *should, ought, good, bad,* and *selfish* to describe themselves and their behaviours. The finding that women with depression frequently use common language to judge themselves against a standard of behaviour demonstrates how cultural messages are translated to the individual level. The inner conflict between what women feel they should be doing, thinking, experiencing, and/or feeling and what they are actually experiencing creates dissonance and stress, a *madness* that fuels depression.

When examining research related to cultural imperatives of the *good woman*, the following five themes convey ubiquitous messages women receive. They include: (1) necessity to prioritize nurturing and caring of others to the extent of being selfless and self-sacrificing (Gilligan; Jack, 1991, 1999a, 1999b, 2011; Schreiber); (2) to be cheerful, strong, and productive while avoiding conflict and the expression of anger (Brown; Schreiber; Simonds); (3) to be autonomous and independent, not smothering others with emotional neediness and not showing vulnerability lest it be interpreted as weakness or failure (Mauthner; McMullen; McMullen and Stoppard); (4) to ensure that a husband is attracted and held and that his emotional and physical needs are met, always prioritizing marital and parenting roles over vocational goals (Brown; Jack 1991, 2011; Scattolon and Stoppard); and (5) to maintain a youthful, slim, and attractive appearance (Dunlap; Jack, 1991, 1999a). For many women, goodness also includes norms and attributes of the achieving, competent superwoman.

Consistent with these perspectives, cultural norms create an assumption that all women want to become mothers. Motherhood is taken for granted as part of a natural role in a woman's life that requires little justification. Janet Stoppard (2000) noted that marriage and motherhood offer escape from what has become a culturally devalued role, that of the single woman. Long before a woman has a child, cultural messages have begun to shape how she will form her identity as a mother, and how this fits with her identity of herself. In fact, Mauthner found that women who experience PPD experienced dissonance between the mothers they expected to be and the mothers they have become and they "describe losing their own voices to those of others –health care professionals, family members, and friends– telling them how they should feel, think, and behave as mothers" (Mauthner 17). The countless parenting books touting solutions to problems and best ways to mother also undermine a mother's own voice and experience.

Moral standards of *good* versus *bad* mothering resonate throughout the research related to PPD. Traits associated with good mothering include being soft-spoken, patient, receptive, nurturing, and enjoying children. With prevailing norms dictating the need for sacrificial mothering, mothering by consistently organizing their lives around their children and spouse as top priorities (O'Reilly), women who do not inherently enjoy infant care, who do not experience positive bonding, or who feel ambivalence about mothering tend to hide this reality from others, lest they be labelled a bad mother (Mauthner) or *mad*. Feminist researchers have argued the bulk of responsibility for children's growth, development, and behaviour rests with the mother, and mothers are often blamed, and blame themselves, for any behavioural problems or faults in their children (Caplan 2000). Deborah Lynne Flores and Victoria Hendrick theorized that sociocultural forces definitively shape a mother's emotional wellbeing. There is little doubt the experience of becoming a mother and motherhood is wrought with social messages.

MULTIFACETED RISK FACTORS

In essence, sociocultural forces are legitimate risk factors for PPD, in as much as biological and psychosocial risk factors are, although sociocultural forces are extremely difficult to research and validate as they are entrenched understandings. Ideologies like the *good woman* and *good mother* are so engrained in our way of being that they cease to exist or to be named. Instead, they are invisible cross-stitches that hem the frays to the pattern of our existence. Visible patterned designs like a woman's psychiatric history, her socio-economic standing, and hormonal changes are easily demarcated and pin-pointable on the patchwork. But, the cross-stitch holding it together—ideas of patriarchy, which promotes individualism, competitiveness, silencing of women's voices, sexism, the unequal division of paid and unpaid labour, and the place and power of women in society—are the way the thread connects design onto fabric. How, then, do we begin to look at the complex patchwork and see women's experience of PPD for all that it is, including cultural discourses that shape the way we believe that the roles in motherhood are immutable? Indeed, a woman's ability to mother becomes the new yardstick with which to measure her worth. Previously it was measured, as Naomi Wolf so aptly described, against the yardstick of her ability to attract men.

PIE CHART CONCEPTUALIZATION

Fox's depiction of PPD in her novel *Dispatches From a Not-So-Perfect Life* and her desire for a pie chart explanation to her experience of PPD, was written tongue in cheek; the view of her own pie chart was as follows:

> 14% cultural pressure to be a perfect mother; 10% dysfunctional family of origin; 8% biochemical tendency to depression; 14% unequal division of household labour with my husband (I did more); 8% alienation from Texas, where I was currently living; 10% sleep deprivation; 8% hormonal imbalances due to breastfeeding; 6% pessimistic temperament; 10% loss of social power; and 12% no good friends in town. (6)

Nevertheless, Fox's notion of the pie chart sums up the multifaceted perspective of risk factors asserted within this chapter. Reconceiving and reconceptualizing PPD includes considering that this pie chart conceptualization underscores the holistic complexity and the confluence of risk factors associated with PPD in each woman's own experience. Depending on a myriad of factors related to stress, anxiety, stressful events and forces, a pie chart conceptualization captures the intricate differences and changes over time for a woman. Reconceiving PPD with such a meta-theoretical view combines categories of biological, psychosocial, and sociocultural risk factors and collapses the *either or* rhetoric in the literature related to PPD, which pits categories of views against each other. Also, while acknowledging that women share many risk factors for PPD, the relative size of the individual pieces of each woman's pie chart will nonetheless be different, given her unique set of circumstances.

BRIEF TREATMENT IMPLICATIONS

A pie chart conceptualization in practice (e.g., counselling women postpartum) would involve, in an egalitarian relationship focused on empowering the client, exploring all categories of risk factors using women's own voices and experiences, including sociocultural forces, which are otherwise often left out of assessment and treatment planning. Using this reconceptualization of PPD, a counsellor would "[take] into account the client's individual circumstances and then [help] her to understand herself within the context of the larger society" (Davis-Gage, Kettmann, and Moel 117) and would challenge the core of negative self-judgments by exploring "the origins of their images of relatedness; how they are tied to gender, inequality, and culture; and how they become moralized" (Jack 1999a: 240). Using these concepts in practice, the counsellor would encourage women with PPD to free themselves from the prescriptive societal expectations of motherhood which assign the majority of the responsibility of child and home care to mothers, while also maintaining respect for the client's cultural values, and to negotiate imbalances of power in her relationships, leading to increased self-concept and a decrease in depressive symptoms (Davis-Gage et al.).

Dana Jack (1999b) presents six ways of listening to the perspectives of women with depression in qualitative research, ways of listening that are directly applicable to the counselling setting (see also Jack 1999a). She advocates avoiding conceptualizing women's depression in the historical understanding steeped in maleness and encourages consideration of the diversity of women's individual experiences and social contexts. *Open listening* (attending to the space between speaker and listener that holds social realities and to the body's emotional discourse therein) and *focused awareness* (attending to word meaning, taking none for granted) occur during the interview or counselling process (Jack 1999b). These two ways of listening exist within a creative tension between the listener, or counsellor, attending simultaneously to her (or his) own experience of the speaker's retelling and to the understanding of the speaker on her (or his) own terms (Jack 1999b). *Attending to moral language* includes listening for moral self-evaluative statements which illustrate the interaction between self-concept and cultural norms and messages—the *should, ought, good* and *bad* type statements (Jack, 1999b). Jack (1999b) defines *attending to inner dialogues* as listening for places in narrative where women talk about their self-experience from two perspectives, or the *divided self. Attending to meta-statements* includes identifying spontaneous statements about the speakers own thoughts, which offer a glimpse as to how a woman experiences herself as she speaks and to how she imagines others hear her (Jack 1999b). Finally, *attending to the logic of the narrative* involves noticing internal consistencies or contradictions in narrative themes (Jack 1999b). These ways of attending occur during the interview or counselling process and also represent systematic ways of analysing the discourse (Jack 1999b). Approaching counselling women with PPD in this way not only benefits the individual client, but also begins to challenge society's long-held beliefs about how women *should* cope with the transition to motherhood.

More generally, when asked, mothers with symptoms of PPD identified they needed someone to listen to their symptoms and concerns, to acknowledge the postpartum period is a difficult time, to affirm they are performing as well as other new mothers do, to normalize their feelings, and to give them hope their symptoms will improve (Letourneau et al.). While some women prefer group support, the researchers found most prefer one-on-one interventions; regardless of support type, a trusting relationship between professional and mother was key (Letourneau et al.). Patricia Leahy-Warren and colleagues encourage those in clinical practice to have an understanding of the social support, both functional (informational, instrumental, emotional and appraisal) and structural (formal and informal), relevant to new mothers, and to empower mothers to mobilize the support available to them.

Additionally, within this reconceptualization of PPD, counselling interventions include the development and enhancement of self-compassion in mothers. As an example, Paul Gilbert developed Compassionate Mind Training, and although it is not specifically for mothers, it has been demonstrated to reduce depression, anxiety, self-criticism, and shame and to increase hope and one's ability to self-soothe in times of distress (Gilbert and Procter). Surely, counsellors utilizing treatment strategies for PPD would benefit from an emphasis on increasing self-compassion in mothers. While a complete discussion of how to cultivate self-compassion is beyond the scope of this chapter, it is worthwhile to note the difference self-compassion would make in managing sociocultural pressures, particularly the pressure in the moral standard to be a *good mother*.

CONCLUSION AND SOCIAL ACTION

A reconception and reconceptualization of PPD illustrated as a pie chart model of the risk factors associated with PPD, including biological, psychosocial, and sociocultural stressors, provides a new lens with which to view PPD and removes the origins of *madness* from the mother, locating it rightfully in the sociocultural landscape that we live within. Understanding risk factors associated with PPD is paramount to enhancing awareness of mechanisms and forces by which mothers become depressed, contributing to strategies for prevention, and in furthering treatment for PPD. Treatment, with respect to sociocultural risk factors involves fighting to interrupt the *good mother* ideology by exposing and normalizing the reality of mothering, which is wrought with a myriad of emotions and experiences—positive, negative, and neutral. Ultimately, "empowering women to weigh the viability of relinquishing societal expectations and the pressure to be 'everything to everyone' may help free women from the burden of depression after childbirth" (Davis-Gage et al. 125).

Similarly, social activism and advocacy to ameliorate effects and bring about change in the conditions of women's lives, is necessary. Depression in women would be reduced if all women had access to social programming, safe, affordable childcare and housing, and other resources. This reconception and reconceptualization of PPD highlights the need to strive to promote gender equality, to encourage full participation of women in economic, social, cultural, and political life in order to improve women's economic autonomy and well-being, to eliminate systemic violence against women and children, and to advance women's human rights. No greater a time than now, in our twenty-first century, will the sociocultural conditions that women bear be more keenly felt and is public policy and advocacy so urgently needed.

REFERENCES

American Psychiatric Association (APA). (n.d.). *Postpartum depression*. Web. <http://healthyminds.org/Main-Topic/Postpartum-Depression.aspx>.

American Psychiatric Association (APA). *Diagnostic and Statistical Manual of Mental Disorders*. 4th ed. Washington, DC: Author, 2000.

Arthur, N. and N. Merali. "Counselling Immigrants and Refugees." *Culture-infused Counselling: Celebrating the Canadian Mosaic*. Eds. N. Arthur and S. Collins. Calgary: Counselling Concepts, 2000. 341-370.

Austin, M. P., D. Hadzi-Pavlovic, L. Leader, K. Saint and G. Parker. "Maternal Trait Anxiety, Depression and Life Event Stress in Pregnancy: Relationships With Infant Temperament." *Early Human Development* 81 (2005): 183-90.

Beck, C. T. "Predictors of Postpartum Depression: An Update." *Nursing Research* 50 (2001): 275-85.

Beck, C. T., R. K. Gable, C. Sakala and E. R. Declercq. "Posttraumatic Stress Disorder in New Mothers: Results from a Two-Stage U.S. National Survey." *Birth: Issues in Perinatal Care* 38 (2011): 216–227.

Bernazzani, O. and A. Bifulco. "Motherhood as a Vulnerability Factor In Major Depression: The Role of Negative Pregnancy Experiences." *Social Science and Medicine* 56 (2003): 1249-60.

Bilszta, J., M. Tang, D. Meyer, J. Milgrom, J. Ericksen and A. Buist. "Single Motherhood Versus Poor Partner Relationship: Outcomes for Antenatal Mental Health." *Australian and New Zealand Journal of Psychiatry* 42 (1) (2008): 56-65.

Bina, R. "The Impact of Cultural Factors Upon Postpartum Depression: A Literature Review." *Health Care for Women International* 29 (6) (2008): 568-592.

Birkeland, R., J. Thompson and V. Phares. "Adolescent Motherhood and Postpartum Depression." *Journal of Clinical Child and Adolescent Psychology* 34 (2) (2005): 292-300.

Bloch, M., P. Schmidt and J. Danaceau. "Effects of Gonadal Steroids in Women With a History of Postpartum Depression." *American Journal of Psychiatry* 157 (2000): 924-930.

Blom, E., P. W. Jansen, F. C. Verhulst, A. Hofman, H. Raat, V. W. Jaddoe, M. Coolman, E. A. Stiegers and H. Tiemeier. "Perinatal Complications Increase the Risk of Postpartum Depression." The Generation R Study. *BJOG: An International Journal of Obstetrics and Gynaecology* 117 (11) (2010): 1390-1398.

Bovier, P. A., E. Chamot and T. V. Perneger. "Perceived Stress, Internal Resources, and Social Support as Determinants of Mental Health Among Young Adults." *Quality of Life Research* 13 (2004): 161-170.

Boyce, P. M. "Risk Factors for Postnatal Depression: A Review and Risk Factors in Australian Populations." *Archives of Women's Mental Health* 6 (2003): 43-50.

Bradley, T., M. E. Cupples and H. Irvine. "A Case Control Study of a Deprivation Triangle: Teenage Motherhood, Poor Educational Achievement and Unemployment." *International Journal of Adolescent Medicine and Health* 14 (2002): 117-23.

Branden, N. *The Six Pillars of Self-Esteem*. London: Bantam, 1994.

Branden, N. *The Psychology of Self-Esteem*. 32nd ed. San Francisco: Jossey-Bass, 2001.

Brown, L. "Gender-Role Analysis: A Neglected Component of Psychological Assessment." *Psychotherapy* 23 (1986): 243-248.

Caplan, P. J. *The New Don't Blame Mother: Mending the Mother-Daughter Relationship*. New York: Routledge, 2000.

Caplan, P. J. *They Say You're Crazy: How the World's Most Powerful Psychiatrists Decide Who's Normal*. Reading, MA: Addison-Wesley, 1995.

Ching-Yu, C. and R. H. Pickler. "Maternal Psychological Well-Being and Salivary Cortisol in Late Pregnancy and Early Post-Partum." *Stress and Health: Journal of the International Society for the Investigation of Stress* 26 (3) (2010): 215-224.

Corwin, E. J., L. E. Murray-Kolb, and L. L. Beard. "Low Hemoglobin Level is a Risk Factor for Postpartum Depression." *Journal of Nutrition* 133 (2003): 4139-42.

Davis-Gage, D., J. Kettmann and J. Moel. "Developmental Transition of Motherhood: Treating Postpartum Depression Using a Feminist Approach." *Adultspan: Theory Research and Practice* 9 (2) (2010): 117-126.

Dearing, E., B. A. Taylor and K. McCartney. "Implications of Family Income Dynamics for Women's Depressive Symptoms During the First Three Years

After Childbirth." *American Journal of Public Health* 94 (2004): 1372-7.

Dennis, C. L., P. A. Janssen and J. Singer. "Identifying Women at-Risk for Postpartum Depression in the Immediate Postpartum Period." *Acta Psychiatrica Scandinavica* 110 (2004): 338-46.

Dennis, C. L. and L. Ross. "Relationships Among Infant Sleep Patterns, Maternal Fatigue, and Development of Depressive Symptomatology." *Birth* 32 (2005): 187-193.

Dennis, C. and L. Ross. "Women's Perceptions of Partner Support and Conflict in the Development of Postpartum Depressive Symptoms." *Journal of Advanced Nursing* 56 (6) (2006): 588-599.

Dørheim, S. K., G. T. Bondevik, M. M. Eberhard-Gran and B. B. Bjorvatn. "Subjective and Objective Sleep Among Depressed and Non-Depressed Postnatal Women." *Acta Psychiatrica Scandinavica* 119 (2) (2009): 128-136.

Dunlap, S. *Counseling Depressed Women.* Louisville, KT: Westminster John Know Press, 1997.

Flores, D. L. and V. C. Hendrick. "Etiology and Treatment of Postpartum Depression." *Current Psychiatry Reports* 4 (2002): 461-466.

Fox, F. *Dispatches From a Not-So-Perfect Life or How I Learned To Love the House, the Man, the Child.* New York: Harmony Books, 2003.

Friedan, B. *The Feminine Mystique.* New York: Dell Publishing, 1963.

Gammel, D. and J. Stoppard. "Women's Experiences of Treatment of Depression: Medicalization or Empowerment?" *Canadian Psychology* 40 (1999): 112-128.

Garabedian, M. J., K. Y. Lain, W. F. Hansen, L. S. Garcia, C. M. Williams and L. J. Crofford. "Violence Against Women and Postpartum Depression." *Journal of Women's Health (15409996)* 20 (3) (2011): 447-453.

Gilbert, P. and S. Procter. "Compassionate Mind Training for People with High Shame and Self-Criticism: Overview and Pilot Study of a Group Therapy Approach." *Clinical Psychology and Psychotherapy* 13 (6) (2006): 353-379.

Gilligan, C. *In a Different Voice: Psychological Theory And Women's Development.* Cambridge, MA: Harvard University Press, 1982.

Golbasi, Z., M. Kelleci, G. Kisacik and A. Cetin. "Prevalence and Correlates of Depression in Pregnancy Among Turkish Women." *Maternal and Child Health Journal* 14 (4) (2010): 485-491.

Goyal, D., C. Gay, and K. A. Lee. "How Much Does Low Socioeconomic Status Increase the Risk of Prenatal and Postpartum Depressive Symptoms in First-Time Mothers?" *Women's Health Issues* 20 (2) (2010): 96-104.

Grigoriadis, S., G. E. Robinson, K. Fung, L. E. Ross, C. Chee, C. Dennis and S. Romans. "Traditional Postpartum Practices and Rituals: Clinical Implications." *Canadian Journal of Psychiatry* 54 (12) (2009): 834-840.

Groer, M. W., M. W. Davis and J. Hemphill. "Postpartum Stress: Current Concepts and the Possible Protective Role of Breastfeeding." *Journal of*

Obstetric, Gynecologic, and Neonatal Nursing 31 (2002): 411–417.

Held, L. and A. Rutherford. "Can't a Mother Sing the Blues? Postpartum Depression and the Construction of Motherhood in Late 20th-Century America." *History of Psychology* 12 December 2011: 1-22. Advance online publication.

Henshaw, C., D. Foreman and J. Cox. "Postnatal Blues: A Risk Factor for Postnatal Depression." *Journal of Psychosomatic Obstetrics and Gynecology* 25 (3-4) (2004): 267-72.

Hiltunen, P., T. Raudaskoski, H. Ebeling and I. Moilanen. "Does Pain Relief During Delivery Decrease the Risk of Postnatal Depression?" *Acta Obstetricia et Gynecologica Scandinavica* 83 (2004): 257-261.

Huang, Y. C. and N. Mathers, "Postnatal Depression – Biological or Cultural? A Comparative Study of Postnatal Women in the UK and Taiwan." *Journal of Advanced Nursing* 33 (2001): 279-87.

Huang, Y. and N. Mathers. "A Comparative Study of Traditional Postpartum Practices and Rituals in the UK and Taiwan." *Diversity in Health and Care* 7 (4) (2010): 239-247. Jack, D. *Silencing the Self: Women and Depression.* Cambridge, MA: Harvard University Press, 1991.

Jack, D. "Silencing the Self: Inner Dialogues and Outer Realities." *The Interactional Nature of Depression: Advances in Interpersonal Approaches.* Eds. T. Joiner and J. C. Coyne. Washington, DC: American Psychological Association, 1999a. 221-246.

Jack, D. "Ways of Listening to Depressed Women in Qualitative Research: Interview Techniques and Analyses." *Canadian Psychology/Psychologie Canadienne* 40 (2) (1999b): 91-101.

Jack, D. "Reflections on the Silencing the Self Scale and its Origins." *Psychology of Women Quarterly* 35 (3) (2011): 523-529.

Jacobs, D. H. and D. Cohen. "Does 'Psychological Dysfunction' Mean Anything? A Critical Essay on Pathology Versus Agency." *Journal of Humanistic Psychology* 50 (3) (2010): 312-334.

Josefsson, A., L. Angelsioo, G. Berg, C. M. Ekstrom, C. Gunnervik, C. Nordin and G. Sydsjo. "Obstetric, Somatic, and Demographic Risk Factors for Postpartum Depressive Symptoms." *Obstetrics and Gynecology* 99 (2002): 223-8.

Kaharuza, F. M., S. Sabroe and O. Basso. "Choice and Chance: Determinants of Short Interpregnancy Intervals in Denmark." *Acta Obstetricia et Gynecologica Scandinavica* 80 (2001): 532-8.

Kendall-Tackett, K. "A New Paradigm for Depression in New Mothers: The Central Role of Inflammation and How Breastfeeding and Anti-Inflammatory Treatments Protect Maternal Mental Health." *International Breastfeeding Journal* 26 (2007): 14.

Kendall-Tackett, K. "Four Research Findings that Will Change What We

Think About Perinatal Depression." *The Journal of Perinatal Education* 19 (4) (2010): 7-9.

Kirjavainen, J., T. Kirjavainen, V. Huhtala, L. Lehtonen, L. H. Korvenrant, and P. Kero. "Infants With Colic Have a Normal Sleep Structure at Two and Seven Months of Age." *Journal of Pediatrics* 138 (2001): 218-23.

Koo, V., J. Lynch and S. Cooper. "Risk of Postnatal Depression After Emergency Delivery." *Journal of Obstetrics and Gynaecology Research* 29 (2003): 246-50.

Kulkarni, S. *Pregnancy Blues: What Every Woman Needs To Know About Depression During Pregnancy.* New York: Bantam Dell, 2005.

Lanes, A., J. L. Kuk and H. Tamim. "Prevalence and Characteristics of Postpartum Depression Symptomatology Among Canadian Women: A Cross-Sectional Study." *BMC Public Health* 11 (4) (2011): 302-400.

Leahy-Warren, P., G. McCarthy and P. Corcoran. "First-time Mothers: Social Support, Maternal Parental Self-Efficacy and Postnatal Depression." *Journal of Clinical Nursing* 21 (3/4) (2012): 388-397.

Leigh, B. and J. Milgrom. "Risk Factors for Antenatal Depression, Postnatal Depression and Parenting Stress." *BMC Psychiatry* 8 (2008): 1-11.

Letourneau, N., L. Duffett-Leger, M. Stewart, K. Hegadoren, C. Dennis, C. Rinaldi and J. Stoppard. "Canadian Mothers' Perceived Support Needs During Postpartum Depression." *Journal of Obstetric, Gynecologic and Neonatal Nursing* 36 (5) (2007): 441-449.

Lyubomirsky, S. and S. Nolen-Hoeksema. "Effects of Self-Focused Rumination on Negative Thinking and Interpersonal Problem Solving." *Journal of Personality and Social Psychology* 69 (1995): 176-190.

Maloney, J. and G. Wong. *Barriers to Self-Compassion: Gender and Perfectionism in the Lives of Women.* Manuscript in preparation, 2012.

Mason, W. A., M. J. Rice, and K. Records. "The Lived Experience of Postpartum Depression in a Psychiatric Population." *Perspectives in Psychiatric Care* 41 (2005): 52-61.

Mauthner, N. "Feeling Low and Feeling Really Bad About Feeling Low: Women's Experiences of Motherhood and Postpartum Depression." *Canadian Psychology* 40 (1999): 143-161.

McBride, C. and M. Bagby. "Rumination and Interpersonal Dependency: Explaining Women's Vulnerability to Depression." *Canadian Psychology* 47 (2006): 184-194.

McKay, K., L. E. Ross and A. E. Goldberg. "Adaptation to Parenthood During the Post-Adoption Period: A Review of the Literature." *Adoption Quarterly* 13 (2) (2010): 125-144.

McMullen, L. "Metaphors in the Talk of 'Depressed' Women in Psychotherapy." *Canadian Psychology* 40 (1999): 102-111.

McMullen, L. M. and J. M. Stoppard, "Women and Depression: A Case

Study of the Influence of Feminism in Canadian Psychology." *Feminism and Psychology* 16 (3) (2006): 273-288.

Miles, S. "Winning the Battle: A Review of Postnatal Depression." *British Journal of Midwifery* 19 (4) (2011): 221-227.

Miller, L. "Linking Evidence and Experience: Postpartum Depression." *Journal of the American Medical Association* 287 (2002): 762-765.

Milman, N. "Postpartum Anemia I: Definition, Prevalence, Causes, and Consequences." *Annals of Hematology* 90 (11) (2011): 1247-1253.

Neff, K. D. "Development and Validation of a Scale to Measure Self-Compassion." *Self and Identity* 2 (3) (2003a): 223-250.

Neff, K. "Self-Compassion: An Alternative Conceptualization of a Healthy Attitude Toward Oneself." *Self and Identity* 2 (2) (2003b): 85.

Neff, K. D. and P. McGehee. "Self-Compassion and Psychological Resilience Among Adolescents and Young Adults." *Self and Identity* 9 (3) (2010): 225-240.

Neff, K. D. and R. Vonk, "Self-Compassion Versus Global Self-Esteem: Two Different Ways of Relating to Oneself. *Journal of Personality* 77 (2009): 23-50.

Nolen-Hoeksema, S., L. E. Parke, and J. Larson. "Ruminative Coping With Depressed Mood Following Loss." *Journal of Personality and Social Psychology* 67 (1994): 92-104.

O'Hara, M. W. "Postpartum Depression: What We Know." *Journal of Clinical Psychology* 65 (12) (2009): 1258-1269.

O'Hara, M. W. and A. M. Swain. "Rates and Risk of Postpartum Depression: A Meta-Analysis." *International Review of Psychiatry* 8 (1996): 37-54.

Olshansky, E. "A Theoretical Explanation for Previously Infertile Mothers' Vulnerability to Depression." *Journal of Nursing Scholarship* 35 (2003): 263-8.

O'Reilly, A. *Rocking the Cradle: Thoughts on Motherhood, Feminism and the Possibility of Empowered Mothering*. Toronto: Association for Research on Mothering, 2006.

Pajulo, M., E. Savonlahti, A. Sourander, H. Helenius and J. Piha. "Antenatal Depression, Substance Dependency and Social Support." *Journal of Affective Disorders* 65 (2001): 9-17.

Parry, B. L., D. L. Sorenson, C. J. Meliska, N. Basavaraj, G. G. Zirpoli, A. Gamst and R. Hauger. "Hormonal Basis of Mood and Postpartum Disorders." *Current Women's Health Reports* 3 (2003): 230-5.

Patchen, L., D. Caruso, and R. Lanzi. "Poor Maternal Mental Health and Trauma as Risk Factors for a Short Interpregnancy Interval Among Adolescent Mothers." *Journal of Psychiatric and Mental Health Nursing* 16 (4) (2009): 401-403.

Patel, R. R., D. J. Murphy and T. J. Peters. "Operative Delivery and Postnatal Depression: A Cohort Study." *British Medical Journal* 330 (7496) (2005): 879.

Payne, J. L., E. S. Fields, J. M. Meuchel, C. J. Jaffe and M. Jha. "Post Adoption

Depression." *Archives of Women's Mental Health* 13 (2) (2010): 147-151.

Posmontier, B. and J. A. Horowitz. "Postpartum Practices and Depression Prevalences: Technocentric and Ethnokinship Cultural Perspectives." *Journal of Transcultural Nursing,* 15 (2004): 34-43.

Raes, F. "Rumination and Worry as Mediators of the Relationship Between Self-Compassion and Depression and Anxiety." *Personality and Individual Differences* 48 (6) (2010): 757-761.

Randolph, M. E. and D. M. Reddy. "Sexual Functioning in Women With Chronic Pelvic Pain: The Impact of Depression, Support, and Abuse." *Journal of Sex Research* 43 (2006): 38-45.

Rapkin, A.J., J. A. Mikacich, B. Moatakef-Imani and N. Rasgon. "The Clinical Nature and Formal Diagnosis of Premenstrual, Postpartum, and Perimeno-pausal Affective Disorders." *Current Psychiatry Reports* 4 (2002): 419-28.

Rich, A. *Of Woman Born: Motherhood as Experience and Institution.* New York: W. W. Norton and Company, 1976.

Ross, L. E., E. M. Sellers, L. Gilbert, S. E. Evans and M. K. Romach. "Mood Changes During Pregnancy and the Postpartum Period: Development of a Biopsychosocial Model." *Acta Psychiatrica Scandinavica* 109 (2004): 457-66.

Rowe-Murray, H. J. and J. R. Fisher. "Operative Intervention in Delivery Is Associated With Compromised Early Mother–Infant Interaction." *BJOG: British Journal of Obstetrics and Gynaecology* 108 (2001): 1068–1075.

Saisto, T., K. Salmela-Aro, J. E. Nurmi and E. Halmesmaki. "Psychosocial Predictors of Disappointment With Delivery and Puerperal Depression." *Acta Obstetricia et Gynecologica Scandinavica* 80 (2001): 39-45.

Scattolon, Y. and J. Stoppard. "Getting On With Life: Women's Experiences and Ways of Coping With Depression." *Canadian Psychology* 40 (1999): 206-219.

Schreiber, R. "Wandering in the Dark: Women's Experiences With Depression." *Health Care for Women International* 22 (2001): 85-98.

Seimyr, L., M. Edhborg, W. Lundh, and B. Sjogren. "In the Shadow of Maternal Depressed Mood: Experiences of Parenthood During the First Year After Childbirth." *Journal of Psychosomatic Obstetrics and Gynecology* 25 (2004): 23-34.

Silverman, M. E. and H. Loudon. "Antenatal Reports of Pre-Pregnancy Abuse Is Associated With Symptoms of Depression in the Postpartum Period." *Archives of Women's Mental Health* 13 (5) (2010): 411-415.

Simonds, S. *Depression and Women: An Integrative Treatment Approach.* New York: Springer Publishing Co., 2001.

Soet, J. E., G. A. Brack and C. D. Dilorio. "Prevalence and Predictors of Women's Experiences of Psychological Trauma During Childbirth." *Birth: Issues in Perinatal Care* 30 (2003): 36-46.

Spasojevic, J. and L. B. Alloy. "Who Becomes a Depressive Ruminator? Developmental Antecedents of Ruminative Response Style." *Journal of Cognitive Psychotherapy* 16 (2002): 405-420.

Smyth, J., M., C. Ockenfels, L. Porter, C. Kirschbaum, D. H. Hellhammer, and A. A. Stone. "Stressors and Mood Measured on a Momentary Basis Are Associated With Salivary Cortisol Secretion." *Psychoneuroendocrinology* 23 (1998): 353-70.

Stoppard, J. "Why New Perspectives Are Needed for Understanding Depression in Women." *Canadian Psychology* 40 (1999): 79-90.

Stoppard, J. *Understanding Depression: Feminist Social Constructionist Approaches.* New York: Routledge, 2000.

Stoppard, J. M. "Moving Towards an Understanding of Women's Depression." *Feminism and Psychology* 20 (2) (2010): 267-271.

Treynor, W., R. Gonzales, and S. Nolen-Hoeksema. "Rumination Reconsidered: A Psychometric Analysis." *Cognitive Therapy and Research* 27 (2003): 247-259.

Van Dam, N. T., S. C. Sheppard, J. P. Forsyth and M. Earleywine. "Self-compassion Is a Better Predictor Than Mindfulness of Symptom Severity and Quality of Life in Mixed Anxiety and Depression." *Journal of Anxiety Disorders* 25 (1) (2011): 123–130.

Watanabe, M., Wada, K., Sakata, Y., Aratake, Y., Kato, N., Ohta, H., and Tanaka, K. "Maternity Blues as Predictor of Postpartum Depression: A Prospective Cohort Study Among Japanese Women." *Journal of Psychosomatic Obstetrics and Gynecology* 29 (3) (2008): 211-217.

Webb, D. A., J. R. Bloch, J. C. Coyne, E. K. Chung, I. M. Bennett and J. Culhane. "Postpartum Physical Symptoms in New Mothers: Their Relationship to Functional Limitations and Emotional Well-Being." *Birth: Issues in Perinatal Care* 35 (3) (2008): 179-187.

Wijngaards-de Meij, L., M. Stroebe, H. Schut, W. Stroebe, J. van den Bout, P. van der Heijden and I. Dijkstra. "Couples At Risk Following the Death of Their Child: Predictors of Grief Versus Depression." *Journal of Consulting and Clinical Psychology* 73 (2005): 617-23.

Wolf, N. *The Beauty Myth.* Toronto: Random House, 1990.

Wylie, L., M. Hollins, G. Marland, C. Martin and J. Rankin. "The Enigma of Post-Natal Depression: An Update." *Journal of Psychiatric and Mental Health Nursing* 18 (1) (2011): 48-58.

Zelkowitz, P., J. Schinazi, L. Katofsky, J. F. Saucier, M. Valenzuela, R. Westreich et al. "Factors Associated With Depression in Pregnant Immigrant Women." *Transcultural Psychiatry* 41 (2004): 445-464.

10.
Postpartum Depression and Caregiving

Beyond the Developmental-Inadequacy Discourse

NICOLE LETOURNEAU AND GERALD F. GIESBRECHT

Postpartum depression (PPD) affects one in seven women (Gaynes et al.; O'Hara and Swain) and is characterized by the disabling symptoms of dysphoria, insomnia or hypersomnia, psychomotor agitation or retardation, fatigue or loss of energy, excessive or inappropriate guilt, reduced concentration or indecisiveness, and recurrent suicidal ideation (APA). Significant anxiety often accompanies PPD (Matthey, Barnett, Howie, and Kavanagh, 2003). In addition to the effects of PPD on mothers, the medical research on the effects of PPD on infants have been well documented (Campbell, Cohn and Myers; Cohn and Tronick; Field 1984; Whiffen and Gotlib; Whiffen, Kerr, and Kallos-Lilly). Scientific discourse of PPD is both implicitly and explicitly mother-blaming in its tone. In its most extreme form, PPD has been described as toxic to children's healthy development (Middlebrooks and Audage). No one should be surprised when many mothers feel added blame and stigma about the links between their symptoms and the reported effects they have on their children. Internalized mother-blame and feelings of inadequacy may even serve to intensify mothers' symptoms of PPD such as inappropriate guilt and anxiety (Letourneau et al. 2007).

This poses a conundrum: While scientific evidence about risks to human development (such as PPD) may help policy makers target funds and resources to support vulnerable families, this discourse simultaneously perpetuates an inaccurate and damaging discourse about mothers with depression that characterizes them as inadequate to support the development of their children. This conundrum is consistent with the work of Susan Penfold and Gillian Walker (1983, 1986) who posit that medicine (psychiatry, in particular) maintains and reinforces women's reduced stature in society; while purporting to help women, paradoxically, it actually socially regulates and oppresses them (Penfold and Walker 1986). Thus the purpose of this chapter is to outline the research that challenges this discourse of developmental-inadequacy among mothers with PPD. In addition, this chapter seeks to examine and to honour the lived experiences of mothers which are often ignored within the scientific and medical discourse.

A CRITIQUE OF THE DEVELOPMENTAL-INADEQUACY DISCOURSE

The developmental-inadequacy discourse[1] perpetuates a view of mothers with depression that fails to describe the many valuable contributions these mothers make to their children's growth and development. To illustrate the basis for the developmental-inadequacy discourse, we highlight some of the documented effects of PPD on the quality of caregiving, including maternal-infant interaction and attachment relationships. As well, the effects of PPD on child development and the challenges of treating women with PPD are delineated. In reviewing this literature, we elucidate some of the social, economic, and relational factors that underlie both depression and child developmental outcomes. We begin with a critique of assumptions that we believe are either unwarranted or create barriers to understanding and meeting the needs of mothers with depression and their children, including (a) mother blaming, (b) constricted conceptu-alizations of caregiving, (c) focusing on inadequacies versus strengths, (d) overlooking child and social contributions, and (e) intergenerational influences on the caregiving relationship.

MOTHER BLAMING

Perhaps the most harmful corollary of the developmental-inadequacy discourse is that women are to blame for the poor developmental outcomes of their children. Identifying PPD as the source of developmental inadequacy unfairly places responsibility for developmental outcomes on women and ignores the fact that PPD is associated with a variety of social, economic, and relational disadvantages that are themselves associated with poor child development. A review of the discourse on the etiology, or cause of PPD demonstrates that mother blaming, whether external or internal, is unhelpful and unwarranted.

Extensive research suggests that PPD arises from multiple factors, usually in combination. Evidence on biological causes, such as alterations in hormones or neurotransmitters following childbirth remains equivocal. Despite the persistence of biological explanations in the medical and lay literatures, there is actually very little evidence to support the notion that PPD can be distin-guished from other forms of depression on the basis of biological factors or that biological factors exert any form of independent causal influence on PPD (Whiffen). A small number of cases of PPD are related to identifiable biological factors such as thyroid dysfunction, triggered or worsened by hormone upheavals surrounding pregnancy and delivery (Ahokas, Aito, and Rimon; Granger and

Underwood; Dennis, Ross and Herxheimer), or increased dopamine sensitivity (Dennis and Stewart).

In contrast, epidemiological studies and meta-analyses of prospective studies have consistently concluded that negative life experiences, such as life stress, child care stress, and marital conflict as well as a lack of social support consistently predict the onset and recovery from PPD (Beck 2001; Dennis and Stewart; Logsdon, Birkimer, and Usui; Logsdon and Usui). Specifically, deficiencies in informational and emotional support have been linked to PPD (Chung and Yue,; Dennis and Chung-Lee; Seguin, Potvin, St-Denis, and Loiselle 1999a, 1999b; Stuchbery, Matthey, and Barnett) and research suggests that mothers with and without depression differ with respect to positive social interactions, number of confidants (Chung and Yue), and perception of social isolation (Nielsen Forman, Videbech, Hedegaard, Dalby Salvig, and Secher). Conflict with people in the social network (e.g., friends and loved ones) increases a mother's risk for developing PPD (Ritter, Hobfall, Lavin, Cameron, and Hulsizer; Seguin et al. 1999a, 1999b) and mothers who perceive less social support present more depressive symptoms than mothers who perceive sufficient support (Brugha et al.; Dankner, Goldberg, Fisch, and DCrum; Logsdon et al.; Ritter et al.). These psychological and social factors, of course, affect biological systems, but the links between psychosocial function, biological systems, and PPD remain speculative.

The idea of "etiology" itself is problematic in the current discussion as such medical language implies that PPD is caused by factors that could be avoided. The term etiology does not lend itself very well to thinking about the complex and overlapping interactions between the range of social and environmental factors that predispose to, but do not cause PPD. Low socioeconomic status and lack of support from a partner, for example, may be unavoidable but nevertheless powerful mediators of maternal PPD *and* poor child developmental outcomes. Moreover, PPD is only one of many risk factors to children's development that relate to social and environmental conditions. Indeed, the risk factors often overlap. Thus, blaming mothers for the developmental outcomes of their children unfairly ignores the complex social and relationship factors that both give rise to symptoms of depression and influence children's development.

CONSTRICTED CONCEPTUALIZATIONS OF CAREGIVING

The developmental-inadequacy discourse promotes a narrow view of caregiving. We acknowledge at the outset that in the vast majority of families, mothers are the primary caregivers of young infants and therefore the majority of infants depend on their mothers to assess their needs and provide the right stimulation at the right time with appropriate intensity and duration. This kind of psychological attunement is precisely what is often, but not always, observed to be wanting in mothers living with depression (Noorlander, Bergink, and van den Berg; Righetti-Veltema, Bousquet, and Manzano; Stanley, Murray, and Stein). For example, mothers with PPD are more likely than mothers without PPD to have negative perceptions of (what others might regard as) normal infant behavior, be less sensitive to their infants' cues, and be less affectionate, positive, and responsive to their infants (Beck 1995; Field 1984; Letourneau, Salmani and Duffett-Leger 2010; Murray and Cooper; Murray, Fiori-Cowley, Hooper and Cooper; Poobalan et al.). These behaviors are taken as evidence that mothers with PPD do not have the ability to meet their infants' needs.

Notwithstanding the fact that in the majority of families, women are the primary caregivers and biologically primed for caregiving (e.g., breastfeeding), the focus on deficient care provided by a mother with depression does not adequately appreciate that infants may receive care from many sources. Fathers, extended family, friends, and loved ones all play a role in the care of infants. Despite such potential for a diversity of capable caregivers, it is mothers who most consistently take responsibility for providing or coordinating care of their infants (Lamb). Numerous studies have pointed out that fathers (Laflamme, Pomerleau, and Malcuit; Magill-Evans, Harrison, Benzies, Gierl, and Kimak; Mezulis, Hyde, and Clark; Tannenbaum and Forehand) and grandparents (Generations United; Kern) play crucial roles in the care and nurturing of children toward developmental success. Mothers with PPD speak of relying on their own mothers, other mothers with children, and partners for support (Dennis and Letourneau, 2007; Letourneau et al. 2007). For example, a recent study of families affected by PPD revealed that fathers' involvement in caregiving during the weekend hours predicted better behavioral development in children (Letourneau, Duffett-Leger, Salmani 2009). These effects were observed until children were 12 years of age. Notably, children whose fathers were more involved in their care had fewer problems with anxiety and depression.

Another important way in which the developmental-inadequacy discourse promotes a narrow view of caregiving is that it is surprisingly non-developmental. Specifically, it relies on a static view of maternal mental health and of children's developmental needs. Unfortunately, the occurrence and reoccurrence of depression becomes more likely over time for many women. For example, fifty percent of mothers with PPD remain clinically depressed at 6 months postpartum and twenty-five percent of untreated mothers remain depressed for over a year (McMahon, Barnett, Kowalenko, and Tennant; Murray, Sinclair, Cooper, Ducournau, and Turner). Mothers who experienced PPD are also three times more likely to experience recurrence of depression following subsequent pregnancies and twice as likely to have a recurrence of depressive symptoms within five to twelve years of onset (Cooper and Murray; Letourneau, Salmani, Duffett-Leger). What is often overlooked in these reports is the fact that the majority of women with PPD *do* improve over time. This is an important point because it suggests that mothers who are unable to provide for all of the developmental needs of their children at one point are likely capable of providing for those needs at other points. Thus, with the right support (e.g., from partners), mothers living with depression can provide adequate care and children can achieve healthy developmental outcomes in spite of PPD.

Healthy development in children is a cumulative process that is less dependent on the quality of care at any given moment than it is on the quality of care over a period of time (Beck, 1995, 1996; Righetti-Veltema et al.; van Doesum, Riksen-Walraven, Hosman, and Hoefnagels). Thus, the developmental time-tables within which healthy cognitive, social, and emotional development may occur are extended enough to allow for improvements in PPD symptoms or to arrange for alternate sources of caregiving. The Bucharest Early Intervention longitudinal study of abandoned children revealed that while there are sensitive periods within human cognitive, social, and emotional development (Nelson, de Haan and Thomas), the window is quite large. Children who were adopted prior to two years of age made significant gains in their IQ, organization of attachment behaviors, and overall brain development (as compared to children who remained in the institution), but children who were adopted after two years of age did not make these gains. These findings suggest that the developmental needs of children are present over a period of time, providing caregivers with opportunities to seek supports and to compensate for temporary periods of poor function.

FOCUS ON INADEQUACIES VERSUS STRENGTHS

The developmental-inadequacy discourse emphasizes the inadequacies of mothers with depression and ignores their strengths. Indeed, most mothers affected by depression have strong desire and motivation to be the "good mother." Nevertheless, and consistent with rates observed for other mental health conditions, approximately 50 percent of mothers with depression do not access available treatments including pharmacologic, psychotherapeutic or support groups (Strass). Chief among the reasons women cite for their lack of seeking psychological treatment include the real fear that they will be labelled "unfit" and their children will be apprehended by the social welfare system (Letourneau et al. 2007). Furthermore, whereas antidepressants effectively reduce the intensity of PPD symptoms by 50 percent, these interventions are refused by 50 percent of mothers who cite concerns about infant health associated with ingesting medications via breast milk, fear of addiction, and the belief that depression will resolve on its own (Battle et al.; Makino, Gold, and Schulkin).

Mothers who opt against using antidepressants to manage their symptoms may be labelled as "difficult" or non-compliant with treatment rather than as competent mothers making informed decisions.

Although these socially sanctioned treatment modalities represent important opportunities for health, they also demand a great deal of women. Women may choose not to participate in these health practices for a variety of reasons including the practical challenges of accessing convenient and affordable treatments (especially in rural communities where anonymity and confidentiality are hard to maintain), the daily hassles of arranging for childcare and transportation, and then actually attending therapy and doing the emotional work associated with recovery. The developmental-inadequacy discourse focuses on the "failure" of these mothers to get treatment without appreciating that finding and engaging in treatment is time consuming and requires a great deal of emotional energy—time and energy that some mothers living with depression choose to focus on their infants.

Furthermore, treatment opportunities are by no means the only pathways toward health. A growing body of research shows that supportive relationships with family and friends can help women overcome the effects of depression (Dennis; Dennis et al.; Dennis and Stewart). For women to fully benefit from support, whatever the source, the evidence of negative effects of depression needs to be recast. Rather than stigmatizing women, the discourse ought to focus on mobilizing societal and health service structures to better support mothers and their families and to eliminate the barriers women face when they seek support.

OVERLOOKING CHILD AND SOCIAL CONTRIBUTIONS

As described by Sara Ruddick, as children grow older, "mothers can neither predict nor control the intellectual skills, moods, tastes, ambitions, friendships" of their children (34). The developmental-inadequacy discourse does not acknowledge that (a) infants arrive with a set of predispositions and modes of engaging their external environment that are not a product of mothering, and (b) because infants act upon and evoke responses from their environments, they contribute to their own development. There is little doubt that PPD, either alone or in combination with social and environmental contextual factors, affects child development (Beck 1998; Grace, Evindar and Stewart), the qualities of the developing relationship between infant and mother, and the security of their attachment (Beck 1995; van Doesum, Hosman, Riksen-Walraven, and Hoefnagels). Nevertheless, PPD is only *one* of many risk factors to children's development. The developmental-inadequacy discourse ignores the infant characteristics that may contribute to PPD and their own development.

Several decades ago, Stella Chess and Alexander Thomas declared that the "blame the mother ideology" has been soundly refuted, largely due to an increased understanding of the influence of children's own behavioral individuality from birth onward in the parent-child interactional process (49). For example, children who cry excessively, who do not give clear signals of their needs, or who are unresponsive to the caregiver's attempts to meet their needs, can interfere with the quality of maternal-infant interaction and predispose a child to less than optimal developmental outcomes, even in the absence of PPD (Barnard et al.). Indeed, difficult infant temperament has been shown to predict maternal depression and not the other way around (Field 1987). Thus the degree to which mothers can be sensitive to their developing infant depends, in part, on infant characteristics. Chess and Thomas described this as "goodness of fit" (see also Thomas, Chess and Birch) between infant characteristics and adult caregiving characteristics. The better the fit in terms of temperamental, affective, and interactive characteristics of caregiver and infant, the better the outcomes expected for the child. Understanding that infants contribute to their relationships with their mothers and consequently to their own development may reduce women's own sense of mother-blame and encourage them to seek appropriate support.

The contributions of social and economic factors on the developmental outcomes of infants of mothers living with PPD have also been ignored. One example can be found in research over the last decade on the association between quality of caregiving and the incidence of children's physical disease and frequency of hospitalization for conditions such as asthma. While children of mothers affected by depression are found to be at risk for developing asthma, the scientific discourse also observed, but downplayed, the role of marital adjustment and parenting problems (Casey et al.; Klinnert et al.; Kozyrskyj et al.; Mrazek et al.; Shalowitz et al. 2006; Shalowitz, Berry, Quinn, and Wolfe,). The developmental-inadequacy discourse has gained considerable ascendance by ignoring or marginalizing the substantial body of literature on the concomitant social and economic conditions, such as income, family stress, and early adversity that give rise to both PPD and children's health problems (Keating and Hertzman; McCain, Mustard, and Shanker). The scientific need to control and predict biases researchers and clinicians to focus on discrete units of behavior and eschew complex social and economic factors that require complex research designs and large budgets.

INTERGENERATIONAL RELATIONSHIP EFFECTS

Both Catherine McMahon et al. and Valerie Whiffen et al. suggest that PPD should be interpreted within attachment theory, as an interpersonal framework that aids understanding of relationship distress in the genesis of PPD. In keeping with this perspective, feminist theorists maintain that women's depression is socially embedded because women's self-concept and self-esteem are strongly connected to the context of their attachment relationships (Stoppard; Whiffen). Furthermore, Whiffen has suggested that pregnancy and childbirth "make a woman especially vulnerable to relationship distress because the baby is a tangible manifestation of her commitment to her partner, and she will be sensitive to any indication that this commitment is not shared" (157). While an intergenerational link between early childhood attachment relationships and women's likelihood of experiencing PPD is beginning to be established (McMahon et al.; Whiffen), the developmental-inadequacy discourse fails to consider the impact of women's own attachment relationships on their adult lives.

To illustrate, secure infant attachment is established when caregivers are consistently sensitive and available (both physically and psychologically) to their infants (Trapolini, Ungerer, and McMahon). When sensitivity and availability are lacking, infants perceive this as stressful and adapt by limiting their exploratory and learning efforts and consequently, their development is compromised (Ainsworth; Cassidy and Shaver). According to Patricia Crittenden's Dynamic Maturational Model of Attachment, these early stressful experiences propagate forward; thus, being reared by a mother with PPD has been directly linked to low attachment security in infants, toddlers (Cicchetti, Rogosch and Toth; Teti, Gelfand, Messinger and Isabella) and preschoolers (Teti et al., 1995). While little is known about the effect of early relationship stress on school aged and adolescent children's attachment security, being reared by a mother with symptoms of depression in infancy predicts an increased incidence of depression and anxiety in school aged and adolescent girls (Halligan, Murray, Martins and Cooper; Letourneau et al. 2006). In adults, McMahon et al. found that 78 percent of mothers with depression were classified as insecure versus only 42 percent of nonsymptomatic mothers. Viewed from this Dynamic Maturational Model perspective, PPD may be viewed as a further propagation of the effects of early attachment experiences on adult life.

Crittenden's Dynamic Maturational Model of Attachment further suggests that healthy adult relationships may attenuate the detrimental effect of early stress and improve attachment security in adulthood. This knowledge, combined with a recognition that an individual's own attachment history contributes to her own likelihood of developing PPD (Whiffen et al.), may empower women to seek help in order to altruistically prevent their daughters from growing up and suffering from PPD as well. Moreover, this knowledge may encourage health professionals to consider more social and psychological forms of care for women with insecure attachment histories.

MOVING BEYOND THE DEVELOPMENTAL-INADEQUACY DISCOURSE

Perhaps the developmental-inadequacy discourse and the Penhold and Walker (1983, 1986) paradox is an unintentional by-product of a genuine desire on the part of researchers and professionals to help women living with depression. In order to be successful in their careers, medical scientists and practitioners must promote their work as both important and effective. A common way to establish the importance of this work is to highlight dysfunction and poor developmental outcomes, often couched in language that is unintentionally pathologizing and mother-blaming. Recognizing that such language may be useful for securing funding and justifying clinical interventions, but is ultimately counterproductive to our understanding of PPD and the women, children, and families it affects, is perhaps a first step toward a more nuanced approach.

If PPD is interpreted not as a medical-biological problem situated within the individual, but rather as a condition that can arise in response to distressing social and environmental conditions interacting with the individual, perhaps mothers' fears of being blamed may be reduced. Stoppard and Gammell (2003) suggest that the medicalization of depression precludes access to more empowering forms of treatment that reflect the understanding of depression as situated within women's social and environmental contexts. Cindy-Lee Dennis and Donna Stewart concluded in their meta-analysis that even with the potential benefits, medication should be accompanied by other interventions to assist in altering the social conditions that often contribute to, or maintain depression. Michael Thase (2003a, 2003b) supports this view by suggesting that social and pharmacotherapeutic intervention combinations are optimal and reduce the likelihood of future depressive episodes. Moving beyond the developmental-inadequacy discourse on mothers with PPD suggests non-judgementally recognizing and valuing the full range of mothers' options.

Psychotherapies and social support interventions address the social and environmental conditions that give rise to PPD. For example, cognitive-behavioral therapy and interpersonal psychotherapy have demonstrated effects comparable to medication (Dobson). Cindy-Lee Dennis and Nicole Letourneau found that women who reported more peer support (from other mothers with children) had fewer symptoms of PPD. In another study of women's treatment preferences for PPD, mothers overwhelmingly reported the need for more accessible support from peers in the social network (Letourneau et al. 2007). Dennis concluded in her 2005 systematic review of social support interventions that peer support interventions (support provided by mothers who experienced PPD) have beneficial effects in treating women who have PPD.

Whatever the form of intervention for PPD, a systematic review revealed that mothers' relationships with their infants and infant developmental outcomes improve in concert with symptom improvement (Poobalan et al.). At the same time, as Janet Stoppard and Deanna Gammell suggest, interventions need to be empowering of women, recognizing the moral obligation to ensure that women, especially vulnerable women, have a voice in shaping the ways that care is offered to them. Interventions need to address the transactions among women's thoughts, world views, support available, and changing relationships. A professional and practical discourse that reframes PPD beyond the developmental-inadequacy perspective could function to reduce stigma and promote mothers' access to help that they perceive to be appropriate and acceptable. In assuming this position, service professionals may be more likely to (a) offer combinations of empowering options that address the range of social and environmental influences that give rise to depressive symptoms and (b) be non-judgemental when a mother declines services or treatments and chooses to self-manage her symptoms.

The developmental-inadequacy discourse assumes that maternal depression results in a (toxic) behavioral organization that poses increased risk of negative consequences for the mother-infant relationship. With support and intervention, however, this organization of cognition, emotion, and behavior may be reorganized to benefit both mothers and infants. Again, empowering mothers to recognize both the limits of their ability to control their children's development (Ruddick) and the potential of interventions to promote maternal-infant interaction and attachment security is essential. This balanced perspective, tempered by recognition of the social and environmental conditions that predispose women to depression, has the potential to encourage women to both free themselves of blame and access the help they desire.

Although the scientific evidence suggests that symptoms and behaviors associated with PPD have negative effects on children's development, their effects should be understood within the broader range of influences on child development. There are limits in the extent to which PPD, and indeed mothers, influence children's development. While PPD exerts an influence on children's development, a balance must be achieved between understanding the ways that PPD affects child development and the ways that children and their environments affect child development and PPD. Women's depression is socially embedded (Stoppard and Gammell) and so is their children's development. With this renewed and more nuanced understanding, perhaps Penfold and Walker's (1983, 1986) paradox may be circumvented.

[1]We coined the term "developmental-inadequacy" to reflect the underlying preoccupation of developmental science on the real and implied deficits in the quality and timing of the stimulation that infants receive from mothers suffering

from PPD, and which putatively constrains their developmental potential. We believe the justification for choosing this term as an accurate description of the majority of research on PPD is made clear within this chapter.

REFERENCES

Ahokas, A., Aito, M., and Rimon, R. "Positive Treatment Effect of Estradiol in Postpartum Psychosis: A Pilot Study." *Journal of Clinical Psychiatry* 61 (3) (2000): 166-169.

Ainsworth, M. D. S. "The Development of Infant-Mother Attachment." *Review of Child Development Research.* Vol. 3. Eds. B. M. Caldwell and H. N. Ricciuti. Chicago: The University of Chicago Press, 1973. 1-94.

American Psychiatric Association (APA). *Diagnostic and Statistical Manual of the Mental Disorders-DSM-IV-TR.* 4th ed. Washington, DC: American Psychiatric Association, 2000.

Barnard, K., M. Hammond, C. Booth, H. Bee, S. Mitchell and S. Spieker. "Measurement and Meaning of Parent-Child Interaction." *Applied Developmental Psychology.* Vol. 3. Eds. F. Morrison, C. Lord and D. Keating. New York: Academic, 1989. 39-80.

Battle, C., C. Zlotnick, T. Pearlstein, I. Miller, H. Howard, A. Salisbury and L. Stroud, "Depression and breastfeeding: Which Postpartum Patients Take Antidepressant Medications?" *Depression and Anxiety* 25 (10) (2008): 888-891.

Beck, C. T. "The Effects of Postpartum Depression on Maternal-Infant Interaction: A Meta-Analysis." *Nursing Research* 44 (5) (1995): 298-304.

Beck, C. T. "Postpartum Depressed Mothers' Experiences Interacting with Their Children." *Nursing Research* 45 (2) (1996): 98-104.

Beck, C. T. The Effects of Postpartum Depression on Child Development: A Meta-Analysis." *Archives of Psychiatric Nursing* 12 (1) (1998): 12-20.

Beck, C. T. "Predictors of Postpartum Depression: An Update." *Nursing Research* 50 (5) (2001): 275-285.

Brugha, T. S., H. M. Sharp, S. A. Cooper, C. Weisender, D. Britto, R. Shinkwin, T. Sherrif and P. H. Kirwan. "The Leicester 500 Project. Social Support and the Development of Postnatal Depressive Symptoms: A Prospective Cohort Survey." *Psychological Medicine* 28 (1) (1998): 63-79.

Campbell, S., J. Cohn, and T. Myers. "Depression in First-Time Mothers: Mother-Infant Interaction and Depression Chronicity." *Developmental Psychology* 31 (3) (1995): 349-357.

Casey, P., S. Goolsby, C. Berkowitz, D. Frank, J. Cook, D. Cutts, M. M. Black, N. Zaldivar, S. Levenson, T. Heeren and A. Meyers. "Maternal Depression, Changing Public Assistance, Food Security, and Child Health Status." *Pediatrics* 113 (2) (2004): 298-304.

Cassidy, J. and P. Shaver, eds. *Handbook of Attachment: Theory, Research and Clinical Applications*. New York,: Guilford Press, 1999.

Chess, S. and A. Thomas. *1983 Annual Progress in Child Psychiatry*. New York: Brunner/Mazel, 1983.

Chung, P. and X. Yue. "Postpartum Depression and Social Support: A Comparative Study in Hong Kong." *Psychologia* 42 (2) (1999):111-121.

Cicchetti, D., F. A. Rogosch and S. L. Toth. "Maternal Depressive Disorder and Contextual Risk: Contributions to the Development of Attachment Insecurity and Behavior Problems in Toddlerhood." *Development and Psychopathology* 10 (2) (1998): 283-300.

Cohn, J. F. and E. Z. Tronick "Mother-Infant Face-to-Face Interaction: The Sequence of Dyadic States At 3, 6, And 9 Months." *Developmental Psychology,* 23 (1) (1987): 68-77.

Cooper, P. J. and L. Murray. "Course and Recurrence of Postnatal Depression. Evidence for the Specificity of the Diagnostic Concept." *British Journal of Psychiatry* 166 (2) (1995): 191-195.

Crittenden, P. *Raising Parents: Attachment, Parenting and Child Safety.* London: Willan, 2008.

Dankner, R., R. P. Goldberg, R. Z. Fisch and R. M. DCrum. "Cultural Elements of postpartum Depression: A Study of 327 Jewish Jerusalem Women." *Journal of Reproductive Medicine* 45 (2) (2000): 97-104.

Dennis, C.-L. "Psychosocial and Psychological Interventions for Prevention of Postnatal Depression: Systematic Review." *British Medical Journal* 331 (7507) (2005): 15.

Dennis, C.-L., and L. Chung-Lee. "Postpartum Depression Help-Seeking Behaviours and Treatment Preferences: A Qualitative Systematic Review." *Birth* 33 (2006): 323-331.

Dennis, C.-L., E. Hodnett, L. Kenton, J. Weston, J. Zupancic, D. E. Stewart and A. Kiss. "Effect of Peer Support on Prevention of Postnatal Depression Among High Risk Women: Multisite Randomised Controlled Trial." *British Medial Journal* 338 (a3064)(2009): 1-9.

Dennis, C.-L., and N. Letourneau. "Global and Relationship-Specific Perceptions of Support and the Development of Postpartum Depressive Symptomatology." *Social Psychiatry and Psychiatric Epidemiology* 42 (5) (2007): 389-395.

Dennis, C.-L. and D. Stewart. "Treatment of postpartum Depression, Part 1: A Critical Review of Biological Interventions." *Journal of Clinical Psychiatry* 65 (9) (2004): 1242-1251.

Dobson, K. "A Meta-Analysis of the Efficacy of Cognitive Therapy for Depression." *Journal of Consulting and Clinical Psychology* 57 (3) (1989): 414-419.

Field, T. "Early Interactions Between Infants and Their Postpartum Depression Mothers." *Infant Behavior and Development* 7 (4) (1984): 517-522.

Field, T. "Affective and Interactive Disturbances in Infants." *Handbook of Infant Development*. Ed. J. Osofsky. New York: John Wiley and Sons, 1987. 972-1005.

Gaynes, B., N. Gavin, S. Meltzer-Brody, K. Lohr, T. Swinson, G. Gartlehner, S. Brody and W. C. Miller. *Perinatal depression: Prevalence, Screening, Accuracy, and Screening Outcomes* (AHRQ Publication No. 05-E006-2; Contract No. 290-02-0016). Research Triangle Park, NC: Agency for Healthcare Research Quality, 2005.

Generations United. *Grandparents and Other Relatives Raising Children: An Intergenerational Action Agenda*. Washington, DC: Author, 1998.

Grace, S. L., A. Evindar and D. E. Stewart. "The Effect of Postpartum Depression on Child Cognitive Development and Behavior: A Review and Critical Analysis of the Literature." *Archives of Women's Mental Health*, 6 (4) (2003): 263-274.

Granger, A. and M. Underwood. "Review of the Role of Progesterone in the Management of Postnatal Mood Disorders." *Journal of Psychosomatic Obstetrics and Gynaecology* 22 (1) (2001): 49-55.

Halligan, S. L., L. Murray, C. Martins and P. J. Cooper. "Maternal Depression and Psychiatric Outcomes in Adolescent Offspring: A 13-Year Longitudinal Study." *Journal of Affective Disorders* 97 (1-3) (2007): 145-154.

Keating, D. and C. Hertzman, eds. *Developmental Health and the Wealth of Nations: Social, Biological, and Educational Dynamics*. New York: Guilford Press, 1999.

Kern, C. W. "Grandparents Who Are Parenting Again: Building Parenting Skills." *Working with Custodial Grandparents*. Eds. B. Hayslip, Jr. and J. H. Patrick. New York: Springer Publishing Co., 2003. 179-193.

Klinnert, M., H. Nelson, M. Price, A. Adinoff, D. Leung and D. Mrazek. "Onset and Persistence of Childhood Asthma: Predictors from Infancy." *Pediatrics* 108 (4) (2001): 69-76.

Kozyrskyj, A., X. Mai, P. McGrath, K. HayGlass, A. Becker and B. MacNeil. "Continued Exposure to Maternal Distress in Early Life Is Associated with an Increased Risk of Childhood Asthma." *American Journal of Respiratory and Critical Care Medicine* 177 (2) (2008): 142-147.

Laflamme, D., A. Pomerleau and G. Malcuit. "A Comparison of Fathers' and Mothers' Involvement in Childcare and Stimulation Behaviors During Free-Play with Their Infants at 9 and 15 Months. "*Sex Roles* 47 (11-12) (2002): 507-518.

Lamb, M., E. *The Role of the Father in Childhood Development*. 3rd ed. New York: John Wiley and Sons, 1996.

Letourneau, N., L. Duffett-Leger and M. Salmani. "The Role of Paternal Support in the Behavioural Development Of Children Exposed to Postpartum Depression." *Canadian Journal of Nursing Research* 41 (3) (2009): 86-106.

Letourneau, N., L. Duffett-Leger, M. Stewart, K. Hegadoren, C. Dennis, C. M. Rinaldi and J. Stoppard. "Canadian Mothers' Perceived Support Needs During Postpartum Depression." *Journal of Obstetric, Gynecologic and Neonatal Nursing* 36 (5) (2007): 441-449.

Letourneau, N., M. Salmani and L. Duffett-Leger. "Maternal Depressive Symptoms and Parenting of Children from Birth to 12 Years." *Western Journal of Nursing Research* 32 (5) (2010): 662-685.

Letourneau, N. L., C. B. Fedick, J. D. Willms, C. L. Dennis, K. Hegadoren and M. J. Stewart. "Longitudinal Study of Postpartum Depression, Maternal-Child Relationships and Children's Behaviour to 8 Years of Age." *Parent-Child Relations: New Research*. Ed. D. Devore. New York: Nova Science Publishers, 2006. 45-63.

Logsdon, M. C., J. C. Birkimer and W. M. Usui. "The Link of Social Support and Postpartum Depressive Symptoms in African-American Women with Low Incomes." *American Journal of Maternal Child Nursing* 25 (5) (2000): 262-266.

Logsdon, M. C. and W. Usui. "Psychosocial Predictors of Postpartum Depression in Diverse Groups of Women." *Western Journal of Nursing Research* 23 (6)(2001): 563-574.

Magill-Evans, J., Harrison, M. J., Benzies, K., M. Gierl, and C. Kimak. "Effects of Parenting Education on First-Time Fathers' Skills in Interactions with Their Infants." *Fathering* 5 (1) (2007): 42-57.

Makino, S., P. W. Gold and J. Schulkin. "Corticosterone Effects on Corticotropin-Releasing Hormone mRNA in the Central Nucleus of the Amygdala and the Parvocellular Region of the Paraventricular Nucleus of the Hypothalamus." *Brain Research* 640 (1,2) (1994): 105-112.

Matthey, S., B. Barnett, P. Howie and D. J. Kavanagh. "Diagnosing Postpartum Depression in Mothers and Fathers: Whatever Happened to Anxiety?" *Journal of Affective Disorders* 74 (2) (2003): 139-147.

McCain, M. N., J. F. Mustard and S. Shanker. *Early Years Study 2: Putting Science into Action*. Toronto: Council for Early Child Development, 2007.

McMahon, C., B. Barnett, N. Kowalenko and C. Tennant. "Psychological Factors Associated with Persistent Postnatal Depression: Past and Current Relationships, Defence Styles and the Mediating Role of Insecure Attachment style." *Journal of Affective Disorders* 84 (1) (2005): 15-24.

Mezulis, A. H., J. S. Hyde and R. Clark. "Father Involvement Moderates the Effect of Maternal Depression During A Child's Infancy on Child Behavior Problems in Kindergarten." *Journal of Family Psychology* 18 (4) (2004): 575-588.

Middlebrooks, J. and N. Audage. *The Effects of Childhood Stress on Health Across the Lifespan*. Atlanta, GA: Centres for Disease Control and Prevention, National Centre for Injury Prevention and Control, 2008.

Mrazek, D., M. Klinnert, P. Mrazek, A. Brower, D. McCormick, B. Rubin, D. Ikle, W. Kastner, G. Larsen, R. Harbeck and J. Jones. "Prediction of Early-Onset Asthma in Genetically At-Risk Children. *"Pediatric Pulmonology* 27 (2) (1999): 85-94.

Murray, L. and P. Cooper. "The Role of Infant and Maternal Factors in Postpartum Depression, Mother-Infant Interactions and Infant Outcome." *Postpartum Depression and Child Development.* Eds. L. Murray and P. J. Cooper. New York: Guilford Press, 1997. 111-135.

Murray, L., A. Fiori-Cowley, R. Hooper and P. Cooper. "The Impact of Postnatal Depression and Associated Adversity on Early Mother-Infant Interactions and Later Infant Outcomes." *Child Development* 67 (5) (1996): 2512-2526.

Murray, L., D. Sinclair, P. Cooper, P. Ducournau and P. Turner. "The socio-emotional Development of Five-Year-Old Children of Postnatally Depressed Mothers." *Journal of Child Psychology and Psychiatry and Allied Disciplines,* 40 (8) (1999): 1259-1271.

Nelson, C., M. de Haan and K. Thomas. *Neuroscience of Cognitive Development: The Role of Experience and the Developing Brain.* Hoboken, NJ: John Wiley and Sons, 2006.

Nielsen Forman, D., P. Videbech, M. Hedegaard, J. Dalby Salvig and N. J. Secher. "Postpartum Depression: Identification of Women at Risk." *British Journal of Obstetrics and Gynaecology* 107 (10) (2000): 1210-1217.

Noorlander, Y., V. Bergink. and M. P. van den Berg. "Perceived and Observed Mother-Child Interaction at Time of Hospitalization and Release in Postpartum Depression and Psychosis." *Archives of Women's Mental Health* 11 (1) (2008): 49-56.

O'Hara, M. W. and A. Swain, "Rates and Risk of Postpartum Depression: A Meta-Analysis." *International Review of Psychiatry* 8 (1996): 37-54.

Penfold, S. and G. Walker. *Women and the Psychiatric Paradox.* Montreal: Eden Press, 1983.

Penfold, S. and G. Walker. "The Psychiatric Paradox and Women." *Canadian Journal of Community Mental Health* 5 (2) (1986): 9-15.

Poobalan, A. S., L. S. Aucott, L. Ross, W. C. S. Smith, P. J. Helms and J. H. G. Williams. "Effects of Treating Postnatal Depression on Mother-Infant Interaction and Child Development: Systematic Review." *British Journal of Psychiatry* 191 (4) (2007): 378-386.

Righetti-Veltema, M., A. Bousquet and J. Manzano. "Impact of Postpartum Depressive Symptoms on Mother and Her 18-Month-Old Infant." *European Child and Adolescent Psychiatry* 12 (2) (2003): 75-83.

Ritter, C., S. E. Hobfoll, J. Lavin, R. P. Cameron and M. R. Hulsizer. "Stress, psychosocial Resources, and depressive Symptomatology During Pregnancy In Low-Income, Inner-City Women." *Health Psychology* 19 (6) (2000): 576-585.

Dennis, C. L., L. Ross and A. Herxheimer. "Oestrogens and Progestins for Preventing and Treating Postpartum Depression. *Cochrane Database of Systematic Reviews* 8 (4) (2008): CD001690.

Ruddick, S. *Maternal Thinking: Toward A Politics of Peace*. Boston: Beacon Press, 1995.

Seguin, L., L. Potvin, M. St-Denis and J. Loiselle. "Depressive Symptoms in the late Postpartum Among Low Socioeconomic Status Women." *Birth* 26 (3) (1999a): 157-163.

Seguin, L., L. Potvin, M. St-Denis and J. Loiselle. "Socio-environmental Factors and Postnatal Depressive Symptomatology: A Longitudinal Study." *Women and Health* 29 (1) (1999b): 57-72.

Shalowitz, M. U., C. A. Berry, K. A. Quinn and R. L. Wolfe. "The Relationship of Life Stressors and Maternal Depression to Pediatric Asthma Morbidity in a Subspecialty Practice." *Ambulatory Pediatrics* 1 (4) (2001): 185-193.

Shalowitz, M. U., T. Mijanovich, C. Berry, E. Clark-Kauffman, K. Quinn and E. Perez. "Context Matters: A Community-Based Study of Maternal Mental Health, Life Stressors, Social Support and Children's Asthma." *Pediatrics* 117 (5) (2006): 940-948.

Stanley, C., L. Murray and A. Stein. "The Effect of Postnatal Depression on Mother-Infant Interaction, Infant Response to the Still-Face Perturbation, and Performance on an Instrumental Learning Task." *Development and Psychopathology* 16 (1) (2004): 1-18.

Stoppard, J. *Understanding Depression: Feminist Social Constructionist Approaches*. New York: Routledge, 2000.

Stoppard, J. and D. Gammell. "Depressed Women's Treatment Experiences: Exploring Themes of Medicalization and Empowerment." *Situating Sadness: Women and Depression in Context*. Eds. J. Stoppard and L. McMullen. New York: New York University Press, 2003. 39-61.

Strass, P. "Postpartum Depression Support." *Canadian Nurse* 98 (3) (2002):25-28.

Stuchbery, M., S. Matthey, and B. Barnett. "Postnatal Depression and Social Supports in Vietnamese, Arabic and Anglo-Celtic Mothers." *Social Psychiatry and Psychiatric Epidemiology* 33 (10) (1998): 483-490.

Tannenbaum, L. and R. Forehand. "Maternal Depressive Mood: The Role of Fathers in Preventing Adolescent Problem Behaviors." *Behaviour Research and Therapy* 32 (3) (1994): 321-325.

Teti, D., D. Gelfand, D. Messinger and R. Isabella. "Maternal Depression and the Quality of Early Attachment: An Examination of Infants, Preschoolers, and their Mothers." *Developmental Psychology* 31 (3) (1995): 364-376.

Thase, M. "Effectiveness of Antidepressants: Comparative Remission Rates." *Journal of Clinical Psychiatry* 64 (2) (2003a): 3-7.

Thase, M. "Evaluating Antidepressant Therapies: Remission as the Optimal

Outcome." *Journal of Clinical Psychiatry* 64 (13): (2003b):18-25.

Thomas, A., S. Chess and H. Birch. *Temperament and Behavior Disorders in Children.* New York University Press, 1968.

Trapolini, T., J. Ungerer and C. McMahon. "Maternal Depression and Children's Attachment Representations During The Preschool Years." *British Journal of Developmental Psychology* 25 (2007): 247-261.

van Doesum, K. T. M., C. M. H. Hosman, J. M. Riksen-Walraven and C. Hoefnagels. "Correlates of Depressed Mothers' Sensitivity Toward Their Infants: The Role of maternal, Child and Contextual Characteristics." *Journal of the American Academy of Child and Adolescent Psychiatry* 46 (6) (2007): 747-752.

van Doesum, K. T. M., J. M. Riksen-Walraven, C. M. H. Hosman and C. Hoefnagels. "A Randomized Controlled Trial of a Home-Visiting Intervention Aimed at Preventing Relationship Problems in Depressed Mothers and Their Infants." *Child Development* 79 (3) (2008): 547-561.

Whiffen, V. "Myths and Mates in Childbearing Depression." *From Menarche to Menopause: The Female Body in Feminist Therapy.* Ed. J. Chrisler. London: Haworth Press Inc., 2004. 151-163.

Whiffen, V. and I. Gotlib. "Comparison of Postpartum and Non-Postpartum Depression: Clinical Presentation, Psychiatric History, and Psychosocial Functioning." *Journal of Consulting and Clinical Psychology* 61 (3) (1993): 485-494.

Whiffen, V., M. Kerr and V. Kallos-Lilly. "Maternal Depression, Adult Attachment, and Children's Emotional Distress." *Family Process* 44 (1) (2005): 93-103.

III. NARRATIVE VOICES:
MAD MOMS

11.
Creating a Space for Mothers
Who Have Lost a Child Through Suicide

DONNA F. JOHNSON WITH HELEN LEVINE

I found the pain in the beginning was unbearable. My therapist once said to me, "Your job is to get through the day," and I remember thinking, how do I survive the next five minutes? You just want to put yourself to sleep for a few months and maybe you'd get through it.

WHEN A MOTHER'S WORST NIGHTMARE is realized through the suicide of her child, she can be overwhelmed with the idea that she is a complete failure as a mother. While guilt is a common reaction in survivors of suicide, the feelings of guilt and failure experienced by the mother of the suicided child can be life-threatening. No existing program for survivors of suicide has been designed specifically to help mothers address their complex emotional and intellectual reactions to their child's suicide. No existing program addresses the cultural prescription for perfection in motherhood that gives rise to feelings of inadequacy in most mothers and which, when a child commits suicide, can lead to despair. This chapter describes how the creation of a feminist space allowed five women to support each other through horrendous loss, and to struggle to an understanding of themselves as real and worthy, and good enough, mothers.

HOW THE GROUP BEGAN

In some ways I[1] am an unlikely person to have become involved in a group like this, for I am not a mother and have never lost a loved one to suicide. In 2005 I began working in the crisis unit of an urban police service. The mandate of the unit is to assist victims of crime and tragic circumstances. We help families through sudden deaths resulting from accidents, homicide, and suicide. We attend a lot of suicides. These deaths are always traumatic, never more so than when the act is completed by a person on the threshold of life. Tragically, suicide is regularly completed by young people of both genders.

185

In my first year with the police I attended numerous suicides of young persons. I began to notice a pattern among the survivors. While everybody in the family was profoundly affected by the suicide, the mothers were often paralyzed. While fathers, stepfathers, and siblings were usually able to get on with their lives after a time, resuming work, school and social activities, many of the mothers were immobilized. Where others in the family felt a measure of guilt, the mothers were often ravaged with guilt and self-loathing, viewing themselves as utter failures as mothers. While others in the family felt deep sadness, the mothers often felt a sorrow of such magnitude their very survival was threatened.

No matter how often friends and professionals tell the mother of a suicided child it is not her fault, no matter how she tries to convince herself of this, she will most likely feel it is very much her fault. Some mothers told me they felt unworthy to walk the earth. Others felt they were going insane, that were it not for their other children they would kill themselves. For the mother, suicidal thoughts can persist for months and even years after her child's suicide.

One afternoon I was visiting with a woman who was deeply depressed following the suicide of her 21-year-old son. I asked if there was anything she could think of that would help. She was already seeing a psychologist. She responded immediately, "I need to meet another mother who has been through this. I need to see what she looks like. I need to see that she has survived … and that she is not a monster."

I searched the community for resources. I found bereavement programs that dealt with suicide as a subtopic, and one program for survivors of suicide in general. No program had been designed specifically to help mothers explore their complex emotional and intellectual reactions to their child's suicide.

My past work had taught me the value of bringing women together in small groups. I approached the manager of the Victim Crisis Unit with the idea of running a pilot project: a 12-week group for mothers who have lost a child to suicide. She threw her support behind the idea. Five women signed up for the group—and I agreed to facilitate.

PROFILES OF THE MOTHERS

The mothers were in their forties and fifties. Two resided in the city, three in small towns. All were employed outside the home: three with the federal government, one as a teacher, another in a local small business. At the time of their child's suicide three of the women were married and living with the child's father and two were divorced and remarried. All had at least one other child. Two were involved with abusive men and were abused before, after, and even, appallingly, during the suicide crisis. The children, two girls and three boys, were aged 16, 16, 18, 21, and 31 when they died. All died by hanging. Four died in their mother's home.

BECOMING VISIBLE TO EACH OTHER

On February 5th 2007, at -28°C, one of the coldest days of the winter, the mothers met in a tiny room inside the police station. They opened up easily, relieved to meet other mothers in the same boat. In quiet tones and with gut-wrenching sorrow they talked about their children's lives and deaths. From the outset the atmosphere in the room was sacred.

The mothers described years of upset preceding the suicide. Years of living on the edge with kids who were unhappy and depressed; trying to get their kids help through doctors, psychiatrists, medication, hospitalization, and sometimes, police and courts. They described how they had walked on eggshells, searching for the balance between compassion and tough love. They described the vacillation between hope and the sickening gut feeling that things were not going to end well. They spoke of ripple effects through the family, of incredible strain on siblings and partners, of never feeling they were parenting adequately. Two of the mothers fully expected their child to complete suicide one day, one was "not surprised," and two were blindsided by the suicide. Three of the mothers found their children and spoke of the image as being permanently etched in their brain.

The mothers spoke powerfully, often poetically, of the anguish of losing a child and their inability to accept the severing of the mother-child bond. They were haunted by thoughts of their child's last moments; by the pain that drove him or her to such a desperate act; by the knowledge that their children had died alone, without their mothers. They spoke of a crushing fatigue, describing themselves as barely functioning, hanging on by a thread. They feared they were not going to make it, yet expressed indifference as to whether they lived or died. They were afraid to show their full grief to family and friends, frightened by their own pain, describing it as a tidal wave that could not be pushed back. They spoke of the pressure, internal and external, to pull themselves together, to pick up their lives, to be the person they were before the tragedy. This, they said, was impossible. The suicide of their child had changed them intrinsically, forever.

IN THEIR OWN WORDS

Francine: I felt I was living outside of my body. My body would move around, I would see people, greet them, talk, make the moves, but my mind was elsewhere. I was disconnected. It's a devastation. I continue to ask myself to this day, "Am

I a good mother?" How can a mother have two kids with depression? Where did I go wrong?" I revisit it all the time. When I hear comments about "oh, my children are involved in sports so they don't get into trouble, my children are doing this and that…, " I feel my inadequacy as a mother. I think there must have been something wrong with me, because it just didn't work out that way.

Nicole: We were troubled with many issues in our home and I think Brett carried all this pain with him. He turned to drugs to try to escape from the emotional pain. As a mother I approached many organizations but the help didn't come fast enough. I believe something happened that particular day. Brett felt he couldn't cope and decided this was the best way out.

Margaret: Before Grant died we all knew, we kind of thought that he might do it, so it wasn't a huge shock … but the devastation! I couldn't eat. I couldn't sleep. In our family no one would talk with each other, and you couldn't get comfort from other people. Other people were sometimes afraid to approach you. You felt like you had a hole in your heart and you put one foot in front of the other every day. Just to survive that day was an incredible feat.

Judy: I started going downhill. Spent my nights walking the house, looking outside for Josh, for his spirit, for his soul. If I saw him I was ready to go with him, because I didn't want him to be alone. Finally, after about three weeks of this I ended up in the hospital having to be sedated.

Mary: I found Shioban and I'm glad. First, no one else had to experience it. Second, it's a profound moment of intimacy. There's something quite unusual about that, the fact that you brought them into the world and you are the first one to see them after they've left it. At the same time it plays to the fact that, yes, I feel totally guilty, so this is what I deserved. I still come back to that place fairly often, that yes, if I had been a good mother … My marriage broke up as well before this happened. If that hadn't happened, if I hadn't worked as hard, if I'd been a stay-at-home mom … all those things that might have prevented her …

Nicole: I also found my son, when I came back from work, and from that moment I was transformed into a different person. I tried to bring Brett back to life. I did CPR on him. And I really thought I had brought him back to life! Working on my own child was so overwhelming, on top of finding him. To have that image of finding your son in that state, it's so heart wrenching, and as a mother that day and the following days I was totally detached emotionally. I felt detached from everyone. I felt alone, I felt angry. I felt the guilt as well. Like all of us I asked, where did I go wrong? What could I have done? Why couldn't I have prevented him from doing this to himself? Regardless of how many people told me not to feel the guilt, I still do after two years. I still feel guilty.

Judy: I felt like a monster. I thought, oh my God, what am I? What kind of mother am I that this could happen to my child, that I couldn't see this coming, that I couldn't prevent it? There are so many "what ifs." And like Nicole said, to go out of the house, it was like I had "loser" stamped on my forehead. I felt that everybody I walked by was looking at me and saying, "Oh, *you're* the mother whose child committed suicide."

Margaret: I lost my sense of motherhood. You blame yourself. What you've done. What you could have done better. After Grant's death I pushed my other children away thinking they don't need me, because obviously I didn't do a very good job.

Mary: As mothers you are usually running the house, fixing everything, finding things, making things right. One of the things I found hardest to accept was that I could not change this story. I couldn't make things right. There was nothing I could do. Everything else I could do something about but this was final. I couldn't bring her back.

Margaret: Losing a child when they're a teenager means they're probably angry with you, they're angry at the world, they don't make sense. So it leaves you with this child that was angry ... it's so unfinished.

Francine: I feel very little. I'm a teacher and I teach young children. Often in the staff room people will share comments about parents not being "good enough" parents ... "look at the children." You know, bad parents equals bad children. Very easy equation. Well, how does that make me feel? Not that Christine was a bad child, but what happened to her is certainly not a happy ending. So I am listening to all of this and I'm thinking, can I even make comments, can I even be part of this group? I feel less than nothing. I just want to disappear. So for the longest time I didn't even go into the staff room. I protected myself. I still feel like an outsider.

Judy: That's how you feel. You feel people are looking at you and judging you. And some people do judge you. Like Francine said, when you go back to work and see someone coming down the hall and they see you and all of a sudden they make a quick u-turn ... it makes you feel so low. I have no self-esteem left. To me being a mother was the biggest joy I had in my life. I loved the fact that I had three boys ... that I could rough around with them when they were kids. I couldn't get them into all sorts of sports when I was divorced. But I tried; they got into some stuff. And I question myself on that too, thinking, well, maybe if I had scrounged some more money and gotten them into something else, Josh would be alive now. But you don't know....

HALF-WAY EVALUATION: BAD MOTHERS

At the end of the fifth week we stopped to assess how the group was going. The mothers described it as a lifeline. The group was the one place where they felt completely understood, free to give vent to the full range of their emotions, to say the unsayable, to rage without fear of judgment or abandonment. They offered each other a depth of caring, a kind of listening, an understanding they could not find anywhere else. There was no question the group had bonded. But I noted the repetition of the themes of guilt and self-blame. Nothing could shake the women's belief that they were directly responsible for their child's suicide through their failure as mothers. As Mary put it: "It doesn't matter how many times a professional or someone who is objective tells you that it's not your fault, you can't tell yourself that until ... I don't know ... I don't know if I'll ever get over that."

I did not know how to deal with this deep and complex, apparently psychological, issue. I decided to consult with Helen Levine, a retired professor of the School of Social Work at Carleton University and the person responsible for introducing feminist counselling into the curriculum in 1980. Helen has thought, written, and taught extensively from a feminist perspective about mothering. She was insightful about the complexities arising from the suicide of a child, suspecting the depth of guilt the women were experiencing was directly tied to internalized patriarchal definitions of motherhood, with their impossible prescription for perfection. I asked Helen to consider joining the group in the capacity of resource person. In the sixth week, with the women's permission, she came on board.

SHIFTING THE GUILT: UNDERSTANDING
THE POLITICS OF MOTHERHOOD

It is difficult to explain how a feminist analysis of motherhood could help a group of grieving women; when you are mourning the loss of a child to suicide a feminist analysis hardly seems relevant. I want to be clear that a feminist analysis didn't alleviate the pain of the mothers' loss. What it did alleviate to some extent was their feelings of self-condemnation.

Helen's respect for women as mothers, her strength-based approach, and her understanding of the politics of motherhood infused the group with vitality and hope. She helped shift the focus from the suicide of the children to the prescription for perfection in mothering that gives rise to feelings of guilt and inadequacy in most women (a friend of mine who was an obstetric nurse used to joke, "Out comes the afterbirth, in comes the guilt!"). Helen helped the mothers take hold of their experience as women and mothers in a world that devalues both. The experience of mothering can be a valuable and joyful part of life; however, the demands and expectations of the role, combined very often with lack of support, exacts a toll on women. When things go haywire in the family, as they inevitably will, it is usually the mother who is held responsible. It is little wonder that when ultimate disaster strikes in the form of her child's suicide, a mother may find herself paralyzed with the feeling that she is responsible.

I have gone back to a monograph Helen co-authored with Alma Estable in 1981, *The Power Politics of Motherhood*, to give an idea of the theory that was woven into the remaining group sessions. Radical in its time, the analysis still strikes a chord with many women. The paper exposed the relentless demands and unspoken assumptions embedded in the institution of motherhood.

> Motherwork is the only labour assumed to be undertaken for love and by one sex exclusively. Motherworkers sign on indefinitely. There are no fixed hours, sick leave, vacation, pension, job security, collective bargaining or unionization. Training is considered unnecessary, and it is assumed there are instinctual blueprints for productivity. When instinct fails or when the "plant" is in trouble, mothers do not enjoy leaves of absence, unemployment insurance or "workman's" compensation. Instead we are labeled inadequate or unfit … (Mothers) are expected, above all else, to maintain the stability of the family. Accordingly, we provide essential psychotherapy in the home. We attempt to mediate conflicts within the family, and between the family and outside institutions. We defuse anger and stress, often by directing it onto ourselves. We are expected to be a steady source of love, of emotional support which needs no refills. (Levine and Estable 6, 12)

Helen Levine and Alma Estable write about the endless giving and accommodating expected of women; about the presumption that women will yield name, mobility, and financial independence in order to become wife and mother; how it is normally expected that women will do most of the domestic and emotional work and nurture relationships in the family; how it is usually mothers who carry the weighty responsibility for child care after separation and divorce; how the painful splits and pulls in women's lives are often glossed over; how when women become unhappy and angry in the attempt to fulfill this impossible prescription they are often pathologized and medicated, expected to control their feelings and behaviour in the interests of the family. They quote a woman who had been on tranquilizers for ten years as saying she used drugs for one purpose and one purpose only—to protect her family from her irritability.

I struggle to express how the shift in energy happened in the group, because it wasn't linear or straightforward, and it certainly wasn't a case of hitting the mothers over the head with theory. It was Helen's self-disclosures about her own struggles and mistakes and periods of being lost. It was gentle conversation and encouragement. It was honouring the mothers for their hard work and devotion to their children. It was making the invisible visible. It was Helen's fierce defense of mothers, protecting and nurturing them as a lioness would her cubs. It was a fragment here, a connection there, an insight, a link. Helen is gifted at making complex feminist theory accessible to women, perhaps because she came to feminism in her own life through painful personal struggles with the institutions of marriage and motherhood. As Laura Mullally noted, "patriarchy is a strong force and Helen Levine effortlessly explains the trickle down and the connection between the political and personal" (1).

As Helen shared her life and perspective, the women began to reflect on their experiences as mothers in a different light. With the exception of Francine's partner, the biological fathers had not been much involved in the raising of the children. They were largely inaccessible as husbands and fathers due to alcohol addiction, controlling and abusive behavior, indifference, or preoccupation with work. They began to consider the huge amount of work and responsibility they had undertaken over the years, parenting with little or no support, sometimes in the face of ill-health and soul-destroying circumstances. They reflected on the sacrifices and accommodations they had made and the injustices they had endured for the sake of their children and for harmony in the home. Embedded in all of this was the loss of self.

During one meeting near to the end, Mary started to weep. She said that she could not figure out what her tears were about. She said she is not a mother who "gave everything." She was, after all, a career woman. She felt perhaps had she devoted more of herself to her kids the outcome would have been different. Margaret said, "I was a stay at home mom and look what happened.... " Francine stated, "I worked half-time and the end result was the same!" The women began to laugh, something they had done rarely since their child's death. They had begun to grasp the complexity of their lives and roles; to honor and appreciate all they had tried to give their children. They had begun to feel compassion for themselves; to let themselves, just a little, off the hook. They had begun to realize, as Nellie McClung put it so long ago, that "a bad old lie has been put over on them" (24). They were not bad mothers at all, but strong and worthy, and good enough, mothers.

It was a beginning. A green shoot, as Helen put it: fragile, but full of potential.

ENDING

At the end of the 12-week pilot, the women did not feel ready to say goodbye. Helen and I continued to meet with the group informally for another six months. The mothers continue to struggle with the loss of their child. Some struggle to balance the reality of the suicide with a refusal to be defined by it. Progress has been uneven, slower for some than others. One or two remain in individual counseling. Where there are ongoing problems in the domestic sphere, the wounds never get a chance to heal.

The group did not change the reality of their child's tragic death. Nevertheless, it did provide a space where each woman could fully process her trauma and loss and evolve in her understanding of herself as a mother. The women describe themselves as having changed fundamentally. In Margaret's words:

> *We changed somehow organically. We are not the same. And not just mentally. Physically, in every way we have changed. We're completely different. For our family to try and understand us … it's beyond them. And you can't share it because you don't even know what has happened to you. Every step of the way we go through stages and we say, oh, Mary went through that, and oh, Nicole was that way for two months, and so you accept these stages and the roller coaster going down into a black hole. At first you think you will never get out of this hole, but as time progresses it gets less deep and less black and you kind of carry forward. But could you have done that by yourself? I couldn't have. The group was a godsend.*

All the mothers expressed the desire to use their experience to help others. Nicole is making presentations to schools, police, and community groups, getting the topic of youth suicide on the table. The mothers have come to speak at my graduate seminar on feminist social work practice. They made an audiotape about their group experience for our presentation at the *Moms Gone Mad* conference (their voices have been transcribed from that tape for this chapter). Margaret has taken up the guitar and has written songs about her experience.

POST SCRIPT

I sent this chapter to the mothers for review and received back the following email:

> *Dear Donna,*
>
> *I have just read the chapter and there is nothing I would change. You have captured in a most poignant way the spirit of the group, the context, and the unbearable gravity of the first months after the suicides. I am very moved by the way you have expressed our experience. I did not know how I would react reading this, but I feel better for having done so. "Being known" is one of the most important blessings of our relationships with others, so that may be what I am experiencing now. You and Helen, by telling our*

stories, have validated us, as mothers, as those who have experienced a painful loss and are still functioning, and just as women who should not feel ashamed of their place in the world. It seems strange to feel and to say this, but after reading this, I feel like I can hold my head a little higher.
    Mary

[1]The "I" in this paper refers to Donna, who got the group off the ground. Helen came on board as a resource person in the sixth week.

REFERENCES

Levine, Helen and Alma Estable. "The Power Politics of Motherhood: A Feminist Critique of Theory and Practice." Occasional Paper. Center for Social Welfare Studies, Carleton University, Ottawa, 1981.

McClung, Nelly. *In Times Like These.* McLeod and Allen, Toronto, 1915.

Laura Mullally. *Reflective Journal # 9* for the course SOWK 5801 Feminist Practice with Individuals, Couples and Families. School of Social Work, Carleton University, Ottawa, 2011.

12.
Daughters of Depression

Breaking Free from the Bell Jar

NANCY GERBER

Pain has an element of blank:
It cannot recollect
When it began, or if there was
A time when it was not.
　　　　　　—Emily Dickinson

HOW DOES IT FEEL to grow up as the daughter of a deeply depressed mother? How does a young girl cope with her mother's sadness as well as her own? For me, as a daughter of "depression," these questions have framed my life as a woman, daughter, scholar, and mother. I have spent the past forty-five years battling a depression that descended sometime during childhood. I have tried writing, meditation, biofeedback, psychotherapy, and medication. I've tried to will myself out of it by trying to ignore it, studying for a doctorate, exercising, and having a positive attitude. At times I have felt that depression has been my most familiar companion.

Recognizing that the experience of maternal sadness and depression, as well as the impact on offspring, is not the same for everyone, this chapter focuses on my own lived experience. In sharing my story it is not my intention to contribute to the mother-blaming literature that inextricably faults mothers for all the ills of their children, as many of the chapters in this collection deconstruct and address. Indeed there are multiple factors that impact children's growth and psychological development. In this chapter, I reveal my own story of struggle with depression, which I believe to have been connected to my mother's depression. I believe it is important to share my experience, which is an empowering process in view of the persistent social stigmas associated with depression that perpetuate shame, guilt, and silence.

My contribution to this book is aimed to empower other mothers to talk about and seek necessary support for their depression and in general to further awareness from a lived perspective. In trying to understand how I came to live with depression, I describe my grandmother's as well as my mother's depressions and reveal the context through which this condition came into their lives. I draw on Sylvia Plath's image of the bell jar, the central metaphor in her novel by that name, to argue that feminist thinking provides alternatives to living with the kind of isolation and silencing Plath invokes in her novel. Lastly, I provide examples of the ways in which feminist scholars and therapists have mapped strategies for fighting against and managing depression.

TRAPPED INSIDE THE BELL JAR

Sylvia Plath compared feelings of depression to being trapped inside a bell jar, a glass dome used by scientists to create a vacuum. A few weeks after her autobiographical novel, *The Bell Jar* (1963), was published, Plath took her life at the age of thirty-three. In February 1963, in the London flat where she lived with her two children following a separation from husband Ted Hughes, Plath locked the kitchen windows and door and turned on the gas (Stevenson). Her children, Frieda and Nicholas, were sleeping in an adjacent ventilated room and survived; however, Nicholas committed suicide in 2009 at the age of forty-seven years.

Plath's image of the bell jar is powerful yet problematic for me. For Plath, to be imprisoned in its airless chamber leads to suffocation, the method Plath chose to end her life. Esther Greenwood, Plath's fictional alter ego in the novel, reflects, "To the person in the bell jar, blank and stopped as a dead baby, the world itself is the bad dream." Alone in a freezing cold flat (that particular winter was one of London's coldest) with two children suffering from colds and flu, Plath must have felt there was no way out, no future that could support her as a mother and a poet.

Phyllis Chesler places the bell jar in a larger socio-cultural context, as a metaphor for patriarchal oppression of women and suffocating gender roles that leave no room for women's artistic creativity and self-expression. She describes Plath as an immensely talented, ambitious young woman without role models, mentors, or community. In Plath's day, men were regarded as the serious artists, while women were relegated to the roles of muse/lover or housekeeper. Women who were mothers were not taken seriously as artists; in addition, the subject of motherhood was not regarded as sufficiently serious or important to be made into art (Ostriker). The feminist consciousness born of the 1960s women's liberation movement had not yet arrived to help women give voice to their desires for personal freedom, agency, autonomy, and creativity.

DEPRESSION'S BEGINNINGS

A full discussion of depression, its causes, and effective treatment is beyond the scope of this personal narrative chapter. Turning back to my own experience, I have sensed that depression in women may enable daughters to remain connected to the mothers they have lost through illness, death, or madness. Mimi Crowell notes the despondency of depressed daughters can be gratifying to them because it preserves the unconscious relationship to the mother. Ironically, as enervating and exhausting as depression is, it may function as an umbilical cord, because a self-destructive connection to a lost or damaged mother enables the daughter to remain attached to her mother without confronting painful feelings of anger or ambivalence (Crowell). Nonetheless, Gina Wong, a Canadian feminist psychologist, often works with women in her counseling practice who are daughters fighting against and successfully managing their own depression because they do not want to reproduce that powerful negative tie to their mothers' depression, nor replicate the same suffering with their own children (personal communication). In this way, Wong notes that the motherline and intergenerational transmission of maternal depression can be interrupted and that *matroreform* (2006, 2010) can be an empowering and transformational process to this change in the generations.

MY STORY: DEPRESSION IN THREE GENERATIONS

On my mother's side, I am the third generation in a motherline of depressed women. My maternal grandmother, who left the Ukraine at the age of sixteen to escape government-sponsored pogroms against Jews, disembarked in Philadelphia alone, without parents, friends, money, or any English. She did not know how to read or write. Like so many immigrant women, my grandmother arrived in this country traumatized by the persecution she had endured in the country of her birth and by the separation from her loved ones. Like many immigrant women, she became depressed.

My grandmother raised three children without any emotional support. She lived under conditions of extreme isolation, poverty, and emotional stress. She was the first generation in her family to leave home and begin marriage and family life far away from those she knew. Her depression became evident to me at some point in my childhood, perhaps when I reached adolescence. My grandmother was known to have a lot of energy: she cooked for everyone, cleaned obsessively, and never seemed to sit down. However, she was also at times lethargic, despondent, melancholy, and withdrawn. And perhaps I recognized these symptoms because I was living with a depressed mother, a woman who lay curled in her bed for several hours every afternoon and forbade me to make noise or even speak to her; a woman who self-medicated her sadness with Librium; a woman whose moods seemed to swing between anxious irritability and explosive anger, often aimed at me.

When I was a child growing up in the sixties, my mother was one of those women suffering from what Betty Friedan called "the problem that has no name." In *The Feminine Mystique*, published in 1963, the same year as Plath's *Bell Jar*, Friedan describes her encounters with suburban middle class women. Friedan was such a woman herself, a mother living in Scarsdale, New York, at the time of the writing. When she asked women to describe their feelings of dissatisfaction with their lives, those she interviewed used words like "tired," "empty," "angry," "incomplete," "sad," "desperate," words that sound very much like the symptoms of depression. Friedan argues that these feelings were an appropriate response to lives filled with the tedium of housework, the isolation of childrearing, and the absence of validation.

Friedan's perspective was certainly descriptive of my mother. In my eyes, she was bored, lonely, and angry. Before her marriage, she worked as a legal secretary in Philadelphia in a law office where she was liked and appreciated. She lived at home, dividing her income between helping her parents with their expenses and maintaining her own independence, an arrangement that gratified her need to feel valued and autonomous. After she married my father, the newlyweds moved to Kew Gardens, Queens, far from friends and family. When I was two years old, my parents left Queens and bought a house in a bedroom community in the suburbs of northern New Jersey. Thus my mother was repeating her own mother's history: in her new home she had no one to turn to for emotional support or reassurance. She lost her identity as a self-sufficient contributor to the household. Unlike my grandmother, who had worked as a seamstress in a shop alongside my grandfather, who was a tailor, my mother was trapped alone in the house with nowhere to go and no one to talk to. For the first few years she did not drive. We were the only Jewish family on the block in an era when most suburban Jews sought communities where other Jews were living, as protection against anti-Semitism. The nasty comments in my eighth grade autograph book—Jewbilee, orange jews—are evidence of such prejudice.

In the sixties, people did not talk about depression. There was too much shame, too much stigma surrounding a condition that was invisible, that could not be measured or quantified on X-rays or other medical tests. When I was growing up, my parents thought it shameful to seek help from psychotherapists. If someone was depressed in the sixties, the alternatives were self-medication through alcohol or drugs like Librium that exacerbate depressive symptoms, electroconvulsive shock (ECT) treatment, or silence and isolation. Depression was regarded as a failure of will: people who were depressed were thought to be weak, self-pitying, or just lazy.

Although I did not have the words to name my feelings as a child, I was depressed, obsessed about my shortcomings and failures, convinced I was unworthy, inadequate and incompetent, worried all the time, afraid of everything—new situations, other people, being alone in the house, walking to school by myself. My mother's volatile temper left me feeling that life was dangerous and out of control. I enjoyed playing across the street with Carol, a girl my age whose mother was more emotionally stable than my own, but the knowledge I would eventually return home to my unpredictable mother made those visits seem compressed and all too short. I envied Carol's comfort and ease with her mother, the way she sought her mother's company. Our mothers were completely different: Carol's seemed to enjoy domestic life; she gardened, sewed, led the local Scouting troop, and played the organ at her church. Such activities did not interest my mother, who craved more intellectual stimulation. Suburban life in those days provided nothing to promote the exchange of ideas and knowledge, and intelligent women must have felt as though their brains were withering away.

It is hard to say at what age I became depressed. My mother's daily afternoon retreats into her bedroom left me feeling that I was the one in charge: responsible for her, my younger brother, and the household. Childhood depression was not acknowledged as an illness and so I suffered alone and silently, trapped inside my own bell jar. I do know that as a child I felt unusually strong attachments to surrogate mother figures. I fell early and intensely in love with my grade school teachers, all women, up to and including the sixth grade. In school, I learned I could win my teachers' approval if I were studious, helpful, and cooperative. At home, no matter how hard I tried, I rarely earned my mother's praise, and her affection was entirely out of reach. I adored my camp counselors and was the only camper who refused to participate in such pranks as putting frogs in their beds or stealing their underwear. By the time I reached thirteen years of age, I felt detached and dissociated from my body, as though it did not really belong to me. I wrote about this sensation in a published prose piece called "Marshmallow Girl":

> The young girl felt she was a marshmallow. Soft and white on the outside, softer and whiter on the inside. She had no core, no center. She could be pulled this way and that, until, maybe, a butterfly would emerge.... But there were no butterflies. Fear lived with the girl, gray and clammy like a wet wool blanket. The fear could enter and stay like an unwelcome guest, indeterminately. Once there, you couldn't order it to leave because it did not obey anyone's orders. She suspected it

had something to do with her mother but was afraid to ask, lest her mother start yelling and cursing. (Gerber 2009)

Depression followed me into adulthood, descending postpartum after the birth of my first child and with even more force after the birth of my second. I suffered frequent panic attacks, which made sleep impossible and daily life overwhelming. I would go to the supermarket, fill my cart with groceries and, feeling too panicky to stand in the check-out line, abandon the cart and walk out the door. The nearest postpartum support group was a 45-minute drive from my home, not far from where my parents' lived. I attended a few of these meetings but never mentioned them to my parents, too ashamed to seem like an incompetent, inadequate mother. I went through my days in a haze of anxiety and exhaustion. Finally, the therapist of a good friend, who had been talking in therapy about her concern for me, called me to say she thought I was suffering from postpartum depression and that I should seek professional help. I was so grateful that someone had put a name to my distress that I called a psychiatrist the next day and began to experience relief through a combination of therapy and anti-depressant medication.

Nancy Graham, a writer who came of age in suburban Toronto at the same time I was growing up in suburban New Jersey, chronicles her experience of living with a severely depressed mother in her memoir, *Afraid of the Day*. Graham employs a powerful, fragmented prose to describe the ECT treatments her mother endured when the author was a child: "the grim-faced reaper on her [mother's] left reaches for the headgear shaped like a huge wishbone, and lowers it into position … head rolls from side to side, eyes screaming in shocked white silence.…" I find Graham's need to bear witness to her mother's suffering profoundly moving. Although Graham was too young to have witnessed the shock treatments first-hand, she clearly suffered an imaginary identification with her mother's pain. I suspect some of the details Graham employs—the electrodes clamped by jelly, the rubber mouth gag, the body in spasms—came from research she conducted later, as an adult who had not stopped thinking about her mother's experience—an adult, who, unlike the child, had access to images of ECT though books, films, and television. I feel a great kinship for Graham, not only because we are the same age, but also because her mother's personal history is so similar to my mother's, that of a shy young woman who lived at home with parents, worked downtown, enjoyed outings with friends, and wanted desperately to be a good wife and mother. Was it something about a particular constellation of character traits, environment, and culture—the early '60s, a time of shifting gender expectations and women's rebellion against traditional female scripts of marriage and domesticity—that predisposed these women—insecure, attached to their parents, afraid to assume the relentless responsibilities of motherhood—to suffer depressive breakdowns? Or is women's depression intractable—persistent, difficult to treat—because of the patriarchal conditions under which women mother? Psychologist Alexandra Kaplan observes that women's psychological development, which centers around connectivity and relationships, is still devalued both at home and in the workplace, creating a culture of invisibility for mothers. Psychologist Janet Stoppard discusses how the figure of "the good woman"—one who puts everyone else's needs before her own—continues to circulate in our culture. Women who model themselves after this figure are prone to losing their sense of autonomy and selfhood in self-silencing.

Nearly 60 years after publication of *The Feminine Mystique*, "the problem that has no name" continues to plague women. According to the U.S. National Institute of Mental Health, women are 70 percent more likely to experience depression than men. In my view, mothering today continues as a practice characterized by social isolation, loneliness, and stress, much as it was during the 1960s in spite of tremendous gains for women. Mothers face new challenges in trying to protect their children—cyberbullying, for instance—for which there are no ready solutions. Access to childcare, paid maternity leave, and health benefits are not universally available in the United States although they are in Canada.

BREAKING FREE FROM THE BELL JAR: STORIES OF EMPOWERMENT

I delivered a version of this chapter at the May 2009 *Moms Gone Mad* conference in New York City, the first time I had ever spoken publicly about my depression. There were about thirty attendees in the room, mostly women, and I felt fortunate to be part of a very supportive, lively discussion. During the question-and-answer period many women in their twenties and thirties spoke openly about their own struggles with depression, postpartum depression, the challenges of raising young children while depressed, the fear of passing along depression to their children. I was tremendously moved by their openness and felt that if we could start a maternal depression support group at that moment, we could have the makings of a movement to empower depressed mothers. One woman, a psychotherapist, commented that her practice was filled with depressed women and suggested that such women are not sick *per se;* rather, our society, which makes impossible demands on women and does not support mothers, is in need of repair. In view of the cultural invisibility of mothering and the silencing of depressed daughters, it is critically important (and the aim of this chapter) that women speak out about their experiences of depression in order to shape public discourse and reduce the sense of isolation and shame experienced by depressed women.

How can depressed daughters heal from depression? Psychologist Gina Wong specializes in maternal mental health and has seen the intergenerational recurrence of depression in mothers. The journey from depression to finding self-compassion and self-acceptance amidst the societal pressures placed on women/mothers in our patriarchal existence is indeed a struggle (personal communication). Wong works with women from a perspective of matroreform (Wong-Wylie 2006, 2010) in changing the script and storyline of intergenerational maternal depression. She recommends books such as Judith Duerk's *Circle of Stones: Woman's Journey to Herself* and Pema Chodron's *Taking the Leap: Freeing Ourselves from Old Habits and Fears* to help women understand the call into the desolate darkness that depression invites, and the echo of self that can be found within that darkness.

Nancy Graham swallowed her mother's depression as surely as if it were mother's milk, battling with alcoholism, bulimia, and other self-destructive behaviors until she finally turned to writing, which allowed her to discover an identity apart from her mother. Writing is one of those paradoxical activities that simultaneously enable the writer to separate and yet remain connected to a depressed mother. Writing about depression—the daughter's, the mother's, or both—gives the daughter much-needed space, enabling her to see that her depression and her mother's are not one and the same. Likewise, Louise DeSalvo observes that writing is a healing activity that leads to experiences of profound insight, strength and power, creativity, and personal wisdom. She also notes the therapeutic aspects of making writing public: "Sharing our work removes us from a solitary brooding ground.... In becoming a witness to our own experience, we offer testimony to a truth that is generally unrecognized or suppressed" (DeSalvo 213). I see the proliferation of mothering blogs as a creative response to mothers' needs to give voice and shape to their lives, to acknowledge the challenges of mothering, and to break free from the isolation and silencing of mothers in patriarchy (Friedman and Calixte).

Many daughters of depression seek healing in psychotherapy, particularly with a feminist therapist sympathetic to gender and women's issues. Psychotherapy offers cognitive and emotional alternatives to the experience of growing up with a depressed mother, reducing the habits of self-attack and withdrawal with which depressed women are often plagued.

In my on-going struggles with depression, I have found friendships with women to be an important source of comfort. These relationships provide welcome respite and relief from self-imposed isolation. Sharing my feelings with supportive, trusted friend helps validate who I am and breaks the silence, shame, and isolation of the bell jar. Through friendship I find the strength to mother myself.

CONCLUSION

Three generations of women in my family have struggled with depression. My grandmother became depressed more than 100 years ago. Today as I write, I am disturbed that women's depression remains so rampant. Societal expectations and cultural pressure to be a "good mother" (Stoppard), economic realities, isolation, and marginalization contribute to the high incidence of depression among contemporary mothers. In the United States, patriarchal culture that prizes rugged individualism and self-reliance leads to self-silencing by depressed women. I have chosen to step outside that place of imprisonment, inscribed by Sylvia Plath in her image of the bell jar, in the hope that other mothers will share their stories of struggle. In breaking down the walls of silence, mothers who speak openly about their depression will empower themselves and other women by creating community, finding their voices, and rewriting the script of withdrawal and isolation and represented by the bell jar.

Feminist work, with it advocacy of collaboration, female empowerment, and recovery of women's experiences and voices, continues to provide a space for women to name the complexities of their lives and speak out against the silencing of patriarchy.

REFERENCES

Chesler, P. *Women and Madness.* New York: Palgrave Macmillan, 2005 [1970].

Chodron, P. *Taking the Leap: Freeing Ourselves from Old Habits and Fears.* Boston: Shambhala, 2009.

Crowell, M. G. "Feminism and Modern Psychoanalysis: A Response to Feminist Critics of Psychoanalysis." *Modern Psychoanalysis* 6 (2) (1981): 221-235.

DeSalvo, L. *Writing as a Way of Healing: How Telling Our Stories Transforms Our Lives.* San Francisco: Harper, 1999.

Dickinson, E. "Pain has an element of blank…." *The Collected Poems of Emily Dickinson.* Introduction by Rachel Wetzsteon. New York: Barnes and Noble, 2003.

Duerk, J. *Circle of Stones: Woman's Journey To Herself.* New York: New World Library, 2004.

Friedan, B. *The Feminine Mystique.* New York: Bantam Books, 1983 [1963].

Friedman, M. and S. Calixte, eds. *Mothering and Blogging: The Radical Act of the Mommyblog.* Toronto: Demeter Press, 2009.

Gerber, N. *Portrait of the Mother-Artist: Class and Creativity in Contemporary American Fiction.* Lanham, MD: Lexington Books, 2003.

Gerber, N. "Marshmallow Girl." *Mamapalooza Magazine.* Eds. Alana Ruben Free and Marjorie Tesser. 2009. Web.

Graham, N. *Afraid of the Day: A Daughter's Journey.* Toronto: Women's Press, 2003.

Kaplan, A. G. "The 'Self-in-Relation': Implications for Depression in Women." *Women's Growth in Connection: Writings from the Stone Center.* Eds. Judith V. Jordan, Alexandra G. Kaplan, Jean Baker Miller, Irene P. Stiver, Janet L. Surrey. New York: Guilford Press, 1991. 206-222.

Ostriker, A. *Writing Like a Woman.* Ann Arbor: University of Michigan Press, 1983.

Plath, S. *The Bell Jar.* New York: Bantam Books, 1971.

Plath, S. *The Collected Poems.* Ed. Ted Hughes. New York: Harper, 2008.

Stevenson, A. *Bitter Fame: A Life of Sylvia Plath.* Boston: Houghton Mifflin, 1989.

Stoppard, J. "Moving Towards an Understanding of Women's Depression." *Feminism and Psychology* 20 (2010): 267-271.

U.S. National Institute of Mental Health. Web. Retrieved 1 September 2012.

Wong-Wylie, G. "Images and Echoes in Matroreform: A Cultural Feminist Perspective." *Journal of the Association for Research on Mothering* 8 (1,2) (2006): 135-146.

Wong-Wylie, G. "Matroreform and Mothering." *Encyclopedia of Motherhood.* Ed. Andrea O'Reilly. Sage Publications. Newbury Park, CA: Sage Publications, 2010. 722-725.

13.
Postpartum Psychosis

A Mother of Madness

GINA WONG AND TERESA TWOMEY

PERIODICALLY THERE IS MEDIA COVERAGE of tragedies involving mothers who kill their children. One notorious and sensationalized story was about Andrea Yates who drowned her five children in Texas on June 20, 2001. Unfortunately, misconceptions about postpartum psychosis continue to exist in social media and among legal and medical professionals. Ms. Yates was first convicted of capital murder and sentenced to life in prison. She was diagnosed with postpartum psychosis and postpartum depression,[1] which prompted the decision to be overturned on appeal. Teresa Twomey shares insights that mothers such as Ms. Yates face a perfect storm:

> These women often face a perfect storm—the confluence of distinct forces that come together to produce tragedy. They suffer a sudden and severe disorder that is often missed or inadequately treated due to a lack of medical recognition. This leads to tragic consequences that are made more turbulent when these women face a legal system where this same lack of DSM recognition leads to a Catch-22 situation. They must demonstrate their actual experience without a recognized diagnosis in a court system that relies on outdated and unscientific approaches to mental illness. Within the legal system they are dependent upon a range of people—from jailers to judges to juries—who are influenced by a society where mental illness is still stigmatized, stereotyped, and misunderstood. (44)

Our cultural dialogue does alarmingly little to inform the general public that ordinary mothers—"mothers who function well domestically and professionally, who do not suspect themselves and whose family and friends do not suspect having a mental disorder—could become so mentally ill after having a baby that they become psychotic, that they might even become homicidal" (Twomey 2). Currently there exists insufficient recognition and understanding of postpartum psychosis from medical, legal, and social perspectives. Postpartum psychosis is often not recognized in mainstream books on women, history, and madness (Twomey).

The good news about postpartum psychosis is that it is recognizable and treatable; and with proper care, women generally recover quickly without harming anyone. Yet tragedies routinely continue to occur. Therefore it is imperative that we focus more attention on understanding, diagnosing, and properly treating women who are unfortunate enough to experience this "mother of madness." In this chapter, we illuminate postpartum psychosis from an understanding and empathetic perspective which contrasts with the system of oppression and judgmental lens through which *mad* mothers are often viewed. We provide awareness about the experience of postpartum psychosis in order to push back against the oppressive forces of stigma, ignorance, and prejudice embodied in social understanding, medicine, and the law and to foster strength and empowerment through educating and giving voice to this illness. We advocate for nothing less than recognizing the full humanity, misfortune, and suffering of women with this illness. To this aim, Gina Wong interviews book author Teresa Twomey on her candid thoughts and reflections from collecting ten stories from other mothers for her seminal book *Understanding Postpartum Psychosis: A Temporary Madness* published in 2009. Teresa is a former litigation attorney who became a maternal mental health advocate after being blindsided by her experience of postpartum mental illness in 1998. When she went looking for information on her experience—which included postpartum psychosis—she found there was almost nothing available for a layperson like herself. She searched on Google but got no hits (now there are hundreds of thousands). None of the books for expectant parents she owned described postpartum psychosis other than to say it was "rare" or "dangerous." As she states in her book, "None of the books described symptoms, frequency, risk factors, treatments, or the like." (Twomey 23)

Teresa then spent years researching postpartum psychosis, talking to experts, and gathering stories. Twomey courageously includes her own story to facilitate wider recognition and comprehension of this terrible—but temporary—mental illness. She continues to be an advocate for women with maternal mental health issues and their families and teaches in a Women and Gender Studies Program.

FURTHERING AN UNDERSTANDING OF POSTPARTUM PSYCHOSIS: THE INTERVIEW
MAY 24, 2010 AT 11:15 AM AT GRAND CENTRAL STATION, NEW YORK, USA

Gina: Teresa, what stands out the most in your experience of writing the book *Understanding Postpartum Psychosis: A Temporary Madness?*

Teresa: There are two things that stand out. First are the intermittent reminders, in the form of phone calls from women and their families and news stories, of the need for more awareness and more accurate information about this illness. Each new tragedy reminded me of that need and really prompted me to keep working on it. Second, was my own healing process in that reading and hearing the stories of other mothers helped me so much. I felt less isolated, less of a "freak," and more encouraged that I would recover 100 percent and be myself again. Even though I was recovered from the illness itself —emotionally, coming to terms with having had this illness, there was still some of the process left to go.

Gina: So how about the process of writing the book. Did it change in any way your understanding and perspectives of postpartum psychosis?

Teresa: Absolutely! I learned as I went. And I'm sure there's more to learn as time goes by. There is still a lot that we don't know. And I think there are aspects of postpartum psychosis we're not even looking at yet... But there are some exciting research projects going on—and new things being learned....

Gina: You teach in a Women and Gender Studies Program. How does this book, this subject, fit with your teaching?

Teresa: It fits very well from my experience. First, it is important to realize that issues around reproduction have historically been central to the oppression of and discrimination against women. And they still are. Additionally, issues around maternal mental health particularly have frequently been used to justify that oppression and discrimination. So it is tempting, as a feminist, to want to distance oneself from these issues. Why give more ammunition to misogynists by acknowledging that, in rare cases, women do experience severe mental health issues accompanying childbirth? So it is problematic in that it fuels the medicalization of women's issues. Fortunately, speaking one's truth is a core feminist belief. And we know if we keep silent for fear of oppression, we are simply doubly oppressed.

However, with that said, I can't say that all feminists see this as I do. I've definitely been criticized for my attempts to spread awareness of postpartum psychosis and postpartum depression.

Gina: Do you find that frustrating? Feeling like this is a feminist issue but having people who would seem to be natural allies opposing your work?

Teresa: Yes, it is very frustrating. But I also understand it. I hear and read lots of judgmental comments about women with postpartum mood disorders. There are attempts to spread awareness, choices of treatment for those disorders—particularly the use of psychotropic pharmaceuticals—and so forth that reinforce a certain understanding of postpartum mood disorders. But I also know that before it happened to me I thought, believed, and advanced much of the same perspective. It has definitely been a learning and humbling experience.

As well, many mental illness advocates I've spoken with do not see much point in distinguishing or providing advocacy, education, and services for an illness that, unlike most mental illnesses, has a specific onset time and generally a temporary, sometimes *very* temporary, duration. That can be frustrating as well. But culturally we don't have a framework for understanding a *temporary* madness.

Gina: You mentioned psychotropic pharmaceuticals, is that something you advocate?

Teresa: I don't advocate for any specific treatment. I am not a medical doctor. I believe it's important to be non-judgmental and support *whatever* approach helps women to recover from this illness. Maybe their thyroid is involved and they need medication for that. Maybe they need antipsychotics and mood stabilizers. Maybe they need Electroconvulsive Therapy (ECT). I'm all for women getting adequate care so that they don't continue to suffer—and believe me, they are suffering—and so they don't kill themselves or someone else. What type of care they receive is not for me to say; that is between them and their doctors. Of course, one hopes their doctors are well informed about postpartum psychosis, which is not always the case unfortunately.

Gina: Yes, I noticed you mentioned that in your book. I was also struck between the difference you bring out in the book about the similarity and differences between postpartum psychosis and postpartum obsessive-compulsive disorder (OCD) and how important it is for doctors to know the difference.

Teresa: It's a problematic situation that a mother reporting OCD symptoms and a mother reporting postpartum psychosis symptoms might sound very similar. For example, you might have a mother who has OCD with intrusive thoughts of her baby being harmed by something or even harmed by her. She may say to her doctor or someone else "I keep having bad thoughts about my child being harmed." Or she may even describe it as "seeing" something bad happen to her child. This is different from having psychotic hallucinations or hearing commands about hurting her child. It's so important to investigate further because on the surface they may sound the same because the fear—harm to the child—may come out sounding identical.

Also, OCD and postpartum psychosis can co-occur. So, I think it's a very problematic thing. And OCD can be very severe. I don't know, and I think it's hard to tell, but my hypothesis is that a number of postpartum suicides are because of OCD, because the mother fears that she is psychotic or she fears she is going to harm her child, she chooses to take her own life instead. So I think we need to do more to be really clear on the diagnosis. And I think we really also need to be very careful when mothers are given medication to be sure that it's being effective. We can't just give a mother an anti-psychotic and three days later let her go home—simply assuming that she's all better. We really need to do more to explore what's going on in these mothers' minds. Psychosis is a break from reality. That mother really has a different relationship to the world. She's seeing, hearing, thinking things that aren't the same as the rest of us, in terms of our understanding of reality. A mother with OCD has intrusive thoughts just like a person with OCD in the regular world. And it comes out of anxiety most of the time. So, from my experience looking back… when I remember the OCD thoughts I remember them as intense, frightening, awful thoughts. When I remember the psychotic hallucinations that I had about my daughter, I remember it very differently. It does not occur to me in my memory as something I thought— it occurs as something that happened—even though, obviously, it did not.

"Urges" Excerpt from *Understanding Postpartum Psychosis: A Temporary Madness:*

> I have sometimes characterized the thought I had as an "urge." When I was a teenager driving on curvy mountain roads I would sometimes imagine steering off a cliff. I would immediately fear that I might actually do it. The thought plus the fear made me think of these experiences as "urges." Yet I knew that I did not want to drive off the road. At the same time I would wonder if a part of me wanted to do it—it was the only explanation I had for why I would have such thoughts. Plus, when I was feeling suicidal as a teen, my reaction was not only fear, it was also the typical thoughts that my death would be a release, a relief. Still, it is important to understand that if I had wanted to go off the cliff, I would have. I didn't. I did not know for a very long time that these intrusive thoughts are characteristic of obsessive-compulsive disorder. I had other indications of this disorder as well, but I did not know it; I simply thought of myself as a "worrywart." (74)

Gina: And it's important to distinguish postpartum OCD and postpartum psychosis because treatment is different?

Teresa: Yes, treatment is different. But also risk is significantly different. Because a mother with OCD, although she may be a threat to herself, almost certainly she is not a threat to her child. She's overly anxious about the wellbeing of her child. A mother with postpartum psychosis could love her child dearly and kill her child through that love—so with postpartum psychosis you can't even say "She's a loving person she would never do anything to hurt her child." She may harm the child BECAUSE she is loving and trying to protect her child.

Treatment for OCD tends to be anti-anxiety medication but again I'm not a medical professional. And a lot of mothers who I know, once they know they have OCD and realize what it is, that alone, knowing that they are not psychotic, knowing they are not a threat to their child, and knowing this comes from anxiety—that alone tends to lessen their anxiety which in turn helps them with the symptoms. And that makes sense because the anxiety fuels the intrusive thoughts, which in turn fuels the anxiety. .

Gina: What about childhood trauma? Do you see any potential association between childhood trauma and postpartum psychosis?

Teresa: I don't know so much about childhood trauma. My personal belief is that a lot of us have latent mental illness potential. Trauma may be more likely to trigger it and bring it out. Like with genetics where something may cause a dormant or unexpressed gene for mental illness to "turn on" and become expressed. I don't know that... that's not based on science, just a hunch. As for myself, were there traumatic things in my past? Absolutely. Was I depressed? Yes, but ... when I first started getting stories of the mothers, I was shocked by the number of people who had either been victims of child abuse or rape, and so early on, one of my thoughts was: "Oh my gosh, do all the mothers with postpartum psychosis have a history of rape?" I've now talked to enough people that it's clear to me that isn't the case. But the numbers certainly were staggering. I probably had at least six or seven stories of mothers who had rape or child sexual abuse in their background before I had talked to other mothers where rape wasn't in the background of their postpartum psychosis. I talked to a mom of a mother who committed suicide who insisted that her daughter had not been raped and the response in my head was "how can you be so sure?" because a lot of women don't even tell their mother. But then I spoke with other mothers with postpartum psychosis who said they were not abuse or rape victims.

Gina: So mothers who come from generally good mental health functioning and don't have any kind of trauma per se in their life—they're home-free?

Teresa: I wish! I wish there was at least some group of mothers, to whom we could say, "Guess what? You get the stamp of approval. You are not at risk for postpartum psychosis." Unfortunately that's not the case. There are mothers who, looking back, had no mental illness, no history in the family and even post recovery no sign of mental illness yet developed postpartum psychosis. I know of one mother who is in the legal system due to the harm she did to her child who is in that very situation. So it's not even that a mother in that situation might get a "small dose of postpartum psychosis." There are mothers who have nothing that would indicate any kind of risk and it still can happen. I wish it were not the case.

Gina: That's one of the things I got from the book—that no one is immune to postpartum psychosis. What about traumatic childbirth, that's something I read in the stories in your book or I don't know if the psychosis is already at play and so brings on the perception of the childbirth as traumatic? Can you say a bit about that?

Teresa: I questioned a lot about that in my experience. I wondered, "is this because I had a bad childbirth experience?" I felt every stitch—and that was as bad as it sounds—and so I thought maybe that was what caused the postpartum psychosis. Plus I heard of other mothers who'd had trauma during childbirth who had postpartum psychosis. So did that help trigger postpartum psychosis? Or maybe it was the lack of support; maybe it was this, maybe it was that… so tempting to try to find the reasons why. Unfortunately, there are just as many mothers who I know who have no "good reason" for their postpartum psychosis…. One example is a mother I recently heard of who is struggling with postpartum psychosis who had no mental illness, perfect childbirth, and it all was out of left field. There are mothers I know who said "I had a great pregnancy and birth. I don't understand how this happened to me."

On a side note: A lot of mothers who have postpartum psychosis—in fact a lot of people with mental illness, seem to fixate on religious ideas and beliefs. Some suddenly seem to become very religious. One mother that I know believed that her son was the new Christ and would be risen again if she killed him. One mother in my book believed that she was the Virgin Mary. Religious delusions show up a lot—seeing devil's eyes in their child, seeing angels. But other things as well … I mean, like paranoia about people spying on her and hidden cameras in the house … espionage … those kinds of things. So, I think there are common symptoms like that which may come into play in postpartum psychosis. But I don't think the religious belief *causes* the postpartum psychosis, just that it is something people fixate on. Perhaps when we experience something outside normal reality it is easy to jump from that to religious beliefs.

Gina: What's the prevalence of postpartum psychosis Teresa?

Teresa: Generally it is reported as occurring in one or two out of 1000 births. From what I've read, that is about the same rate as Down Syndrome. There are some people who believe if you include "postpartum mania" and "postpartum depression with psychotic features" and so forth that the number would be higher. It is a poorly defined illness within the medical guidelines—the DSM (the *Diagnostic and Statistical Manual*)—so it is difficult for me to know for certain. But Jane Honikman, the founder of Postpartum Support International, assured me that the one or two out of 1000 is accurate.

Actually this is probably a good time to note that "postpartum psychosis" is not treated as a distinct separate illness in the DSM, that is, you won't find the term "postpartum psychosis" in the index of the DSM-IV-TR. That does not mean women do not experience this illness or it does not exist. The DSM notes that postpartum mood disorders with psychotic features DO occur but instead of a separate diagnosis, it uses a "postpartum onset specifier" for these episodes. Furthermore, the DSM recognizes that there are unique aspects to the postpartum period. That said, without a specific name for this experience, it seems many doctors are not trained to spot it and that leaves courts and juries free to decide whether they think this illness even exists. This does great disservice to the women who face our legal system due to this illness and is one of the reasons I wrote the book.

Gina: What's your conceptual understanding of how postpartum psychosis develops and how it's best treated?

Teresa: I don't know what causes it. My guess is that there is a chemical disorder in the brain. I think that we often want to blame social circumstances—and symptoms often give us a good excuse to do so because our delusions may reflect our circumstances—but I don't think that is a cause. I do think circumstances may contribute to risk of harm, however. I believe women with postpartum psychosis should be treated with tender, loving care. They are so vulnerable. They need supervision. Medication can be helpful as well. And for some, ECT as I talked about earlier can be a saving grace—a wonderful thing to have available. But it seems most people fear that and only use it as a last resort, if at all. I've often wondered: if the doctors had insisted on the use of ECT, would Andrea Yates still just be a stay-at-home mom of five kids?

Gina: With proper treatment how soon before a mother is better?

Teresa: That varies of course. With ECT, that can sometimes help immediately and is the reason behind why some people believe it should be done sooner. I want to back up and say what's often done now. Many women I've been in touch with have been kept for a few days in the general population of a mental institution or psych ward and then sent home even though they may not be recovered. In the psych ward they often feel traumatized. They may go to group therapy and feel like they don't fit. I've heard from more than one woman that she was required to go to group sessions for alcohol and drug addiction because they did not have a group more suited to her illness. So, that's some of what I hear from mothers about what happens. What would be nicer to have happen is for these mothers to be in more home-like settings but in a secure facility where they can be monitored and it's not as traumatic. If she could be treated with kid gloves rather than being treated as if she's a criminal, that would be much better. Mothers are aware of the harsh treatment and it often traumatizes them further. We do this with a lot of mentally ill people—as if they don't experience pain. Some mothers dislike it so much they will lie to get out and pretend to be better. Some of the mothers who I've talked to admitted to pretending to get well so they could be released in order to attempt suicide. Often these women are (or feel they are) treated more harshly than what is warranted.

Gina: Can postpartum psychosis resolve on its own without treatment or intervention?

Teresa: Certainly it can resolve on its own. But if there's an underlying disorder such as depression or bipolar disorder, that likely won't just go away. Or, as I like to say, "If you have an underlying disorder, having postpartum psychosis won't cure it." But there is a huge risk to trying to let it resolve on its own. I'm often asked about this because I did not receive treatment. But I would never intentionally choose to forego treatment for postpartum psychosis—it is just too risky. If someone is considering that, I would say, "Can you live with the worst case scenario? Are you willing to risk infanticide or suicide?" Because although that is rarely the outcome, every family that has had a tragic outcome that I've spoken with has said they simply did not believe it could happen to them. I can't even imagine the horror of living with something like that.

So, a word about why I didn't receive treatment. I think I had a mild case, although it was the worst thing I've ever experienced. To put that into perspective, I've been raped, I've gone through breast cancer, chemotherapy, and all that. And still, postpartum psychosis was, by far, the worst thing I ever experienced. I knew there was something wrong with me. I tried to tell everybody who would listen that I couldn't cope, that I needed help. I think most people thought it was because of the physical problems I was having or maybe they thought I was overreacting—or any number of things. But, even the medical providers that we went to, when they asked how I was doing and I would collapse into a blubbering mess … they would just do a physical. No one ever did a mood check on me to see what was going on. And my husband and I, like most, were uninformed about postpartum psychosis. Also, I wouldn't have believed something like that could happen to me. We were very lucky that mine resolved very quickly and was very mild. I now know that I do have an underlying disorder but it is pretty mild.

Gina: How long did it last?

Teresa: From beginning to end for the psychosis, it's hard to say. I had post-traumatic stress disorder (PTSD) and OCD as well. My guess is probably, maybe, a month. But it's all so foggy it's hard to say and nobody documented it or really knew so it could have been two months. I don't even know. After that I went into a very deep, deep depression and that lasted until I got pregnant with my twins (22 months later).

Gina: I know this is hard; but, can you take me back to the worse day or days? I'm curious specifically what you were feeling, thinking, and doing.

Teresa: So, in terms of the worse. When I think about the things that felt the worst to me was that I had really horrific nightmares and visions. I thought I was a horrible mother to have those thoughts. Like every time I passed the stairs, I thought about throwing my daughter down the stairs. I saw in my mind's

213

eye throwing her down the stairs. The nightmares often times involved sexual images—my husband wants to make love and is chasing me and then is either using a knife or having his penis turn into a knife. I'm sure that was because of a combination of the rape and the traumatic birth … those two elements together. But those were symptomatic of the PTSD and OCD. As far as the psychosis goes, it was very scary because I knew something was wrong with me but I didn't know what. In my head I was hearing things—like people talking and laughing, like there was a party going on in a different room. Or sometimes it was more sinister—specifically in a room just north of my bedroom. And I knew it wasn't real, even when it was happening, because there was no room there! And I *knew* there was no room there. And I still heard these people. It was very weird—both thinking and believing—that I was hearing people and yet, at the same time, knowing that it couldn't be happening. Another thing happened repeatedly: I'd hear the front door unlock and I'd hear the door open and I'd hear the footsteps and I'd hear the thunk of a suitcase being put down on the couch and the click click of the latch of the briefcase opening. I'd hear rustling of papers and I'd think it was my husband so I'd call down the stairs. Of course, no one would answer. And I would call my husband at work to say that someone was in the house and he had to come home to check it out. He'd come home and of course there wouldn't be anybody there. He thought I was hearing squirrels. I didn't tell him what I was hearing specifically. And it didn't occur to me, until much later, to wonder why in the world would an intruder come into a house and put down a briefcase and start going through papers!? (*laughs*) But, at the time that didn't matter because it seemed real. Every time it happened, my poor husband had to come home. He would be upset—which I interpreted as being upset and annoyed at me. Plus I was starting to get paranoid about my relationship with my husband so his upset only furthered my paranoia. I also experienced being unable to read and I noticed that I couldn't follow a plot on TV or even distinguish a commercial from the main show.

The worst of it, the very worst thing was I had a hallucination that I killed my daughter. I don't know if I can do this without tears….

I was with her on the bed. She was maybe a month old, not even, very young. And I saw myself pick up this pair of scissors and plunge them into her, starting at her pubis and then cut all the way to her neck. Then I thought, "Oh, that's awful I'm having one of *those* (the OCD) thoughts." At the same time, I knew it didn't feel like another one of *those* thoughts but I *wanted* it to be one of those bad thoughts. Because what I really feared was that it was real. And so I gathered up all the sharp things I could find in the room—all the while not looking at her and telling myself that it couldn't have happened, it couldn't have happened. I took all the items I gathered to another room and hid them at the back of the closet. I had to get a chair to reach the back of the closet, thinking that if I was ever tempted to do something like that I wouldn't be able to get to the stuff easily and I would have time to "come back to myself" before I could do something awful. I was also thinking about the laws in England. There's an infanticide law that if you kill your child within the first year after birth it is assumed that it is due to "imbalance of mind" and it is handled as manslaughter, not murder. I thought if we had laws like that maybe I could tell somebody what was going on with me. But I was in U.S. I thought: what if I got treatment but the treatment didn't work, and then I did do something to her? Then it would be seen as premeditated because I sought help. I might get the electric chair. So I thought I better not tell anyone. Plus I believed my husband would just jump on a chance to put me away for life. Later it occurred to me how twisted my thinking was. For one thing, I would lay down my life for my daughter in a heartbeat. And later I thought, "that isn't what would happen in the U.S— that help-seeking would be used to show premeditation—is it?" But unfortunately that was pretty accurate regarding the handling of this illness by the U.S. justice system in these cases—particularly regarding help-seeking. Many women who are now in prison for infanticide did seek help and that help-seeking was used against them in court.

Gina: The complexities are enormous. Your insights Teresa are powerful and enlightening. So, back to that day … so the thoughts are around state laws and wanting to make as many barriers as you could by putting sharp things away…

Teresa: So then I'm thinking those things and walking back into the room and thinking about wanting to seek help but not being able to tell anybody. And thinking in my head that this is just a bad thought—isn't it?. It has to be, I couldn't do something like that to my child—could I?. But then when I went back to the room what I saw was her cut open on the bed with blood everywhere. I thought I killed her (*tearful*). I don't know how long that lasted. I don't know what I did. I was alone in the house. I don't think I screamed. All I remember is coming in and seeing that and then the next thing I remember is blackness… and then a sort of coming out of that blackness but I didn't pass out, I was still standing there. So, the blackness thing was just in my head. And I saw that she was just sleeping peacefully on the bed—thank goodness! But, it was horrible. When I saw her with the blood everywhere it never occurred to me that it wasn't real. Like earlier when I saw myself cut her I went away and thought it was just one of those thoughts even though it didn't feel the same. I wanted it to be one of those thoughts because I didn't want to believe I could do something like that. And I didn't know anything about hallucinating. Then when I came back into the room, it was like "Oh my gosh, I really did do it, it really did happen" and I believed then that I really did do it and I had only been trying to fool myself that it hadn't happened. I thought it was 100 percent real. Then when I kind of came to and saw she was okay, it didn't occur to me at all that that couldn't be real either. It was just as real to me as the hallucination had been.

Gina: So then what?

Teresa: I don't remember what happened the rest of the day, I don't know what time of day that was. I don't know when my husband came home. I don't know how many days after that it was … I don't remember anything else that day.

Gina: And you say you feel you had postpartum psychosis mild (*laughs*)?!

Teresa: Yeah, compared to intensity, duration, degree of behavior that a lot of other mothers whose stories are in my book had, I look at mine and see that it was pretty short and my behavior wasn't that bizarre—because nobody noticed. I'm not saying emotionally it wasn't severe because it was, incredibly. But it wasn't the same bizarre level some other mothers experience.

Gina: Thank you for sharing this gut-wrenching experience Teresa. It just grips at my heart. You describe it so well in your book and how it's like a memory that actually happened.

Teresa: Thank *you* for your interest in and attention to this illness, Gina. I truly believe that awareness is the best way to prevent the tragedies associated with this illness.

Gina: What were family members' perceptions of you at the time?

Teresa: It's a little hard to say what their ideas were. I don't think any of them knew I was that ill. I think my family saw me as being over sensitive, over dramatic, high maintenance. I wanted someone to be with me 24/7, I tried to get my mom to come and help. I wanted someone to be there because it seemed like when there were people around the symptoms weren't as severe and I wouldn't have the opportunity to hurt the baby. When I was alone, the symptoms got more out of control. But, none of them thought I was mentally not well. They thought I was upset and not coping well and demanding and unreasonable. But, I think that was how I was seen before and that they thought: this is just Teresa and just a little more so… I had my share of moments in the past when I'd acted badly so I don't think they really thought it was anything more than me going through similar stuff. I wasn't telling people that I would hear people talk in another room that I knew wasn't there. I was worried that if I did, they would take my daughter and have me locked up in a mental institution for the rest of my life. So I only expressed my desperation by saying things like "I'm not a good mom. I'm a bad mom. I can't cope. I need help…." But I wouldn't share anything specific about *why* I felt that way.

"Perception of Normal" Excerpt from *Understanding Postpartum Psychosis: A Temporary Madness:*

> It's hard to give a complete picture of my postpartum period. Much of it is fuzzy now. I can think of no better word than desperate. Deeply,

darkly desperate. Yet I know that I smiled and joked. I changed di-
apers and cooed at my baby. I did dishes and returned phone calls. I
don't really remember doing that, but I must have. If I hadn't, surely
someone would have noticed something seriously wrong.

But I hid it. No one knew that I could not really follow a television
program. I liked having the TV on. When I would hear things that
I recognized as auditory hallucinations I would blame them on the
TV and even when I knew they were not coming from the TV. I also
could not read. The letters would be readable for a few words or so,
but then they began to look like hieroglyphs—I could not read them;
no matter how hard I tried, I could not make sense of them. That was
particularly scary because I had never heard of such a thing before. (76)

I did think of running away. A lot: like daily. I struggled almost every morning to not leave the family. But I thought if I left I would need to hide out. I
thought I'd have to be in disguise for the rest of my life. I thought if I left I
could never see any of my friends or family ever again. I'd go around the house
looking for cash so I could go live that life. Luckily we didn't keep much cash
around, so I never left. But, the feeling that my family would be much better
without me was there. Fortunately, suicide did not occur to me as the way out.

Postpartum psychosis and depression affected my perception of bonding. For
the first two years of my daughter's life I felt we were not properly bonding.
And I felt guilt and despair about whether that affected her in any particular
way. I remember a period of time when I felt invisible. Nobody knew me and
I would look at myself in the mirror and not recognize myself. I would look
at my eyes and it was like I wasn't there. And I didn't know if I'd ever come
back. There was someone who worked at the post office and whenever I would
come in he would recognize me and say "Hi, how are you?" He was just this
pleasant guy. One day I desperately needed to know that I could be seen, that
I was recognizable to someone. I wrote a letter so I could take it to the post
office and I drove to the post office but he wasn't there that day. I went out in
my car and put my daughter in the backseat and sat in the driver's seat and
sobbed my eyes out. I just sat there and cried and cried and cried. Then my
daughter started crying. In that moment, I felt we were bonding a little—or
were at least in sync—and yet it was so sad.

Gina: How are things now with the completion and the success of your book?

Teresa: Well, my marriage survived; my daughter is great. And I feel that I
was lucky ... so I wanted to write this book to help others and hopefully, help
to save lives. If a mother who is incarcerated wrote a book like this it would
probably be perceived as self-serving, like she has an agenda. But, I have nothing
to gain from coming forward and could just have easily hidden and gone on

with my merry life rather than risk facing stigma and even discrimination for this. This book isn't going to be a "best seller." I'd like to add that I'm grateful to Praeger Publishing that they saw the value in this book and chose to publish it.

For me, this book is a bit like "giving back" in gratitude for having been spared from the fate of so many women who have this illness. Plus, the book has been such a blessing to me. It is enormously satisfying to know that something you created has brought hope and healing to others. I know of defense attorneys using it successfully in cases involving women with postpartum psychosis and it has even been credited with saving lives. So I'm so grateful to have been able to actually have it out there for others to use. That is very rewarding.

Gina: Thanks so very much Teresa. You are a gift and I know in fact that you have and will save many mothers' and children's lives as a result of your advocacy on postpartum psychosis. This is an incredibly meaningful experience for me to meet with you and talk with you. Thank you for all that you're doing on this front.

Teresa: Thank you, Gina. I hope you are aware that, through this, you too are doing something important to help prevent future tragedies.

[1]Mothers with postpartum psychosis are not always depressed although these experiences often occur together.

REFERENCES

American Psychiatric Association. *Diagnostic and Statistical Manual of Mental Disorders*. 4th ed. Washington, DC: Author, 2000.

Twomey, T. *Understanding Postpartum Psychosis: A Temporary Madness*. Westport, CT: Praeger Publishers, 2009.

14.
Envious Mothers, Beautiful High-Spirited Daughters

The First Step Towards Woman's Inhumanity to Woman

PHYLLIS CHESLER

I AM HONORED TO BE HERE with you today. I have also been waiting a long, long time to have a group of beautiful and high-spirited women who want to discuss what I've called *Woman's Inhumanity to Woman*. I have written a book with that title which has just been published in a 2009 edition with a new "Introduction."

Before I focus only on "envious mothers and high spirited daughters," allow me to frame this relationship more broadly. I began the research for *Woman's Inhumanity to Woman* (originally published in 2001) right after another woman sabotaged me in a way that was to have lasting consequences. She was a friend and a colleague and I had not seen it coming. When I finally picked myself up off the floor, I began asking other women whether anything like this had ever happened to them. The floodgates of memory, both theirs and mine, opened up to reveal worlds of previously unspoken pain.

Women's aggression is both direct (physical) and indirect. "Indirect aggression" is characterized by a clique of girls or women who exert power "indirectly" by bullying, gossiping about, slandering, and shaming one girl or woman so that she will be shunned by her female intimates, thrown out of her college sorority, perhaps fired from her job, divorced by her husband, and definitely dropped from the A-list of partygoers. Gossip is a chief weapon of indirect aggression. Slandering another girl or woman ("she's a slut," "she's ... different," "she really thinks she's something") leads to her being ostracized by her female friends and peers, a punishment that girls and women experience as being put into solitary confinement or as a social death.

This experience at the hands of other girls and women, as opposed to being bullied by boys or men, is what most accounts for female conformity, cautiousness, and "two-facedness." It is too dangerous to share exactly what you think or feel (the ebullience does not die completely. You will hear it rise again whenever two or three female friends laugh together or riotously exchange secrets).

Women rarely admit that they themselves are harder on women than on men, that they hold higher and different standards for women than they do for men, and that they often never forgive each other for a single lapse or for the kinds of betrayals for which women routinely forgive men. Most women could not admit or even remember how they themselves might have betrayed or joined in shunning other women. The most profound amnesia often prevails.

Like men, women have internalized sexist values. They do not always respect, trust, or even like other women. Like men, women are, unsurprisingly, human beings and thus are capable of both compassion and cruelty, cooperation and competition, selfishness and altruism. This is hardly surprising since women grow up in the same culture that men do and are not immune to that culture. We live on the same planet; women are not an alien species. To the extent that women are oppressed, we have also internalized the prevailing misogynist ideology which we uphold both in order to survive and in order to improve our own individual positions vis-a-vis all other women.

Researchers in Europe, North America, and Australia have found that verbal and indirect aggression among girls and women includes name-calling, insulting, teasing, threatening, shutting the other out, becoming friends with another as revenge, ignoring, gossiping, telling bad stories behind a person's back, and trying to get others to dislike that person. Additionally, the formation of exclusive female dyads and cliques begins early in life. Author Nancy Friday notes that "boys try the macho, aggressive form of bullying; with girls, bullying means exclusion from their friendship group."

In the United States the psychologist Gloria Cowan has been studying women's hostility to women. Such hostility includes a refusal to believe that women are economically discriminated against or are the victims of sexual violence. Cowan's subjects are young and middle-aged, Hispanic-, Native-, Asian-, African-, and white-Americans. She found that a woman's political or economic philosophy does not predict whether she will be hostile toward women. Rather, such hostility is correlated with the believer's own satisfaction or dissatisfaction with herself. That is, women with low self-esteem are more hostile to other women. Cowan added that women who are hostile toward other women don't feel good about themselves. They were found to have lower personal self-esteem, optimism, sense of self-efficacy, life satisfaction, and higher objectified body consciousness compared to non-hostile women.

Most women do not hate women; only some do. Most women in fact depend upon other women for emotional and social companionship. But, as men do, women either idealize or demonize women. Most women unconsciously expect other women to mother them and feel betrayed when a woman fails to meet their ideal standards. Most women are no more realistic about women than men are. To a woman other women are (supposed to be) Good Fairy Godmothers, and if they are not they may swiftly become their dreaded Evil Stepmothers.

Getting women to talk about this is very hard. I once raised this issue at a workshop. One woman immediately protested. She said, "No, you are absolutely wrong. Women are very supportive of each other." She immediately looked around for support.

Within an hour, this woman grew tearful. She admitted, "My mother was my lifelong enemy. She refused to touch me. Now as she lies dying she wants me to be her body servant. I can't do it." Another workshop member said, "My grandmother used to physically hit my mother. My mother pretended this was not happening." Women want to believe that they and other women are "safe." Hence, a woman cannot afford to notice that a woman—her own mother no less—is hitting her.

The feminist therapist conference in 1990 could not accept what I said about women's inhumanity to women. Likewise, one of my adult students described her mother as an "eternally competitive sister." She said, "Mom was always happy when people mistook her for my sister. She still is. She kept pushing me to succeed, comparing me, negatively, to relatives who were child prodigies. But she was the one who was holding me back. She made disparaging remarks to me about myself every day, every hour."

We now understand that a mother may verbally, physically, sexually, and psychologically abuse her daughter. She may allow her husband to do so too, and she may eject her victimized daughter, not her violent husband. A "good enough" mother may also humiliate and reject her daughter, treat her coldly, try to break her spirit. In some instances, otherwise good enough mothers also envy and persecute their younger, prettier, talented, and ambitious daughters.

Mothers have been scapegoated for the crimes of men for a long time. I do not wish to do that here. Most mothers are "single" mothers since the responsibility for child care almost always falls entirely on their shoulders. Given that this is so, most mothers have done very well by the human race in terms of physical survival. Psychological survival is something else entirely. However, mothers, who are women, are also too-quickly psychiatrically diagnosed and I do not want to follow suit.

The mother-daughter relationship is our primary love and often blood bond. It shadows our every subsequent relationship. Until very recently, most women minimize or deny that their relationships with their one-and-only mothers have been embattled, fierce, bitter, ambivalent or dangerous. If they admit anything, they might first blame themselves, thus, choosing to view themselves as failures rather than risk viewing their mothers in this way.

It is very frightening to think of one's mother as a Scary Lady/Evil Stepmother, as dangerous, destructive, perhaps even infanticidal. Most daughters deny that they have envious mothers who may have wished to keep them at home by making them feel stupid, ugly, sick, selfish, totally unlovable. Mothers are meant to provide safety, security, protection, and love. What does it say about a daughter whose mother has not done so? Instead, women will "forget" about the emotional coldness, the non-stop verbal criticism, the rages, the beatings, the painful punishments.

The Greek myth about Demeter and Persephone and the Greek plays about Queen Clytemnestra and her matricidal daughter Electra is one way to help women understand what the *normal* but unconscious mother-daughter dynamics are about. The Earth Goddess Demeter demands a merged Persephone-Kore daughter. Electra can never leave home, or at least, not for long. Princess Electra—and we are all Electra's daughters, think about *that*—cannot abide her mother, Queen Clytemnestra, as a sexual woman who has ordered the death of her equally adulterous husband, Electra's father Agamemnon—who, by the way, sacrificed Clytemnestra's younger daughter, Iphighenia, to the Gods, to ensure his military triumph over the Trojans. To become her own Queen, Clytemnestra needs to "murder" her mother. Today, many women may need to "murder" their mothers psychologically in order to avoid their fates.

In *Woman's Inhumanity to Woman*, I use these ancient myths to help us understand the embattled relationship between the poet Sylvia Plath and her mother, Aurelia; Linda Sexton Gray's embattled relationship with *her* mother, the poet Anne Sexton (Gray wrote about it); the pathological relationship between Bette Davis and her daughter B. D. Hyman (at least from B.D.'s point of view); the educator and writer Jill Kerr Conway's embattled relationship with her "raging" and "paranoid" mother; Christina Crawford's relationship with her sadistic mother, the actress, Joan Crawford.

I also write about great love affairs between mothers and daughters. And about how all daughters long for their mother's love, approval, protection: Hence, the importance to us of Fairy Godmothers. But that is another discussion.

Can a "Good Enough" mother persecute her talented daughter? Yes, and here are some things she can do:

•Constant criticism and monitoring of appearance.
•Generalized criticism. Maternal denial that the criticism is important, maternal insistence that the criticism is actually a proof of love. An envious mother can bully and berate her daughter constantly about her choice of friends, spouse, career, ideas, etc.
•Criticism of her daughter to her daughters' friends, spouse, employer, etc.
•The silent treatment. Both psychotherapist and writer, Kim Chernin, and writer Daphne Merkin wrote about very cold mothers who, when their daughters tried to fight back against the non-stop criticism, encountered the silent treatment for days, even weeks at

a time—until they, the daughter, apologizes and cries and begs her mother to forgive her.
•The medicalizing and pathologizing of a healthy daughter.
•Beating, whipping, solitary confinement.

South African novelist Olive Schreiner (1855-1920) was seriously and routinely beaten by her mother as was feminist writer, Charlotte Perkins Gilman, (1860-1935), revolutionary and writer Agnes Smedley (1894-1950), and the contemporary writers bell hooks and Bertha Harris.

•Mothers' preference for a son

This prejudice blew many talented women right out of the water, including Sylvia Plath and Doris Lessing.

•Sexual surveillance.
•Collaboration with incest.
•Maternal envy.

Envious mothers can engage in all the above behaviors too. Girls and women rarely acknowledge the possibility that their own mothers may envy them. Such knowledge is terrifying and threatens the symbiotic connection. Psychotherapist Betsy Cohen suggests that the daughter of an envious mother wished to "deny the obvious, to protect herself from a truth that is too painful to bear." The daughter still needs her mother—"precisely because she never had a nurturing mother." In my view, maternal envy teaches many daughters how not to be a threat to other women. In addition, maternal envy teaches daughters to be passive, fearful, conformist, obedient—as well as similarly cruel to other women. Cohen's women patients say: "I'm afraid to be powerful because my mother might retaliate." Or, "Right in my own home, I was taught that success is not safe."

In addition, aging mothers in an ageist culture are being rapidly phased out. Husbands acquire second, younger wives, daughters become vital just as mothers view themselves as fading. Even in an era of plastic surgery, envious mothers may consciously and unconsciously envy their daughters' youth, fertility, sexual opportunities, career opportunities. By the way, race, class, and religion may lead to different kinds of mother-daughter relationships. That too is another discussion.

Envious mothers may fear that the world will treat their ambitious, i.e. reckless, daughters badly and are only trying to save them. I do not agree with this view but thought I'd mention it anyway.

In my book I discuss the talented, persecuted daughters including the British founder of Nursing, Florence Nightingale; the great American novelist Edith Wharton; the great French sculptor, Camille Claudel; the acclaimed American actress, Frances Farmer; the twentieth century Greek-American opera star, Maria Callas—to name a few. I hope you have the opportunity to read *Woman's Inhumanity to Woman*.

Revised and Reprinted 2009 Keynote Speech for the Moms Gone Mad Conference, New York, May 2009.

REFERENCES

Chesler, P. *Woman's Inhumanity to Woman.* Chicago: Lawrence Hill Books, 2009.

Contributor Notes

Kathryn Bell is a Master's in Counselling Graduate from the Graduate Centre in Applied Psychology with Athabasca University. She is currently, together with her husband, raising her young children in Edmonton, Alberta, Canada and both working and publishing in the field. She enjoys semi-professional hobby photography, gardening, and working to support new or young mothers.

Grace B. Nyamongo is a lecturer in the Department of Gender and Development Studies at Kenyatta University. She is Chair of the Board of Governors of Mogongo Girls High School in the Nyamira County of Western Kenya. Grace is actively engaged in sensitization programs for empowering rural women, and mentoring of girls and boys on various issues including poverty eradication strategies, HIV/AIDS, lifestyle, education, Female Genital Mutilation (FGM), and gender-based violence among others. Her research interests include women and work in Sub-Saharan Africa, violence against women and girls, gender issues, and African sexuality. Grace is currently residing in Nairobi, Kenya with her spouse and their three teenage children who have been greatly inspired by their parents' passion for the countryside community development activities.

Paula J. Caplan is a clinical and research psychologist, activist, nonfiction author of 12 books, including *Don't Blame Mother: Mending the Mother-Daughter Relationship*, and a playwright, screenwriter, actor, and director. She is a Fellow in Harvard Kennedy School's Women and Public Policy Program and an Associate in the DuBois Institute at Harvard University. She became interested in mother-daughter relationships in the late 1970s both because they are important and also because the study of them helped illuminate the socially-constructed barriers between women that could impede women's alliances with each other to build the Second Wave of the Women's Movement. Over time, she came to understand that much of mother-blame is frankly hate speech, with all that that entails, and that some of the Perfect Mother myths and Bad Mother myths about which she wrote in *Don't Blame Mother* are mutually exclusive because of serving the function of ensuring that whatever a mother does, she can be demeaned and scapegoated by those with more power. Most recently, her interest in mothers has related to the various relationships between mothers and the military. One of her favorite mothers in her award-winning play, CALL ME CRAZY, is Amalia Freud (mother of Sigmund), whom she played in its New York production.

Phyllis Chesler is an Emerita Professor of Psychology and Women's Studies at City University of New York. She is a bestselling and influential author, a legendary feminist leader, and a psychotherapist and expert courtroom witness. She currently resides in Manhattan. Phyllis is co-founder of the Association for Women in Psychology (1969) and co-founder of the National Women's Health Network (1974). Phyllis's fifteen books and thousands of articles and speeches have inspired countless people. Her books include: the classic *Women and Madness* (1972); *With Child: A Diary of Motherhood* (1979); *Mothers on Trial: The Battle for Children and Custody* (1986); *Sacred Bond: The Legacy of Baby M* (1988); and *Woman's Inhumanity to Woman* (2002). Her work has been translated into many European languages and into Japanese, Chinese, Korean, and Hebrew. Since 9/11, Phyllis has focused on the rights of women, dissidents, and gays in the Islamic world; on anti-Semitism; the psychology of terrorism; the nature of propaganda, and honor-related violence. She has testified for Muslim and ex-Muslim women who are seeking asylum or citizenship based on their credible belief that their families will honor kill them. Her archives reside at Duke University. There are over 4 million references to Phyllis's work online. She may be reached at her website <www.phyllis-chesler.com>.

Regina M. Edmonds, Ph.D., is a licensed clinical psychologist and a Professor of Psychology at Assumption College, Worcester, MA. U.S.A. Some of her research focuses on discovering the qualities that characterize successful mother-daughter relationships. One objective of this research is to gain insight into the processes that promote joy within mother-daughter relationships and to use these insights to both counter the persistence of mother-blame within psychological theory and to help heal more troubled mother-daughter bonds. Another goal is to celebrate the contributions mothers make to the development of daughters, as well as to reflect on the impact mothering has on the development and identity formation of women themselves. Regina's other specialties within the field of clinical psychology include the treatment of eating difficulties, the amelioration of self-injurious behavior, and the exploration of the impact of trauma upon the development of the self. Regina has also served, for over a decade, as the director of Assumption's Women's Studies Program which addresses the concerns of women in America as well as within the global context. This interdisciplinary program is designed to raise awareness about the challenges women and families face as a consequence of globalization, the unequal distribution of wealth, and other factors which deeply disadvantage many mothers. Regina resides in central Massachusetts with her spouse and is the extraordinarily proud (and perhaps—at times—mad) mother of two adult daughters.

Nancy Gerber received a Ph.D. in Literatures in English from Rutgers University. For eight years she taught in the English and Women's Studies departments at Rutgers-Newark. Since 2008 she has been a student in the psychoanalytic training program at the Academy of Clinical and Applied Psychoanalysis in Livingston, New Jersey. She is the author of *Losing a Life: A Daughter's Memoir of Caregiving* (2005), which chronicles the impact of her father's stroke. Her writing has appeared in scholarly and literary journals, including the *Journal of the Association of Research on Mothering*, *Journal of Aging, Humanities, and the Arts*, *The Mom Egg*, *Hip Mama*, and others. She is the mother of two sons, ages 27 and 21, and is just beginning to understand that mothering is a lifelong process.

Gerald F. Giesbrecht, Ph.D., is a Registered Psychologist and Assistant Professor in the Department of Paediatrics at the University of Calgary. Gerry's interest in maternal depression derives primarily from his experiences as a therapist to families that struggle to achieve adequate conditions for healthy child development. His research deals principally with the effects of maternal mental health on fetal and infant development. He is particularly interested in the pathways by which depression, anxiety, and stress may alter development and the possibility that high-quality postnatal mother-child interactions can reverse these effects. Because the nature of his research sometimes leads to criticism about the potential for mother-blaming, he has become interested in the ways that the scientific enterprise can unintentionally harm the individuals we wish to understand and help.

Donna F. Johnson is a sessional lecturer in the School of Social Work at Carleton University. She worked for over 20 years in the anti-violence movement, where she gained extensive experience facilitating feminist groups. She continues to work as a police service crisis counselor.

Nicole Letourneau is full professor in the Faculties of Nursing and Medicine (Pediatrics) and holds the Norlien/Alberta Children's Hospital Foundation

Chair in Parent-Infant Mental Health at the University of Calgary. She is also the RESOLVE Alberta Research Coordinator, engaged with partners across the Prairies in research and education on family violence and abuse prevention. Until 2011, she was the Canada Research Chair in Healthy Child Development at the University of New Brunswick where she also co-founded the New Brunswick Health Policy Laboratory. She has received many honours including the Nurses Association of New Brunswick Merit Award in Research in 2011, named to Canada's Top 40 Under 40 and to "Who's Who in Canada" in 2008, named Canada's premier young investigator for receiving the Peter Lougheed New Investigator award from CIHR in 2007, received the Outstanding New Investigator in Research Award from the Canadian Association for Nursing Research in 2003 and finally, received the Alumni Horizon Award for early achievement from the University of Alberta in 2003. She has published results of her research in over 80 refereed journals and books. She was also a member of the Canadian Institute for Advanced Research New Investigator Network and served on CIHR's Institute of Gender and Health Institute Advisory Board, and CIHR's Population Health Review Committee. Currently, she serves on the board of the International Association for the Study of Attachment, Scientific Advisory Panel of Assistant Human Reproduction Canada, board of the New Brunswick Health Research Foundation, chairs CIHR's Standing Committee on Ethics and is a member of CIHR's Nominating and Governance Committee.

Helen Levine is a retired social worker and professor. At the School of Social Work at Carleton University she introduced women's issues and feminist perspectives into the curriculum for the first time. She received the Governor General's Award in Commemoration of the Persons Case for advancing the equality of women in Canada. She has published essays on mothering and was featured in the NFB film *Motherland: Tales of Wonder*, a feature-length documentary that casts a critical eye at the North American experience of mothering.

Joanne C. Minaker, Ph.D., is an Assistant Professor in the Sociology Department at Grant MacEwan University in Edmonton, Alberta. Joanne's work is about care, connection, mothering, and social (in)justice. Her passion to bring attention to social injustices affecting children, youth, and their families stems from her experiences sharing a life of love, learning, and laughter with her amazing academic husband and their inspiring children—sons Ayden (nine) and Taryk (six), and daughter Maylah (two). Among her recent publications include a book, co-authored with Bryan Hogeveen, *Youth, Crime, and Society: Issues of Power and Justice* and various articles on mothering. Joanne's current research project explores the challenges, barriers, and opportunities marginalized young mothers encounter in their experiences of mothering at the margins of mainstream society. She is also working on an edited collection (with Bryan Hogeveen), *Criminalized Mothers:Criminalizing Motherhood* with Demeter Press. Joanne can be also found practicing yoga, running, or on Twitter @ JoanneMinaker.

Marina Morrow, Ph.D. is an Associate Professor and Director of the Centre for the Study of Gender, Social Inequities and Mental Health in the Faculty of Health Sciences at Simon Fraser University. Marina's research interests are in mental health with foci on gender and intersectional analyses, access to health services, critical health policy and health reform. In her work Marina strives to better understand the social, political and institutional processes through which health and mental health policies and practices are developed and how social and health inequities are sustained or attenuated for different populations. Marina strongly supports public scholarship and collaborative research partnerships with community-based organizations, people with lived experience of mental health and substance use problems, health care practitioners, advocates and policy decision makers. Marina has published a wide range of reports and academic journal articles. She is the lead editor on *Women's Health in Canada: Critical Perspectives on Theory and Policy* (2007).

Roblyn Rawlins is Associate Professor of Sociology and past Director of Women's Studies at The College of New Rochelle, New York. She has published and presented research on mothers' clubs, the history of childrearing advice books, scientific and popular understandings of early intellectual development in children, the ways in which childrearing experts discipline mothers, gender, national identity and experiences of public harassment among college students studying abroad, the motivations and practices of home cooks, and the ways in which young women negotiate issues of food, identity and family. She lives, cooks, and mothers on the banks of the Delaware River in Hunterdon County, New Jersey, with her husband and her infant son, Samuel.

Jules E. Smith, MA, worked in the area of depression and anxiety during pregnancy, after the birth of a baby or adoption of a child for nearly 10 years, both as a clinical counsellor and as a researcher with university affiliations. Her understanding of emotional distress during pregnancy and after a baby evolved through listening to women's own stories on becoming mothers. This intersected with her own experience of becoming a mother and how her orientation to everything—identity, work, relationships, everyday activities, public life, etc., was radically altered. Jules recently left this field to work in a regional campus as the student and community counsellor in the small rural community where she lives with her partner and daughter. She still finds many opportunities to continue sharing stories on the experience of mothering.

Teresa M. Twomey, JD, a former litigation attorney, is an activist for maternal mental health (which includes serving as Legal Resources Coordinator, and for almost ten years, as a state Co-coordinator for Postpartum Support International). She teaches in the Women and Gender Studies department of Southern Connecticut State University, including a course on Representations of Motherhood. Her book, *Understanding Postpartum Psychosis: A Temporary Madness* was published by Praeger in 2009. Teresa has published chapters, articles and essays in a variety of media and on a variety of topics. One recent example is an article in an international business journal, *Competitiveness Review*, titled, "Revealing the Role of Privilege in Free Markets, Equality-Under-Law and Sustainability" (with Drew Harris). Teresa resides in Cheshire, Connecticut, U.S. with her spouse and their three amazing daughters. She is currently in the early stages of creating a business which incorporates her various passions and her commitment to making a positive difference in the world.

Alison Watts is currently completing her Ph.D. and is a sessional academic in the School of Arts and Social Sciences at Southern Cross University, Lismore, Australia. Her thesis draws from thirty-one mothers' mental patient files, including a family member, from one mental institution in Melbourne, Australia from the interwar years: 1920 to 1936. This research uses feminist, historical approaches to investigate the relationship between gender, motherhood, and mental disorder in twentieth century, Australian context. Alison is a single mother and resides in Lismore, New South Wales, Australia with her teenage son

Gina Wong, Ph.D., is a Registered Psychologist, Associate Professor, and Chair in the Graduate Centre for Applied Psychology at Athabasca University. She is a board member with MIRCI and an Alberta Co-Coordinator with Postpartum Support International. Gina directs a limited counselling practice supporting adolescent girls and women through life transitions. She specializes in maternal mental health and wellness and publishes/presents on related issues from feminist and cross-cultural perspectives. Gina has an active program of research in the area of Matroreform. As a feminist psychologist, the intersection of multiple perspectives as an academic, researcher, theorist, and counselling practitioner culminates with her own experiences of being a feminist mother. She resides in Edmonton, Alberta, Canada with her partner, and their children.